Cloud Security and Privacy

Cloud Security and Privacy

Tim Mather, Subra Kumaraswamy, and Shahed Latif

O'REILLY®

Beijing · Cambridge · Farnham · Köln · Sebastopol · Taipei · Tokyo

Cloud Security and Privacy

by Tim Mather, Subra Kumaraswamy, and Shahed Latif

Copyright © 2009 Tim Mather, Subra Kumaraswamy, and Shahed Latif. All rights reserved.
Printed in the United States of America.

Published by O'Reilly Media, Inc., 1005 Gravenstein Highway North, Sebastopol, CA 95472.

O'Reilly books may be purchased for educational, business, or sales promotional use. Online editions are also available for most titles (*http://my.safaribooksonline.com*). For more information, contact our corporate/institutional sales department: 800-998-9938 or *corporate@oreilly.com*.

Editor: Mike Loukides	**Indexer:** Lucie Haskins
Production Editor: Sarah Schneider	**Cover Designer:** Karen Montgomery
Copyeditor: Audrey Doyle	**Interior Designer:** David Futato
Proofreader: Kiel Van Horn	**Illustrator:** Robert Romano

Printing History:

September 2009:   First Edition.

ISBN: 978-0-596-80276-9

[SB]

[3/10]

1267806252

CONTENTS

PREFACE

IN FEBRUARY 2008, I RAN INTO SUBRA KUMARASWAMY, OF SUN MICROSYSTEMS, at the quarterly meeting of the Electronic Crimes Task Force put on by the San Francisco office of the U.S. Secret Service. Subra and I have attended a number of these meetings, and we knew each other from similar, previous professional events. Both of us are information security practitioners, and that is a small world in Silicon Valley, where we both have lived and worked for many years. Subra asked what I was up to, and I told him I was considering writing a book on cloud computing and security.

Even in February 2008, the hype about cloud computing was very evident in Silicon Valley. Similarly, lots of concerns were being voiced about the apparent lack of (information) security provided in cloud computing. As Subra and I discussed, though, at that time no substantive or articulate information was available on this topic—hence my musings about writing a book on the subject. Subra told me that he too was spending time researching cloud computing and had failed to find any substantive or articulate information on the topic. I asked Subra whether he was interested in helping me write such a book, and he responded yes. (Having been through the anguish of writing a book previously, I was looking for some very competent help, and Subra certainly fits that description.) So began our book odyssey.

Originally, our effort was intended to be one chapter in another O'Reilly book on cloud computing. However, after we went substantially over the O'Reilly guideline on length for not just one but two chapters, we pitched the idea of an entire book on cloud security and privacy. O'Reilly accepted our proposal, and what we thought was going to be a 20-page effort became a 200-page effort. That was no small increase in the amount of work we needed to complete—and quickly, if ours was to be one of the first such books to market.

In late 2008, Subra and I started giving a series of presentations to different technically savvy audiences in Silicon Valley outlining our findings on cloud computing and security. We were excited about the reaction we got from these audiences. No one felt we were off the mark technically, and the audiences were hungry for more information and more detail. After one such meeting, a KPMG employee said he wanted to talk with us further about cloud computing and auditing. Still in need of good material for the book, Subra and I readily agreed to a meeting.

Well, the meeting wasn't quite what we were expecting. We were hoping to get some information from KPMG about concerns and trends around auditing of cloud-based services. Instead, one of the partners, Shahed Latif, asked whether he could join our book effort. Subra and I talked it over and agreed to let him join. We needed good audit information, and Shahed certainly brings credibility to the subject. (In addition to his other extensive audit experience, Shahed is the KPMG partner for providing a number of services for a major cloud service provider that Subra and I were already aware of, given that we had some fairly extensive discussions with senior information security personnel for that same cloud service provider. Additionally, I knew Shahed professionally. I have been on the pointed end of the KPMG audit spear three times in my career: at Apple, VeriSign, and Symantec. In fact, while I was chief information security officer at Symantec, Shahed was the KPMG IT audit partner. So, Shahed was a known entity to us.

With three authors now, we were off and running to complete the book in a timely manner, and hopefully be first to market.

—Tim Mather

Who Should Read This Book

Anyone interested in cloud computing should read this book. Although it focuses on security, privacy, and auditing of cloud-based services, we did not write it strictly for information security professionals, though we certainly expect that many of them will find it helpful. We wrote this book for technically savvy business personnel who are, or who are considering, using cloud computing and are interested in protecting their information. Data is king, and today the confidentiality, integrity, and availability of data is more important than ever. Therefore, security, privacy, and auditing of cloud-based services should be of interest to our readers.

What's in This Book

In this book, we will define cloud computing in a systematic manner and examine security and privacy issues that this new model raises. Here is a short summary of the book's chapters and what you'll find inside:

Chapter 1, *Introduction*

Introduces the concept of cloud computing and the evolution of computing into cloud computing.

Chapter 2, *What Is Cloud Computing?*

Defines cloud computing as having the following five attributes: multitenancy (shared resources), massive scalability, elasticity, pay as you go, and self-provisioning of resources. However, the term *cloud computing* has multiple definitions, because this is a nascent and rapidly changing arena. For example, a recent study noted more than 22 different definitions of cloud computing.* In this chapter, we discuss the largely agreed-upon types of services offered through cloud computing, because some of them are important enabling technologies, such as virtualization.

Chapter 3, *Infrastructure Security*

Describes the IT infrastructure security capabilities that cloud services generally offer. IT infrastructure security refers to the established security capabilities at the network, host, and application levels.

Chapter 4, *Data Security and Storage*

Examines the current state of data security and the storage of data in the cloud, including aspects of confidentiality, integrity, and availability.

Chapter 5, *Identity and Access Management*

Explains the identity and access management (IAM) practice and support capabilities for authentication, authorization, and auditing of users who access cloud services.

Chapter 6, *Security Management in the Cloud*

Depicts security management frameworks and the standards that are relevant for the cloud.

Chapter 7, *Privacy*

Introduces privacy aspects to consider within the context of cloud computing, and analyzes the similarities and differences with traditional computing models. Additionally, in this chapter we highlight legal and regulatory implications related to privacy in the cloud.

Chapter 8, *Audit and Compliance*

Reveals the importance of audit and compliance functions within the cloud, and the various standards and frameworks to consider.

---

* Vaquero, Luis M., Luis Rodero-Merino, Juan Caceres, et al. "A Break in the Clouds: Towards a Cloud Definition." *ACM SIGCOMM Computer Communication Review* archive, Volume 39, Issue 1 (January 2009).

Chapter 9, *Examples of Cloud Service Providers*

> Provides information on some examples of cloud service providers (CSPs), including who some of the major CSPs are (in terms of size and influence) and what services they provide.

Chapter 10, *Security-As-a-[Cloud] Service*

> Looks at a different facet of cloud computing security: security delivered as a service unto itself through the cloud. This security-as-a-[cloud] service (SaaS) is also an emerging space, and in this chapter we look at what some of those cloud security services are.

Chapter 11, *The Impact of Cloud Computing on the Role of Corporate IT*

> Looks at the impact of cloud computing on organizational IT departments as they exist today. Although some may feel that cloud computing provides an important complement to IT departments today, the view from IT departments might be that cloud computing replaces much of what IT is responsible for.

Chapter 12, *Conclusion, and the Future of the Cloud*

> Summarizes the concepts presented in the book and provides some thoughts on the future of the cloud.

This book also includes a glossary of terms, as well as three appendixes that discuss relevant audit formats (SAS 70 Type II and SysTrust) and provide one model of the relationships between audit controls relevant to cloud computing.

Conventions Used in This Book

The following typographical conventions are used in this book:

Italic

> Indicates new terms, URLs, and email addresses

`Constant width`

> Used to refer to language and script elements

> **NOTE**
>
> This icon signifies a tip, suggestion, or general note.

Using Code Examples

This book is here to help you get your job done. In general, you may use the code in this book in your programs and documentation. You do not need to contact us for permission unless you're reproducing a significant portion of the code. For example, writing a program that uses several chunks of code from this book does not require permission. Selling or distributing a CD-ROM of examples from O'Reilly books *does* require permission. Answering a question by citing this book and quoting example code does not require permission. Incorporating a significant amount of example code from this book into your product's documentation *does* require permission.

We appreciate, but do not require, attribution. An attribution usually includes the title, author, publisher, and ISBN. For example: *"Cloud Security and Privacy, by Tim Mather, Subra Kumaraswamy, and Shahed Latif. Copyright 2009 Tim Mather, Subra Kumaraswamy, and Shahed Latif, 978-0-596-80276-9."*

If you feel your use of code examples falls outside fair use or the permission given above, feel free to contact us at *permissions@oreilly.com*.

Safari® Books Online

Safari Books Online is an on-demand digital library that lets you easily search over 7,500 technology and creative reference books and videos to find the answers you need quickly.

With a subscription, you can read any page and watch any video from our library online. Read books on your cell phone and mobile devices. Access new titles before they are available for print, and get exclusive access to manuscripts in development and post feedback for the authors. Copy and paste code samples, organize your favorites, download chapters, bookmark key sections, create notes, print out pages, and benefit from tons of other time-saving features.

O'Reilly Media has uploaded this book to the Safari Books Online service. To have full digital access to this book and others on similar topics from O'Reilly and other publishers, sign up for free at *http://my.safaribooksonline.com*.

How to Contact Us

Please address comments and questions concerning this book to the publisher:

O'Reilly Media, Inc.
1005 Gravenstein Highway North
Sebastopol, CA 95472
800-998-9938 (in the United States or Canada)
707-829-0515 (international or local)
707-829-0104 (fax)

We have a web page for this book, where we list errata, examples, and any additional information. You can access this page at:

http://oreilly.com/catalog/9780596802769

To comment or ask technical questions about this book, send email to:

bookquestions@oreilly.com

For more information about our books, conferences, Resource Centers, and the O'Reilly Network, see our website at:

http://oreilly.com

Acknowledgments

We want to thank the many people from cloud service providers who took the time to talk with us about security and privacy in the cloud. Even though a significant amount of that material was told to us on a non-attribution basis, it was nevertheless invaluable for us to understand the providers' perspectives on this topic. We also spoke with several customers of cloud computing services and got some great insights into their real-world concerns and experiences.

In putting this book together, we felt it was important to capture the latest solutions and trends in the market. To this end, we met with a number of companies to understand the current trends. Organizations we talked to included Microsoft, the National Institute of Standards and Technology, Salesforce.com, and Sun Microsystems. With that in mind, we would like to thank the following people who helped us: John Dutra, John Howie, Peter Mell, Izak Mutlu, and Rajen Sheth.

We also owe a big thank you to several people who took the time to review our manuscript and keep us accurate technically, as well as helping us with readability. Thank you specifically to Dan Blum, Robert Fly, Tim Grance, Chris Hoff, Jim Reavis, Laura Robertson, and Rodney Thayer. Although any errors or omissions in the book are strictly our own responsibility, these individuals helped ensure that we made fewer of them.

Several KPMG employees also helped us significantly in our efforts, and we need to recognize them. They did everything from providing content and helping with graphics, to putting together the glossary, coordinating our meetings, and handling a number of other tasks that made our work easier. Thank you very much to Graham Hill, Vijay Jajoo, Mark Lundin, Bob Quicke, Ismail Rahman, Doron Rotman, and Nadeem Siddiqui.

Finally, there is a saying in Silicon Valley about "eating your own dog food." Marketing personnel generally translate this phrase to "using your own products." Well, when it came to writing this book, we endeavored to eat our own dog food—that is, we used cloud services wherever possible in this effort. We used cloud-based email, calendaring, and our own cloud-based website for document and graphics management, as well as for coordinating with our editor at O'Reilly (thanks, Mike Loukides!), our reviewers, our contributors, and Lasselle-Ramsay, which helped significantly in making our material presentable.

From Tim Mather

I would like to thank Diva, Penny, Tiramisu, and Sam for all of their support, and for allowing me to repurpose a huge number of affection hours over the past year to book writing. Thanks to my cats for their support and understanding.

From Subra Kumaraswamy

I am fortunate to have the love and support of my family, especially for putting up with me on the many lost weekends over the past year. A big thank you goes to my wife, Preethika, and my two children, Namrata and Nitin. I also owe thanks to my manager, Leslie Lambert (CISO of Sun Microsystems), for her support and encouragement in this endeavor. Also, I appreciate all the gestures from friends and colleagues who volunteered to review my material and spread the word.

From Shahed Latif

I would like to thank my family for the support and love they gave me when I had to spend many weekends, bank holidays, and long evenings completing this book. A special thanks to Moni, my wife, and Ayaz, my son, for their understanding and support.

CHAPTER ONE

Introduction

"Mind the Gap"

IF YOU HAVE EVER RIDDEN THE LONDON UNDERGROUND, YOU ARE FAMILIAR WITH the phrase "Mind the gap." You are implored to mind the gap between the platform and the moving Underground cars. The subway platform and the car doors should line up horizontally and vertically, but they usually do not. In some places the gap between the two can be significant. So, you need to watch your step.

We could use the concept of minding the gap as an operative phrase about cloud computing and its security. Ideally, these two concepts, cloud computing and the security that it affords, should align, but they usually do not. It has become a common mantra in the high-technology industry to chant "cloud computing good" while at the same time saying "cloud security bad." But what does that really mean? Exactly what is wrong with security in cloud computing?

The purpose of this book is to answer those questions through a systematic investigation of what constitutes cloud computing and what security it offers. As such, this book also explores the implications of cloud computing security on privacy, auditing, and compliance for both the cloud service provider (CSP) and the customer. Is security in cloud computing a bad thing? The answer depends on what you use cloud computing for, and your expectations. If you are a large organization with significant resources to devote to a sophisticated information security program, you need to overcome a number of security, privacy, and compliance challenges that we explore later in the book. However, if you are a small to medium-size business (SMB), the security of cloud computing might look attractive, compared to the resources you can afford to spend on information security today.

The Evolution of Cloud Computing

To understand what cloud computing is and is not, it is important to understand how this model of computing has evolved. As Alvin Toffler notes in his famous book, *The Third Wave* (Bantam, 1980), civilization has progressed in waves (three of them to date: the first wave was agricultural societies, the second was the industrial age, and the third is the information age). Within each wave, there have been several important subwaves. In this post-industrial information age, we are now at the beginning of what many people feel will be an era of cloud computing.

In his book *The Big Switch* (W.W. Norton & Co., 2008), Nicholas Carr discusses an information revolution very similar to an important change within the industrial era. Specifically, Carr equates the rise of cloud computing in the information age to electrification in the industrial age. It used to be that organizations had to provide their own power (water wheels, windmills). With electrification, however, organizations no longer provide their own power; they just plug in to the electrical grid. Carr argues that cloud computing is really the beginning of the same change for information technology. Now organizations provide their own computing resources (power). The emerging future, however, is one in which organizations will simply plug in to the cloud (computing grid) for the computing resources they need. As he puts it, "In the end the savings offered by utilities become too compelling to resist, even for the largest enterprises. The grid wins." In fact, Part 2 of his book is about "living in the cloud" and the benefits it provides. (Carr also discusses at length some of the perceived negative consequences to society of this big switch, specifically some of the darker aspects this change brings to society.)

Carr is not alone in arguing for the benefits of cloud computing, but he has put forth what is arguably the most articulate statement of those benefits thus far. And although he focuses specifically on the economic benefits of cloud computing, he does not discuss information security problems associated with "the big switch." We do, and that is the purpose of this book: to articulate security and privacy issues associated with "the big switch" to cloud computing.

As we noted earlier, within each wave there are subwaves, and there have already been several within the information age, as Figure 1-1 shows. We started with mainframe computers and progressed to minicomputers, personal computers, and so forth, and we are now entering cloud computing.

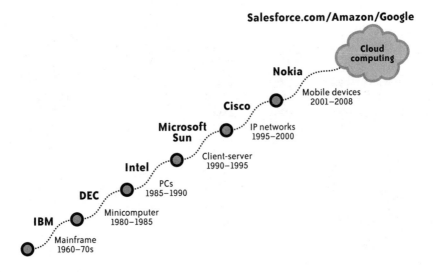

FIGURE 1-1. Subwaves within the information age

Another view illustrates that cloud computing itself is a logical evolution of computing. Figure 1-2 displays cloud computing and cloud service providers (CSPs) as extensions of the Internet service provider (ISP) model.

In the beginning (ISP 1.0), ISPs quickly proliferated to provide access to the Internet for organizations and individuals. These early ISPs merely provided Internet connectivity for users and small businesses, often over dial-up telephone service. As access to the Internet became a commodity, ISPs consolidated and searched for other value-added services, such as providing access to email and to servers at their facilities (ISP 2.0). This version quickly led to specialized facilities for hosting organizations' (customers') servers, along with the infrastructure to support them and the applications running on them. These specialized facilities are known as *collocation facilities* (ISP 3.0). Those facilities are "a type of data center where multiple customers locate network, server, and storage gear and interconnect to a variety of telecommunications and other network service provider(s) with a minimum of cost and complexity."* As collocation facilities proliferated and became commoditized, the next step in the evolution was the formation of application service providers (ASPs), which focused on a higher value-added service of providing specialized applications for organizations, and not just the computing infrastructure (ISP 4.0). ASPs typically owned and operated the software application(s) they provided, as well as the necessary infrastructure.

---

* Wikipedia definition of collocation facility: *http://en.wikipedia.org/wiki/Co-location_facility.*

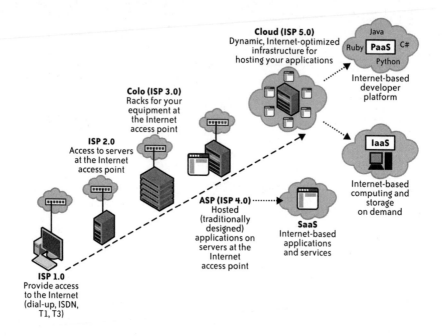

FIGURE 1-2. Evolution of cloud computing

Although ASPs might appear similar to a service delivery model of cloud computing that is referred to as software-as-a-service (SaaS), there is an important difference in how these services are provided, and in the business model. Although ASPs usually provided services to multiple customers (just as SaaS providers do today), they did so through dedicated infrastructures. That is, each customer had its own dedicated instance of an application, and that instance usually ran on a dedicated host or server. The important difference between SaaS providers and ASPs is that SaaS providers offer access to applications on a *shared*, not dedicated, infrastructure.

> **NOTE**
>
> The acronym "SaaS" is used for both software-as-a-service and security-as-a-service, which is discussed in Chapter 10. However, all uses of "SaaS" in this book, with the exception of Chapter 10, are to software-as-a-service.

Cloud computing (ISP 5.0) defines the SPI model, which is generally agreed upon as providing *S*aaS, platform-as-a-service (*P*aaS), and infrastructure-as-a-service (*I*aaS). For more information about these service models, see Chapter 2.

With increasing attention, some would say hype, now being paid to cloud computing, companies are increasingly claiming to be "cloudy." Suddenly, many companies are claiming to operate "in the cloud." Serious cloud washing is underway. Similarly, a number of computing groups have announced their efforts to promote some facet of cloud computing. Some of these groups are established (e.g., the National Institute of Standards and Technology efforts to promote standardization in cloud computing), and some of them are brand new, having emerged only with the appearance of this new computing model (e.g., the Cloud Security Alliance's promotion of security in cloud computing, or the Open Cloud Manifesto's promotion of cloud interoperability). Many other groups have also announced efforts dedicated to cloud computing, such as the Distributed Management Task Force (DMTF); the Information Technology Association of America, a high-technology industry association; and the Jericho Forum, an international information security thought leadership association, among many others.

Summary

Cloud computing is a nascent and rapidly evolving model, with new aspects and capabilities being announced regularly. Although we have done our best in the forthcoming chapters to provide a comprehensive and timely look at these issues, no doubt there are areas that we have not addressed or aspects that might have changed already. With that in mind, we encourage your feedback. We also invite you to participate in an ongoing discussion with us about the issue of cloud computing at *http://www.cloudsecurityandprivacy.com*.

CHAPTER TWO

What Is Cloud Computing?

IF YOU LOOK BACK TO THE INDUSTRIAL REVOLUTION AND ITS IMPACT ON THE world economy, the revolution itself did not take place overnight, but through waves of changes. If you move forward to the adoption of the Internet, the Internet has also developed through waves of changes. Cloud computing has the potential to be the next disruptive wave.

This chapter describes:

- Cloud computing technology components
- Cloud services delivery
- Cloud varieties
- Key drivers for adopting the cloud
- The impact of cloud computing on the continuum of users
- The impact of cloud computing on application developers
- Key enablers that must evolve to break down current barriers for cloud computing to succeed

Cloud Computing Defined

Our definition of cloud computing is based on five attributes: multitenancy (shared resources), massive scalability, elasticity, pay as you go, and self-provisioning of resources.

Multitenancy (shared resources)
> Unlike previous computing models, which assumed dedicated resources (i.e., computing facilities dedicated to a single user or owner), cloud computing is based on a business model in which resources are shared (i.e., multiple users use the same resource) at the network level, host level, and application level.

Massive scalability
> Although organizations might have hundreds or thousands of systems, cloud computing provides the ability to scale to tens of thousands of systems, as well as the ability to massively scale bandwidth and storage space.

Elasticity
> Users can rapidly increase and decrease their computing resources as needed, as well as release resources for other uses when they are no longer required.

Pay as you go
> Users pay for only the resources they actually use and for only the time they require them.

Self-provisioning of resources
> Users self-provision resources, such as additional systems (processing capability, software, storage) and network resources.

One of the attributes of cloud computing is *elasticity* of resources. This cloud capability allows users to increase and decrease their computing resources as needed, as Figure 2-1 illustrates. There is always an awareness of the baseline of computing resources, but predicting future needs is difficult, especially when demands are constantly changing. Cloud computing can offer a means to provide IT resources on demand and address spikes in usage.

Interest in the cloud is growing because cloud solutions provide users with access to supercomputer-like power at a fraction of the cost of buying such a solution outright. More importantly, these solutions can be acquired on demand; the network becomes the supercomputer in the cloud where users can buy what they need when they need it. Cloud computing identifies where scalable IT-enabled capabilities are delivered as a service to customers using Internet technologies.

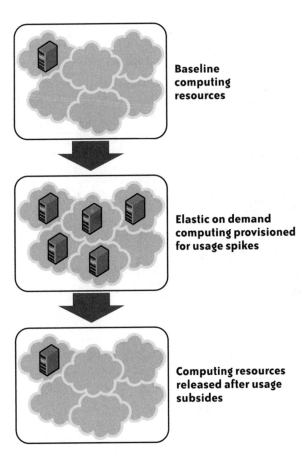

Baseline computing resources

Elastic on demand computing provisioned for usage spikes

Computing resources released after usage subsides

FIGURE 2-1. Attribute of elasticity

Cloud computing has generated significant interest in the marketplace and is forecasted for high growth, as illustrated in Figure 2-2, which highlights the recent notable cloud launches and the current and projected revenues for cloud-based services.

Recent notable cloud launches

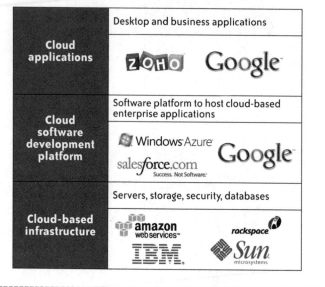

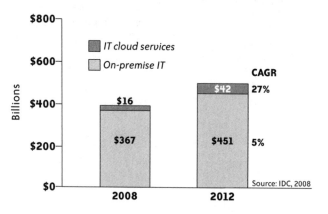

FIGURE 2-2. Recent notable cloud launches (top) and spending on cloud-based services (bottom)

Cloud computing is expected to be a significant growth driver in worldwide IT spending. In fact, cloud services are expected to grow at a compound annual growth rate (CAGR) of 27% and reach $42 billion by 2012; spending on non-cloud IT services is expected to grow at a CAGR of 5%, according to IDC.

The SPI Framework for Cloud Computing

A commonly agreed upon framework for describing cloud computing services goes by the acronym "SPI." This acronym stands for the three major services provided through the cloud: software-as-a-service (*SaaS*), platform-as-a-service (*PaaS*), and infrastructure-as-a-service (*IaaS*). Figure 2-3 illustrates the relationship between services, uses, and types of clouds.

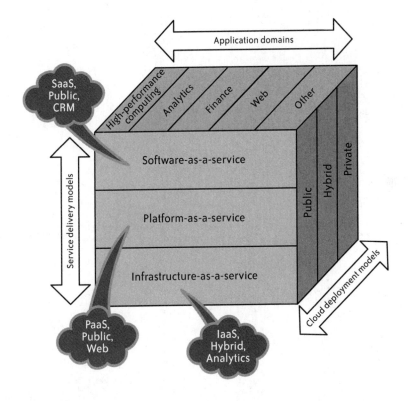

FIGURE 2-3. SPI service model

We will now explore each of these components in detail.

Relevant Technologies in Cloud Computing

Cloud computing isn't so much a technology as it is the combination of many preexisting technologies. These technologies have matured at different rates and in different contexts, and were not designed as a coherent whole; however, they have come together to create a technical ecosystem for cloud computing. New advances in processors, virtualization technology, disk storage, broadband Internet connection, and fast, inexpensive servers have combined to make the cloud a more compelling solution.

Figure 2-4 illustrates the relevant technologies.

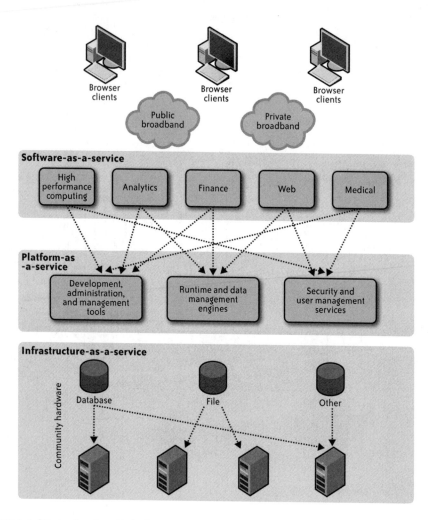

FIGURE 2-4. Architecture for relevant technologies

Cloud access devices

The range of access devices for the cloud has expanded in recent years. Home PCs, enterprise PCs, network computers, mobile phone devices, custom handheld devices, and custom static devices (including refrigerators) are all online. Interestingly, the growth of the iPhone and the proliferation of applications available from its App Store illustrate an improvement in terms of access to the cloud. This greater access is resulting in greater use and growth of services within the cloud. For example, you can now use Skype through the iPhone, thus bringing this peer-to-peer network much closer to users, and Salesforce.com has introduced an application that allows users to access its services from the iPhone, as well as many other vendors.

Browsers and thin clients

Users of multiple device types can now access applications and information from wherever they can load a browser. Indeed, browsers are becoming increasingly sophisticated. Enterprise applications, such as SAP and Oracle, can be accessed through a browser interface—a change from when a client (a so-called "fat") application needed to be loaded onto the desktop. The general population has become more familiar with the browser function and can use a discrete application, where the context is intuitive, without requiring training or user guides.

High-speed broadband access

A critical component of the cloud is the broadband network, which offers the means to connect components and provides one of the substantial differences from the utility computing concept of 30 years ago. Broadband access is now widely available, especially in global metropolitan areas. Nearly pervasive wireless access (e.g., WiFi, cellular, emerging WiMAX) is available, which has established mobile devices as entry points to the IT resources of the enterprise and the cloud.

Data centers and server farms

Cloud-based services require large computing capacity and are hosted in data centers and server farms. These distributed data centers and server farms span multiple locations and can be linked via internetworks providing distributed computing and service delivery capabilities.

A number of examples today illustrate the flexibility and scalability of cloud computing power. For instance, Google has linked a very large number of inexpensive servers to provide tremendous flexibility and power. Amazon's Elastic Compute Cloud (EC2) provides virtualization in the data center to create huge numbers of virtual instances for services being requested. Salesforce.com provides SaaS to its large customer base by grouping its customers into clusters to enable scalability and flexibility.

Storage devices

Decreasing storage costs and the flexibility with which storage can be deployed have changed the storage landscape. The fixed direct access storage device (DASD) has been replaced with storage area networks (SANs), which have reduced costs and allowed a great deal more flexibility in enterprise storage. SAN software manages integration of storage devices and can independently allocate storage space on demand across a number of devices.

Virtualization technologies

Virtualization is a foundational technology platform fostering cloud computing, and it is transforming the face of the modern data center. The term *virtualization* refers to the abstraction of compute resources (CPU, storage, network, memory, application stack, and database) from applications and end users consuming the service. The abstraction of infrastructure yields the notion of resource democratization—whether infrastructure, applications, or information—and provides the capability for pooled resources to be made available and accessible to anyone or anything authorized to utilize them via standardized methods.

Virtualization technologies enable multitenancy cloud business models by providing a scalable, shared resource platform for all tenants. More importantly, they provide a dedicated resource view for the platform's consumers. From an enterprise perspective, virtualization offers data center consolidation and improved IT operational efficiency. Today, enterprises have deployed virtualization technologies within data centers in various forms, including OS virtualization (VMware, Xen), storage virtualization (NAS, SAN), database virtualization, and application or software virtualization (Apache Tomcat, JBoss, Oracle App Server, WebSphere).

From a public cloud perspective, depending on the cloud services delivery model (SPI) and architecture, virtualization appears as a shared resource at various layers of the virtualized service (e.g., OS, storage, database, application).

Figure 2-5 illustrates OS virtualization and the layers of the virtualization environment as defined by Sun Microsystems. IaaS providers including Amazon (EC2), ServePath (GoGrid), and Sun Cloud employ this type of virtualization, which enables customers to run instances of various operating system flavors in a public cloud. The virtualization platform shown in Figure 2-5 is the Sun xVM hypervisor environment that virtualizes shared hardware resources for the guest or virtual server operating systems (Linux, Solaris, and Microsoft Windows) hosted on the hypervisor. The hypervisor is a small application that runs on top of the physical machine hardware layer. It implements and manages the virtual CPU (vCPU), virtual memory (vMemory), event channels, and memory shared by the resident virtual machines (VMs). It also controls I/O and memory access to devices.

In Xen, as well as Sun xVM (which is based on the work of the Xen community), a VM is called a *domain*, whereas in the VMware virtualization product it is referred to as a *guest OS*. In Figure 2-5, the VMs are labeled as dom0 and domU1, domU2, and domU3. Dom0 is used to manage the other user domains (domU1, etc.). VMware employs a similar mechanism, and calls it as "service console." Management through dom0 or the service console consists of creating, destroying, migrating, saving, or restoring user domains. An operating system running in a user domain is configured so that privileged operations are executed via calls to the hypervisor.

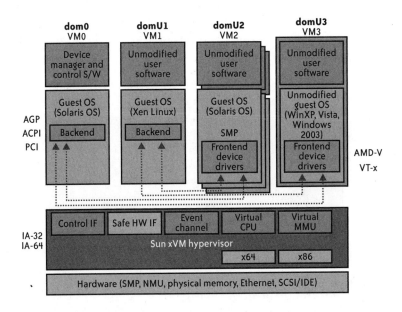

FIGURE 2-5. Sun xVM hypervisor environment

In addition to OS and storage virtualization, SaaS and PaaS service providers are known to have implemented software and database virtualization whereby customers share the software application stack and database resources. For example, Salesforce.com is known to have virtualized both the software and the database stack. In that model, all customers share every single layer of the delivery infrastructure.

APIs

A suitable application programming interface (API) is another enabler for the cloud computing services delivery model (see Figure 2-6). APIs empower users by enabling features such as self-provisioning and programmatic control of cloud services and resources. Depending on the type of cloud services delivery model (SPI), an API can manifest in different forms, ranging from simple URL manipulations to advanced SOA-like programming models. APIs also help to exploit the full potential of cloud computing and mask the complexity involved in extending existing IT management processes and practices to cloud services.

APIs offered by IaaS cloud service providers (CSPs) such as Amazon EC2, Sun Cloud, and GoGrid allow users to create and manage cloud resources, including compute, storage, and networking components. In this case, use of the API is via HTTP. The GET, POST, PUT, and DELETE requests are used, although most tasks can be accomplished with GET and POST. In some cases, resource representations are in JavaScript Object Notation (JSON). For example, Sun's cloud specification of the Sun Cloud API includes:

- Common behaviors that apply across all requests and responses
- Resource models, which describe the JSON data structures used in requests and responses
- Requests that may be sent to cloud resources, and the responses expected

All *aaS developers need to become familiar with specific APIs to deploy and manage software modules to the *aaS platform. SaaS services typically do not offer APIs other than for basic export and import functionality using browsers or scripts that use HTTP(S) and web URI manipulation methods.

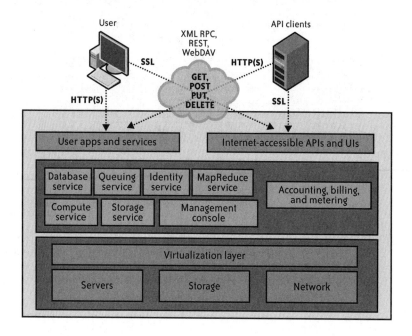

FIGURE 2-6. API enabler for cloud computing

Today, one of the key challenges that cloud customers face is the fact that each CSP has a unique API. As a result, cloud applications are not portable across clouds, and it is very difficult to achieve interoperability among applications running across clouds (including your private cloud). Since APIs are unique to a cloud service, architects, developers, and data center staff members must become familiar with platform-specific features.

Although there is no cloud API standard, standardization efforts are mushrooming and are driven by vendor as well as user communities. One such effort is Universal Cloud Interface (UCI), an attempt to create an open and standardized cloud interface for the unification of various cloud APIs. The UCI forum claims that the goal is to achieve a singular programmatic point of contact that can encompass the entire infrastructure stack, as well as emerging cloud-centric technologies, all through a unified interface. As of this writing, we are not aware of any concerted effort by CSPs to develop a ubiquitous and consistent API across clouds—and that makes porting an application and sharing data across clouds a monumental task. It is also important to realize that market incentives for CSPs are geared toward locking their customers into their cloud offerings. This may make easy interoperability difficult to achieve.

The Traditional Software Model

Traditional software applications are based on a model with large, upfront licensing costs and annual support costs. Increasing the number of users can raise the base cost of the package due to the need for additional hardware server deployments and IT support. Licensing costs are often based on metrics that are not directly aligned with usage (server type, number of CPUs, etc., or some physical characteristic) and are not virtual. A typical enterprise software package requires hardware deployment, servers, and backup and network provisioning to accommodate the number of users on- and off-campus. Security architecture is also taxed in an effort to protect this valuable resource from unauthorized access. Traditional software applications tend to be highly customizable, which comes at a cost—in both dollars and manpower.

The Cloud Services Delivery Model

As we noted earlier, a cloud services delivery model is commonly referred to as an SPI and falls into three generally accepted services (see Figure 2-7).

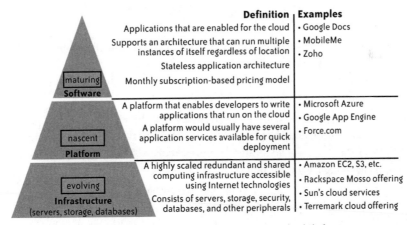

While cloud-based software services are maturing, cloud platform and infrastructure offerings are still in their early stages

FIGURE 2-7. Cloud services delivery model

The Software-As-a-Service Model

Traditional methods of purchasing software involved the customer loading the software onto his own hardware in return for a license fee (a capital expense, known as *CapEx*). The customer could also purchase a maintenance agreement to receive patches to the software or other support services. The customer was concerned with the compatibility of operational systems, patch installations, and compliance with license agreements.

In a SaaS model, the customer does not purchase software, but rather rents it for use on a subscription or pay-per-use model (an operational expense, known as *OpEx*). In some cases, the service is free for limited use. Typically, the purchased service is complete from a hardware, software, and support perspective. The user accesses the service through any authorized device. In some cases, preparatory work is required to establish company-specific data for the service to be fully used and potentially integrated with other applications that are not part of the SaaS platform.

Key benefits of a SaaS model include the following:

- SaaS enables the organization to outsource the hosting and management of applications to a third party (software vendor and service provider) as a means of reducing the cost of application software licensing, servers, and other infrastructure and personnel required to host the application internally.

- SaaS enables software vendors to control and limit use, prohibits copying and distribution, and facilitates the control of all derivative versions of their software. SaaS centralized control often allows the vendor or supplier to establish an ongoing revenue stream with multiple businesses and users without preloading software in each device in an organization.

- Applications delivery using the SaaS model typically uses the one-to-many delivery approach, with the Web as the infrastructure. An end user can access a SaaS application via a web browser; some SaaS vendors provide their own interface that is designed to support features that are unique to their applications.

- A typical SaaS deployment does not require any hardware and can run over the existing Internet access infrastructure. Sometimes changes to firewall rules and settings may be required to allow the SaaS application to run smoothly.

- Management of a SaaS application is supported by the vendor from the end user perspective, whereby a SaaS application can be configured using an API, but SaaS applications cannot be completely customized.

A typical SaaS offering is SaaS over a public network, in which a SaaS-based application is delivered via the Internet to the organization's firewall.

The single most important architectural difference between the traditional software model and the SaaS model is the number of tenants the application supports. The traditional software model is an isolated, single-tenant model, which means a customer buys a software application and installs it on a server. The server runs only that specific application and only for that single customer's end user group. The SaaS model is a multitenant architecture model, which means the physical backend hardware infrastructure is shared among many different customers, but logically is unique for each customer.

Multitenant architecture design maximizes the sharing of resources across tenants, but is still able to securely differentiate data belonging to each tenant. For example, when a user at one company accesses customer information by using a SaaS Customer Relationship Management (CRM) application, the application instance that the user connects to can accommodate users from dozens, or even hundreds, of other companies—all completely unbeknownst to any of the other users.

SaaS solutions are very different from application service provider (ASP) solutions. There are two main explanations for this:

- ASP applications are traditional, single-tenant applications, but are hosted by a third party. They are client/server applications with HTML frontends added to allow remote access to the application.

- ASP applications are not written as Net-native applications. As a result, their performance may be poor, and application updates are no better than self-managed premise-based applications.

By comparison, SaaS applications are multitenant applications that are hosted by a vendor with expertise in the applications and that have been designed as Net-native applications and are updated on an ongoing basis.

The Platform-As-a-Service Model

In a platform-as-a-service (PaaS) model, the vendor offers a development environment to application developers, who develop applications and offer those services through the provider's platform. The provider typically develops toolkits and standards for development, and channels for distribution and payment. The provider typically receives a payment for providing the platform and the sales and distribution services. This enables rapid propagation of software applications, given the low cost of entry and the leveraging of established channels for customer acquisition.

PaaS is a variation of SaaS whereby the development environment is offered as a service. The developers use the building blocks (e.g., predefined blocks of code) of the vendor's development environment to create their own applications.

PaaS solutions are development platforms for which the development tool itself is hosted in the cloud and accessed through a browser. With PaaS, developers can often build web applications without installing any tools on their computer, and can then deploy those applications without any specialized system administration skills.

PaaS systems are useful because they enable lone developers and start-up companies to deploy web-based applications without the cost and complexity of buying servers and setting them up. The benefits of PaaS lie in greatly increasing the number of people who can develop, maintain, and deploy web applications. In short, PaaS offers to democratize the development of web applications in much the same way that Microsoft Access democratized the development of the client/server application.

Today, building web applications requires expert developers with three highly specialized skill sets:

- Backend server development (e.g., Java/J2EE)
- Frontend client development (e.g., JavaScript/Dojo)
- Website administration

PaaS offers the potential for general developers to build web applications without needing specialized expertise, which allows an entire generation of Microsoft Access, Lotus Notes, and PowerBuilder developers to build web applications without too steep a learning curve.

The alternative to PaaS is to develop web applications using desktop development tools, such as Eclipse or Microsoft Access, and then manually deploy those applications to a cloud-hosting provider, such as Amazon Web Services (AWS).

At a minimum, a PaaS solution should include the following elements:

- A PaaS development studio solution should be browser-based.
- An end-to-end PaaS solution should provide a high-productivity integrated development environment (IDE) running on the actual target delivery platform so that debugging and test scenarios run in the same environment as production deployment.
- A PaaS solution should provide integration with external web services and databases.
- A PaaS solution must provide comprehensive monitoring of application and user activity, to help developers understand their applications and effect improvements.
- Scalability, reliability, and security should be built into a PaaS solution without requiring additional development, configuration, or other costs. Multitenancy (the ability for an application to automatically partition state and data to service an arbitrary number of users) must be assumed without additional work of any sort.
- A PaaS solution must support both formal and on-demand collaboration throughout the entire software life cycle (development, testing, documentation, and operations), while maintaining the security of source code and associated intellectual property.
- A PaaS solution should support pay-as-you-go metered billing.

Table 2-1 illustrates the different components of a typical PaaS offering.

TABLE 2-1. PaaS components

Client capabilities	Browser-based development tools: Google Web Toolkit, Google Gears, Mashup Editor, Google Gadgets, etc.
Cloud computing services	Cloud-based runtime: EC2, Google App Engine, etc.
General purpose support services	Web services tools: Simple Storage Service, Simple DB, MTurk, GAE Datastore, GDate, Google Accounts, Social Graph API, etc.

PaaS platforms also have functional differences from traditional development platforms, including:

Multitenant development tools

> Traditional development tools are intended for a single user; a cloud-based studio must support multiple users, each with multiple active projects.

Multitenant deployment architecture

> Scalability is often not a concern of the initial development effort and is left instead for the system administrators to handle when the project deploys. In PaaS, scalability of the application and data tiers must be built-in (e.g., load balancing and failover should be basic elements of the developing platform).

Integrated management

> Traditional development solutions (usually) are not associated with runtime monitoring, but in PaaS the monitoring ability should be built into the development platform.

Integrated billing

> PaaS offerings require mechanisms for billing based on usage that are unique to the SaaS world.

Table 2-2 compares the flexibility offered by in-house development platforms and PaaS.

TABLE 2-2. Comparison of in-house and PaaS development platforms

Supported area	In-house development platform	PaaS
Endpoints: desktops, browsers, mobile devices	Most endpoints and clients are supported	Mostly browser-based
Business logic	Multiple vendors are supported	Restricted by PaaS model
Application development framework	Java Platform, Enterprise Edition (Java EE), .NET, etc.	Restricted by PaaS model
Application servers	Multiple vendors are supported	Provided by PaaS
Databases	Multiple vendors are supported	Provided by PaaS
Servers and VMs	Multiple vendors are supported	Provided by PaaS
Storage	Multiple vendors are supported	Provided by PaaS

The Infrastructure-As-a-Service Model

In the traditional hosted application model, the vendor provides the entire infrastructure for a customer to run his applications. Often, this entails housing dedicated hardware that is purchased or leased for that specific application. The IaaS model also provides the infrastructure to run the applications, but the cloud computing approach makes it possible to offer a pay-per-use model and to scale the service depending on demand. From the IaaS provider's perspective, it can build an infrastructure that handles the peaks and troughs of its customers' demands and add new capacity as the overall demand increases. Similarly, in a hosted application model, the IaaS vendor can cover application hosting only, or can extend to other services (such as application support, application development, and enhancements) and can support the more comprehensive outsourcing of IT.

The IaaS model is similar to utility computing, in which the basic idea is to offer computing services in the same way as utilities. That is, you pay for the amount of processing power, disk space, and so on that you actually consume. IaaS is typically a service associated with cloud computing and refers to online services that abstract the user from the details of infrastructure, including physical computing resources, location, data partitioning, scaling, security, backup, and so on. In cloud computing, the provider is in complete control of the infrastructure. Utility computing users, conversely, seek a service that allows them to deploy, manage, and scale online services using the provider's resources and pay for resources the customer consumes. However, the customer wants to be in control of the geographic location of the infrastructure and what runs on each server.

Features available for a typical IaaS system include:

Scalability
> The ability to scale infrastructure requirements, such as computing resources, memory, and storage (in near-real-time speeds) based on usage requirements

Pay as you go
> The ability to purchase the exact amount of infrastructure required at any specific time

Best-of-breed technology and resources
> Access to best-of-breed technology solutions and superior IT talent for a fraction of the cost

Cloud Deployment Models

The term *cloud* is a metaphor for the Internet and is a simplified representation of the complex, internetworked devices and connections that form the Internet. Private and public clouds are subsets of the Internet and are defined based on their relationship to the enterprise. Private and public clouds may also be referred to as *internal* or *external* clouds; the differentiation is based on the relationship of the cloud to the enterprise.

The public and private cloud concepts are important because they support cloud computing, which enables the provisioning of dynamic, scalable, virtualized resources over Internet connections by a vendor or an enterprise IT organization to customers for a fee. The end users who use the services offered via cloud computing may not have knowledge of, expertise in, or control over the technology infrastructure that supports them.

The majority of cloud computing infrastructure consists of reliable services delivered through data centers and built on servers with different levels of virtualization technologies. The services are accessible anywhere that access to networking infrastructure is available. The cloud appears as a single point of access for all consumer computing needs. Commercial offerings should meet the quality of service requirements of customers and typically offer service-level agreements (SLAs). Open standards are critical to the growth of cloud computing, and open source software has provided the foundation for many cloud computing implementations (e.g., the use of Xen in AWS).

Public Clouds

Public clouds (or external clouds) describe cloud computing in the traditional mainstream sense, whereby resources are dynamically provisioned on a fine-grained, self-service basis over the Internet, via web applications or web services, from an off-site, third-party provider who shares resources and bills on a fine-grained, utility-computing basis.

A public cloud is hosted, operated, and managed by a third-party vendor from one or more data centers. The service is offered to multiple customers (the cloud is offered to multiple tenants) over a common infrastructure; see Figure 2-8.

In a public cloud, security management and day-to-day operations are relegated to the third-party vendor, who is responsible for the public cloud service offering. Hence, the customer of the public cloud service offering has a low degree of control and oversight of the physical and logical security aspects of a private cloud.

Private Clouds

Private clouds and *internal clouds* are terms used to describe offerings that emulate cloud computing on private networks. These (typically virtualization automation) products claim to deliver some benefits of cloud computing without the pitfalls, capitalizing on data security, corporate governance, and reliability concerns. Organizations must buy, build, and manage them and, as such, do not benefit from lower upfront capital costs and less hands-on management. The organizational customer for a private cloud is responsible for the operation of his private cloud.

FIGURE 2-8. Public cloud

Private clouds differ from public clouds in that the network, computing, and storage infrastructure associated with private clouds is dedicated to a single organization and is not shared with any other organizations (i.e., the cloud is dedicated to a single organizational tenant). As such, a variety of private cloud patterns have emerged:

Dedicated

Private clouds hosted within a customer-owned data center or at a collocation facility, and operated by internal IT departments

Community

Private clouds located at the premises of a third party; owned, managed, and operated by a vendor who is bound by custom SLAs and contractual clauses with security and compliance requirements

Managed

Private cloud infrastructure owned by a customer and managed by a vendor

In general, in a private cloud operating model, the security management and day-to-day operation of hosts are relegated to internal IT or to a third party with contractual SLAs. By virtue of this direct governance model, a customer of a private cloud should have a high degree of control and oversight of the physical and logical security aspects of the private cloud infrastructure—both the hypervisor and the hosted virtualized OSs. With that high degree of control and transparency, it is easier for a customer to comply with established corporate security standards, policies, and regulatory compliance.

Hybrid Clouds

A hybrid cloud environment consisting of multiple internal and/or external providers is a possible deployment for organizations. With a hybrid cloud, organizations might run non-core applications in a public cloud, while maintaining core applications and sensitive data in-house in a private cloud (see Figure 2-9).

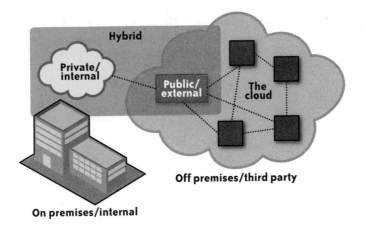

FIGURE 2-9. Hybrid cloud

Figure 2-10 lists some examples of CSPs.

	Cloud providers	What they offer	Target cloud product segment	
	Amazon AWS	Cloud-based infrastructure hosting including storage, Virtual Private Clouds (VPC)	Infrastructure-as-a-service	Service-centric
	Salesforce AppExchange	Cloud-based application hosting	Platform-as-a-service	
Established organizations	IBM	Cloud infrastructure hosting and related value-added services	Cloud infrastructure	Products and services
	Microsoft	Cloud-based software platform	Application development platform	
	Sun	Cloud infrastructure hosting and related value-added services	Cloud infrastructure	
	Engine Yard	Platform to run Ruby on Rails applications	Platform-as-a-service	Niche services
New entrants	FlexiScale	Cloud hosting platform similar to Amazon's EC2 platform – aimed towards start-ups	Infrastructure-as-a-service	
	CohesiveFT	Offers a cloud-based VPN security solution	Cloud security management service	Niche management services
	RightScale	Cloud management platform; capable of managing cloud infrastructure from multiple providers	Clound infrastructure management service	

FIGURE 2-10. CSP examples and their respective offerings

Services provided through the integration of cloud components are evolving, barriers are being overcome, and enablers are being developed. A major concern is to trust that a company's or an individual's information is both secure and private. Establishing this trust is a major milestone in the adoption of the full range of cloud computing; see the next section for more details.

Key Drivers to Adopting the Cloud

This section further articulates the cloud's impact on IT users. To compare client/server computing and cloud computing, Table 2-3 illustrates some of the benefits cloud computing offers: lower IT costs, faster time to go live, and reduced complexity. However, with cloud computing it is critical to understand how to integrate the cloud solution into existing enterprise architecture.

TABLE 2-3. Cloud computing: A customer's perspective

Dedicated/traditional IT	Cloud computing
High upfront IT investments for new builds	Low upfront IT investments; pay-for-use model
High cost of reliable infrastructure	Reliability built into the cloud architecture
High complexity of IT environment	Modular IT architecture environments
Complex infrastructure	No infrastructure

The following subsections describe a number of compelling reasons to move operations toward cloud computing.

Small Initial Investment and Low Ongoing Costs

Public cloud computing can avoid capital expenditures because no hardware, software, or network devices need to be purchased. Cloud usage is billed on actual use only, and is therefore treated more as an expense. In turn, usage-based billing lowers the barrier to entry because the upfront costs are minimal. Depending on the contract being signed, most companies can terminate the contract as preferred; therefore, in times of hardship or escalating costs, cloud computing costs can be managed very efficiently.

Economies of Scale

Most development projects have a sizing phase during which one attempts to calculate the storage, processing power, and memory requirements during development, testing, and production. It is often difficult to make accurate estimates; under- or overestimating these calculations is typical. The lead time for acquiring the equipment to support these estimates can sometimes be lengthy, thus adding to the time necessary to complete the project. With the flexibility that cloud computing solutions offer, companies can acquire computing and development services as needed and on demand, which means development projects are less at risk of missing deadlines and dealing with the unknown.

Open Standards

Some capabilities in cloud computing are based on open standards for building a modular architecture that can grow rapidly and can change when required. Open source software is defined as computer software that is governed by a software license in the public domain, or that meets the definition of *open source*, which allows users to use, change, and improve the software. The flexibility to alter the source code is essential to allow for continued growth in the cloud solution. Open source software is the foundation of the cloud solution and is critical to its continued growth.

Sustainability

CSPs have invested considerable expense and thought into creating a resilient architecture that can provide a highly stable environment. Traditionally, companies have periodically struggled to maintain IT services due either to single points of failure in the network or to an inability to keep pace with business changes in both volume and the nature of transactions. Cloud computing allows companies to rely on the CSP to have limited points of failure, better resilience via clustering, and the ability to invest in state-of-the-art resilience solutions.

The Impact of Cloud Computing on Users

This section describes the impact of cloud computing on different types of users:

- Individual consumers
- Individual businesses
- Start-ups
- Small and medium-size businesses (SMBs)
- Enterprise businesses

Individual Consumers

Many computer-savvy individuals today are already major users of cloud computing. Although PCs have their own storage, they rely on cloud computing providers for many of their storage and computing requirements.

Any reasonably savvy computer user stores personal email in the cloud, stores photos in the cloud, buys music from a CSP, stores profiles and information to support collaboration on social networking sites (e.g., Facebook, LinkedIn, MySpace), finds driving and walking directions in the cloud, develops websites in the cloud, and collaborates with others in the cloud (we used Google Sites while writing this book). Consumers may arrange tennis games and golf tee times, track adherence to fitness programs, make purchases, perform searches, make phone calls, communicate via video, and search the Internet to learn the latest news, determine the origin of a quotation, or find the profile of a new acquaintance. Tax returns are now prepared through the cloud and stored in the cloud. A tremendous amount of personal data resides in the cloud. Many of the terms and conditions that we routinely accept present privacy risks that could be a concern to individuals. Of course, there is also the concern of accidental loss, or fraudulent access unauthorized by a CSP.

The focus of this book is not consumer cloud computing; however, current consumer use predicts the expectations for technology from consumers who are expected to become organizational users.

Individual Businesses

Inspired by the low entry costs for cloud services, technically savvy consumers are now using cloud-based tools to develop their businesses. The expectation is that software should be nearly free of charge, and that users should pay only for additional services or some extra capacity. Consumers can host a website to attract customers, use eBay or Craigslist to sell and market individual items, use virtual marketing to spread the word, place ads with search engine providers, engage with online banks to manage funds, supervise online accountancy services to manage finances, and use office assistants to book trips and arrange appointments. All of this computing power can reside in the cloud.

Start-ups

When a business owner starts up a new business, he wants to set up operation in a scalable, flexible fashion. Building an IT department is a low priority compared to marketing the product, investing in research and development, or securing the next round of funding. In the past, a mature IT infrastructure was a sign that a start-up company was ready for an initial public offering (IPO). A company would demonstrate scalability by implementing a robust enterprise resource planning (ERP) solution and hosting it on the premises. Currently, a more common approach is to outsource the majority of IT and maintain a lean IT shop. The challenge now becomes getting locked into provider contracts and the levels of service that the CSP will face. Critical success factors are the ability to scale the infrastructure as volume increases, and rapidly modify the service for new product lines, channels, markets, or business models. One potential model is a mixed model based on the classic definition of *core* and *context*, with control for context maintained internally. The evolution depends on the interoperability across platforms that are internal or are in the cloud. Start-ups have less legacy data and fewer processes and applications than established companies, and they pioneer some of the cloud computing services for an integrated business.

Small and Medium-Size Businesses (SMBs)

There may be as many definitions of *SMB* as there are definitions of *cloud computing*. Often, the SMB category is defined by revenue, but when discussing technology requirements, it's equally important to think about the number of products, number of channels, countries of operation, and integration of the supply chain with third parties. In short, saying something is a "small business" is a measure of the business's complexity. Many small businesses grow through acquisition, or are born as a spin-off from a larger business. The SMB age is a critical component in understanding the maturity and entrenchment of legacy processes and data. The requirements for data security and privacy are no less onerous than for a larger enterprise. One generalization about SMBs is that their IT departments are smaller, and are therefore less diverse in skills and knowledge, than those of larger enterprise businesses. Significant IT projects can become difficult to justify and investment in IT can decline, IT infrastructure becomes outdated, and the IT group can have difficulty responding to business needs in a timely manner. Decision making in an SMB is often concentrated among fewer individuals than in a larger enterprise. Depending on the specific scenario, the SMB environment has some essential characteristics that can accelerate growth in the broad use of cloud computing. We may see complex SMBs as the vanguard of cloud computing with no in-house infrastructure and IT services delivered from a combination of CSPs.

Enterprise Businesses

Mature enterprise businesses are broadening their use of cloud-enabled computing. At a minimum, this could mean allowing users to access services beyond the corporate firewall. Broader usage of cloud services includes using knowledge tools to support personal productivity, such as online research or travel services. Companies may use corporate applications, such as employee work surveys that use the company's directory to populate broad characteristics but that don't include personally identifiable information. Mature businesses adopting cloud computing may also use cloud applications in business-critical departments and functions, such as Salesforce.com applications, document management, purchasing, and logistics. In these cases, the users access applications and store in the cloud data that includes personal and sensitive information. In evaluating an application run in-house or a cloud-based service, security and privacy concerns could trump costs. An important consideration is redundancy of data between the CSP and the traditional enterprise applications. Vendor lock-in to a proprietary architecture or solution would kill the cost, flexibility, and extensibility arguments. The compelling argument for a cloud solution is time to market, where a cloud application is the only feasible alternative, given cost and time constraints.

Governance in the Cloud

Figure 2-11* illustrates the impact of cloud computing on the governance structure of IT organizations. Traditionally, most IT organizations govern the five technology layers shown in the figure. The two on-premises models indicate that IT has total control over (and responsibility for) all five technology layers. However, as we move from IaaS to PaaS to SaaS, the IT organization's level of control diminishes and the CSP's level of control increases. However, although control increases for the CSP, responsibility remains with the IT organization. It is critical for IT organizations to develop strong monitoring frameworks over the SPI delivery model to ensure that their service levels and contractual obligations are met.

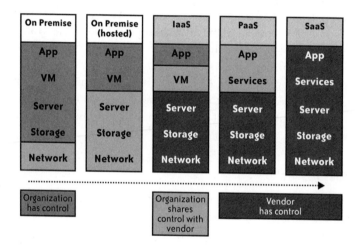

FIGURE 2-11. Impact of cloud computing on the governance structure of IT organizations

Barriers to Cloud Computing Adoption in the Enterprise

Although there are many benefits to adopting cloud computing, there are also some significant barriers to adoption. Two of the most significant barriers to adoption are security and privacy, and we discuss them extensively in the following chapters. However, it is important to at least call out what some of the other barriers to adoption are, and we discuss those in the following sections. The other barriers, besides security and privacy, are significant, but are outside the scope of this book.

---

* Governance in the Public Cloud © Dan Blum, "Cloud Computing Security in the Enterprise," Burton Group, Inc., July 2009; 12.

Security

Because cloud computing represents a new computing model, there is a great deal of uncertainty about how security at all levels (e.g., network, host, application, and data levels) can be achieved. That uncertainty has consistently led information executives to state that security is their number one concern with cloud computing. The subsequent chapters present a detailed examination of those concerns to determine whether they are grounded.

Privacy

The ability of cloud computing to adequately address privacy regulations has been called into question. Organizations today face numerous different requirements attempting to protect the privacy of individuals' information, and it is not clear (i.e., not yet established) whether the cloud computing model provides adequate protection of such information, or whether organizations will be found in violation of regulations because of this new model.

Connectivity and Open Access

The full potential of cloud computing depends on the availability of high-speed access to all. Such connectivity, rather like electricity availability, globally opens the possibility for industry and a new range of consumer products. Connectivity and open access to computing power and information availability through the cloud promotes another era of industrialization and the need for more sophisticated consumer products.

Reliability

Enterprise applications are now so critical that they must be reliable and available to support 24/7 operations. In the event of failure or outages, contingency plans must take effect smoothly, and for disastrous or catastrophic failure, recovery plans must begin with minimum disruption. (See the Cloud Computing Incidents Database at *http://wiki.cloudcommunity.org/wiki/ CloudComputing:Incidents_Database*.) Each aspect of reliability should be carefully considered when engaging with a CSP, negotiated as part of the SLA, and tested in failover drills. Additional costs may be associated with the required levels of reliability; however, the business can do only so much to mitigate risks and the cost of a failure. Establishing a track record of reliability will be a prerequisite for widespread adoption.

Interoperability

The interoperability and portability of information between private clouds and public clouds are critical enablers for broad adoption of cloud computing by the enterprise. Many companies have made considerable progress toward standardizing their processes, data, and systems through implementation of ERPs. This process has been enabled by scalable infrastructures to create single instances, or highly integrated connections between instances, to manage the consistency of master and transaction data and produce reliable consolidated information. Even with these improved platforms, the speed at which businesses change may still outpace the ability of IT organizations to respond to these changes. SaaS applications delivered through the cloud provide a low-capital, fast-deployment option. Depending on the application, it is critical to integrate with traditional applications that may be resident in a separate cloud or on traditional technology. The standard for interoperability is either an enabler or a barrier to interoperability, and permits maintenance of the integrity and consistency of a company's information and processes.

Independence from CSPs

Examples exist of IT outsourcing contracts that have effectively locked a customer into a service that does not meet current or evolving needs at a speed and cost that are acceptable to meet business goals. This could be caused by a number of factors, and is a concern if limited options exist for quickly engaging an alternative provider supplier to meet the needs without large transition or penalty costs. A CSP may hold valuable data and business rules that cannot be easily migrated to a new provider. Standards to enable migration and plug and play of cloud components can help. For example, companies today depend less on the browser provider, but may depend on a proprietary data-based structure. Separating storage IaaS providers from processing providers can help with provider flexibility. There are downsides to going to a componentized approach, because the customer may become the integrator of these services. However, these may be the skills that enterprises should develop to balance the scalability of cloud computing with acceptable price performance and risk.

Economic Value

The growth of cloud computing is predicated on the return on investment that accrues. It seems intuitive that by sharing resources to smooth out peaks, paying only for what is used, and cutting upfront capital investment in deploying IT solutions, the economic value will be there. There will be a need to carefully balance all costs and benefits associated with cloud computing—in both the short and long terms. Hidden costs could include support, disaster recovery, application modification, and data loss insurance. There will be threshold values whereby consolidating investments or combining cloud services makes sense; for example, it might not be efficient or cost-effective to utilize multiple autonomous SaaS applications. Each may contract for disaster recovery program services. There is a point where economies of scale mean these functions should be combined in a similar service. Application usage may begin with a low volume of transactions that can be supported with semi-automated master data management. As usage expands and interoperability requirements for the business process become more onerous, a new approach is needed. This evolution may be the most cost-effective approach; however, there is a risk that the business transition costs from one solution to another may change the cost and benefit equation, and hence the solution that should be employed.

IT Governance

Economic value is an aspect of IT governance. Effective governance processes that align IT and the business are critical to set the appropriate context for making investment decisions and to balance short-term and long-term needs.

Changes in the IT Organization

The IT organization will be affected by cloud computing, as has been the case with other technology shifts. There are two dimensions to shifts in technology. The first is acquiring the new skill sets to deploy the technology in the context of solving a business problem, and the second is how the technology changes the IT role. During the COBOL era, users rarely programmed, the expectations of the user interface varied, and the adaptability of the solution was low. Training was delivered in separate manuals and the user used the computer to solve problems only down predefined paths. With the advent of fourth-generation languages, roles within IT, such as system analyst and programmer, became merged into analyst/programmer, users started to write their own reports, and new applications, including operational data stores, data entry, and query programs, could be rapidly deployed in weeks. IT's role will change once again (as we discuss in Chapter 12): the speed of change will impact the adoption of cloud technologies and the ability to decompose mature solutions from hype to deliver real value from cloud technology; and the need to maintain the controls to manage IT risk in the business will increase.

Political Issues Due to Global Boundaries

In the cloud computing world, there is variability in terms of where the physical data resides, where processing takes place, and from where the data is accessed. Given this variability, different privacy rules and regulations may apply. Because of these varying rules and regulations, by definition politics becomes an element in the adoption of cloud computing, which is effectively multijurisdictional.

For cloud computing to continually evolve into a borderless and global tool, it needs to be separated from politics. Currently, some major global technological and political powers are making laws that can have a negative impact on the development of the global cloud. For example, as a result of the USA Patriot Act, Canada has recently asked that its government not use computers in the global network that are operating within U.S. borders, fearing for the confidentiality and privacy of the Canadian data stored on those computers. Cloud computing depends largely on global politics to survive. Imagine if the telecommunications companies in the United States get their way and do away with the current Internet standard of network neutrality completely. Having data throttled and information filtered goes against the basic concept of cloud computing and global knowledge. You can't have a working cloud of information and services to draw from and build on if someone or something is constantly manipulating the data held within it, or worse, if something is blocking it from your view to achieve a hidden agenda. Politics are affecting the scalability of the Internet, the availability of Internet access, the free flow of information, and the cloud-based global economy on a daily basis. We already know the concept works; it was instrumental in crunching the massive amounts of data needed to complete the Human Genome Project. That project has netted answers to the question of where hundreds of diseases and traits come from, and would not have been possible in such a short time without the computer sharing allowed by cloud computing and available via the Internet.

Summary

With all of the hype around cloud computing, and multiple definitions of cloud computing, it is difficult to discern exactly what constitutes "cloud computing." This problem is made more difficult as vendors rush to claim that they are now cloud computing companies, or at least "cloud-friendly." Suddenly, the entire technology sector has become "cloudy"—similar to the dot-com stampede of the late 1990s. In this chapter, we attempted to provide some basic information on the now-standard delivery model, SPI, and types of clouds. We also provided information on some of the benefits of using cloud computing, as well as some of the barriers to adoption. The goal here was to ensure that the reader has a basic understanding of how we define cloud computing and what we view as its benefits to more fully discuss security, privacy, and audit considerations in the following chapters.

CHAPTER THREE

Infrastructure Security

IN THIS CHAPTER, WE DISCUSS THE THREATS, CHALLENGES, AND GUIDANCE ASSOCIATED with securing an organization's core IT infrastructure at the network, host, and application levels. Information security practitioners commonly use this approach; therefore, it is readily familiar to them. We discuss this infrastructure security in the context of SPI service delivery models (SaaS, PaaS, and IaaS). Non-information security professionals are cautioned not to simply equate infrastructure security to infrastructure-as-a-service (IaaS) security. Although infrastructure security is more highly relevant to customers of IaaS, similar consideration should be given to providers' platform-as-a-service (PaaS) and software-as-a-service (SaaS) environments, since they have ramifications to your customer threat, risk, and compliance management. Another dimension is the cloud business model (public, private, and hybrid clouds), which is orthogonal to the SPI service delivery model; what we highlight is the relevance of discussion points as they apply to public and private clouds. When discussing public clouds the scope of infrastructure security is limited to the layers of infrastructure that move beyond the organization's control and into the hands of service providers (i.e., when responsibility to a secure infrastructure is transferred to the cloud service provider or CSP, based on the SPI delivery model). Information in this chapter is critical for customers in gaining an understanding of what security a CSP provides and what security you, the customer, are responsible for providing.

Infrastructure Security: The Network Level

When looking at the network level of infrastructure security, it is important to distinguish between public clouds and private clouds, as we explained in Chapter 2. With private clouds, there are no new attacks, vulnerabilities, or changes in risk *specific to this topology* that information security personnel need to consider. Although your organization's IT architecture may change with the implementation of a private cloud, your current network topology will probably not change significantly. If you have a private extranet in place (e.g., for premium customers or strategic partners), for practical purposes you probably have the network topology for a private cloud in place already. The security considerations you have today apply to a private cloud infrastructure, too. And the security tools you have in place (or should have in place) are also necessary for a private cloud and operate in the same way. Figure 3-1 shows the topological similarities between a secure extranet and a private cloud.

However, if you choose to use public cloud services, changing security requirements will require changes to your network topology. You must address how your existing network topology interacts with your cloud provider's network topology. There are four significant risk factors in this use case:

- Ensuring the confidentiality and integrity of your organization's data-in-transit to and from your public cloud provider
- Ensuring proper access control (authentication, authorization, and auditing) to whatever resources you are using at your public cloud provider
- Ensuring the availability of the Internet-facing resources in a public cloud that are being used by your organization, or have been assigned to your organization by your public cloud providers
- Replacing the established model of network zones and tiers with domains

We will discuss each of these risk factors in the sections that follow.

Ensuring Data Confidentiality and Integrity

Some resources and data previously confined to a private network are now exposed to the Internet, and to a shared public network belonging to a third-party cloud provider.

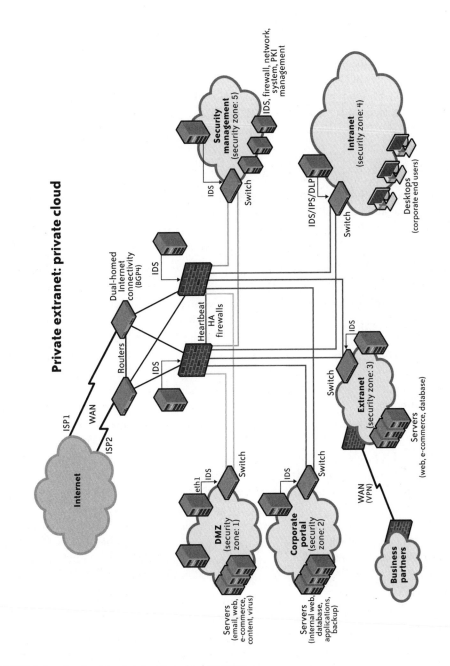

FIGURE 3-1. Generic network topology for private cloud computing

An example of problems associated with this first risk factor is an Amazon Web Services (AWS) security vulnerability reported in December 2008.* In a blog post, the author detailed a flaw in the digital signature algorithm used when "... making Query (aka REST) requests to Amazon SimpleDB, to Amazon Elastic Compute Cloud (EC2), or to Amazon Simple Queue Service (SQS) over HTTP." Although use of HTTPS (instead of HTTP) would have mitigated the integrity risk, users not using HTTPS (but using HTTP) did face an increased risk that their data could have been altered in transit without their knowledge.

Ensuring Proper Access Control

Since some subset of these resources (or maybe even all of them) is now exposed to the Internet, an organization using a public cloud faces a significant increase in risk to its data. The ability to audit the operations of your cloud provider's network (let alone to conduct any real-time monitoring, such as on your own network), even after the fact, is probably non-existent. You will have decreased access to relevant network-level logs and data, and a limited ability to thoroughly conduct investigations and gather forensic data.

An example of the problems associated with this second risk factor is the issue of reused (reassigned) IP addresses. Generally speaking, cloud providers do not sufficiently "age" IP addresses when they are no longer needed for one customer. Addresses are usually reassigned and reused by other customers as they become available. From a cloud provider's perspective this makes sense. IP addresses are a finite quantity and a billable asset. However, from a customer's security perspective, the persistence of IP addresses that are no longer in use can present a problem. A customer can't assume that network access to its resources is terminated upon release of its IP address. There is necessarily a lag time between the change of an IP address in DNS and the clearing of that address in DNS caches. There is a similar lag time between when physical (i.e., MAC) addresses are changed in ARP tables and when old ARP addresses are cleared from cache; an old address persists in ARP caches until they are cleared. This means that even though addresses might have been changed, the (now) old addresses are still available in cache, and therefore they still allow users to reach these supposedly non-existent resources. Recently, there were many reports of problems with "non-aged" IP addresses at one of the largest cloud providers; this was likely an impetus for an AWS announcement of the Amazon Elastic IP capabilities in March 2008.† (With Elastic IP addresses, customers are given a block of five routable IP addresses over which they control assignment.) Additionally, according to Simson Garfinkel:

---

* This issue was reported on the blog of Colin Percival, "Daemonic Dispatches," on December 18, 2008. See "AWS signature version 1 is insecure" (*http://www.daemonology.net/blog/2008-12-18-AWS-signature -version-1-is-insecure.html*). There was no public acknowledgment of this issue on the AWS website, nor any public response to Percival's blog posting.

† See "Announcing Elastic IP Addresses and Availability Zones for Amazon EC2" (*http://aws.amazon.com/ about-aws/whats-new/2008/03/26/announcing-elastic-ip-addresses-and-availability-zones-for-amazon-ec2/*). Though announced in March 2009, the Elastic IP service became available October 22, 2008.

A separate ongoing problem with the load balancers causes them to terminate any TCP/IP connection that contains more than 2^{31} bytes. This means that objects larger than 2GB must be stored to S3 in several individual transactions, with each of those transactions referring to different byte ranges of the same object.[‡]

However, the issue of "non-aged" IP addresses and unauthorized network access to resources does not apply only to routable IP addresses (i.e., resources intended to be reachable directly from the Internet). The issue also applies to cloud providers' internal networks for customer use and the assignment of non-routable IP addresses.[§] Although your resources may not be directly reachable from the Internet, for management purposes your resources must be accessible within the cloud provider's network via private addressing. (Every public/Internet-facing resource also has a private address.) Other customers of your cloud provider may not be well intentioned and might be able to reach your resources internally via the cloud provider's networks.[||] As reported in *The Washington Post*, AWS has had problems with abuses of its resources affecting the public and other customers.[#]

Some products emerging onto the market[*] will help alleviate the problem of IP address reuse, but unless cloud providers offer these products as managed services, customers are paying for yet another third-party product to solve a problem that their cloud provider's practices created for them.

Ensuring the Availability of Internet-Facing Resources

Reliance on network security has increased because an increased amount of data or an increased number of organizational personnel now depend on externally hosted devices to ensure the availability of cloud-provided resources. Consequently, the three risk factors enumerated in the preceding section must be acceptable to your organization.

BGP[†] prefix hijacking (i.e., the falsification of Network Layer Reachability Information) provides a good example of this third risk factor. Prefix hijacking involves announcing an

[‡] See Section 3.3, "An Evaluation of Amazon's Grid Computing Services: EC2, S3 and SQS," by Simson L. Garfinkel; TR-08-07, Computer Science Group, Harvard University, Cambridge, Massachusetts.

[§] See RFC 1918, "Address Allocation for Private Internets," for further information.

[||] For example, see "Instance Addressing and Network Security" in the *Amazon Elastic Compute Cloud Developer Guide* (API Version 2008-12-01).

[#] "Amazon: Hey Spammers, Get Off My Cloud!" reported in *The Washington Post*, July 1, 2008.

[*] An example is CohesiveFT's VPN-Cubed, but this product is not available as a cloud provider service from most cloud providers—which would mean yet another third-party solution to integrate into your cloud environment. However, cloud provider AWS does offer this product as a service.

[†] Border Gateway Protocol is an interdomain routing protocol used in the core of the Internet. You can find more information about BGP in RFC 4271, "A Border Gateway Protocol 4 (BGP-4)."

autonomous system‡ address space that belongs to someone else without her permission. Such announcements often occur because of a configuration mistake, but that misconfiguration may still affect the availability of your cloud-based resources. According to a study presented to the North American Network Operators Group (NANOG) in February 2006, several hundred such misconfigurations occur per month.§ Probably the best known example of such a misconfiguration mistake occurred in February 2008 when Pakistan Telecom made an error by announcing a dummy route for YouTube to its own telecommunications partner, PCCW, based in Hong Kong. The intent was to block YouTube within Pakistan because of some supposedly blasphemous videos hosted on the site. The result was that YouTube was *globally* unavailable for two hours.‖

In addition to misconfigurations, there are deliberate attacks as well. Although prefix hijacking due to deliberate attacks is far less common than misconfigurations, it still occurs and can block access to data. According to the same study presented to NANOG, attacks occur fewer than 100 times per month. Although prefix hijackings are not new, that attack figure will certainly rise, and probably significantly, along with a rise in cloud computing. As the use of cloud computing increases, the availability of cloud-based resources increases in value to customers. That increased value to customers translates to an increased risk of malicious activity to threaten that availability.

DNS# attacks are another example of problems associated with this third risk factor. In fact, there are several forms of DNS attacks to worry about with regard to cloud computing. Although DNS attacks are not new and are not directly related to the use of cloud computing, the issue with DNS and cloud computing is an increase in an organization's risk at the network level because of increased external DNS querying (reducing the effectiveness of "split horizon" DNS configurations*) along with some increased number of organizational personnel being more dependent on network security to ensure the availability of cloud-provided resources being used.

‡ According to RFC 1930, "Guidelines for Creation, Selection, and Registration of an Autonomous System (AS)," an autonomous system is a connected group of one or more IP prefixes run by one or more network operators that has a single and clearly defined routing policy.

§ See "Short-Lived Prefix Hijacking on the Internet" by Peter Boothe, James Hiebert, and Randy Bush, presented at NANOG 36 in February 2006.

‖ For example, see "Pakistan Cuts Access to YouTube Worldwide" in *The New York Times*, February 26, 2008.

DNS stands for Domain Name System. See RFCs 1034, "Domain Names—Concepts and Facilities," and 1035, "Domain Names—Implementation and Specification."

* That is not to say that internal DNS systems are entirely free of attacks—just that they are safer than external DNS systems and queries using them. For example, see the paper "Corrupted DNS Resolution Paths: The Rise of a Malicious Resolution Authority," written by members of the faculty of the Georgia Institute of Technology.

Although the "Kaminsky Bug"[†] (CVE-2008-1447, "DNS Insufficient Socket Entropy Vulnerability") garnered most of the network security attention in 2008, other DNS problems impact cloud computing as well. Not only are there vulnerabilities in the DNS protocol and in implementations of DNS,[‡] but also there are fairly widespread DNS cache poisoning attacks whereby a DNS server is tricked into accepting incorrect information. Although many people thought DNS cache poisoning attacks had been quashed several years ago, that is not true, and these attacks are still very much a problem—especially in the context of cloud computing. Variants of this basic cache poisoning attack include redirecting the target domain's name server (NS), redirecting the NS record to another target domain, and responding before the real NS (called *DNS forgery*).

A final example of problems associated with this third risk factor is denial of service (DoS) and distributed denial of service (DDoS) attacks. Again, although DoS/DDoS attacks are not new and are not directly related to the use of cloud computing, the issue with these attacks and cloud computing is an increase in an organization's risk at the network level because of some increased use of resources external to your organization's network. For example, there continue to be rumors of continued DDoS attacks on AWS, making the services unavailable for hours at a time to AWS users.[§] (Amazon has not acknowledged that service interruptions are in fact due to DDoS attacks.)

However, when using IaaS, the risk of a DDoS attack is not only external (i.e., Internet-facing). There is also the risk of an internal DDoS attack through the portion of the IaaS provider's network used by customers (separate from the IaaS provider's corporate network). That internal (non-routable) network is a shared resource, used by customers for access to their non-public instances (e.g., Amazon Machine Images or AMIs) as well as by the provider for management of its network and resources (such as physical servers). If I were a rogue customer, there would be nothing to prevent me from using my customer access to this internal network to find and attack other customers, or the IaaS provider's infrastructure—and the provider would probably not have any detective controls in place to even notify it of such an attack. The only preventive controls other customers would have would be how hardened their instances (e.g., AMIs) are, and whether they are taking advantage of a provider's capabilities to firewall off groups of instances (e.g., AWS).

[†] The Kaminsky Bug was named after the security researcher who discovered the problem, Dan Kaminsky of IOActive. A good non-technical explanation of the bug and of attempts to mitigate it through efforts with the vendor community is available in the article "Fresh Phish," published in the October 2008 issue of IEEE's *Spectrum* magazine.

[‡] For example, see US-CERT Vulnerability Note VU#800113, "Multiple DNS implementations vulnerable to cache poisoning." As of December 31, 2008, the National Vulnerability Database lists 312 vulnerabilities for the DNS protocol and implementations of DNS. The National Vulnerability Database is sponsored by the U.S. Department of Homeland Security's US-CERT, and NIST.

[§] For example, see "Rumor: Amazon Hit With Denial-of-Service Attack, Again," posted June 6, 2008 at *http://www.appscout.com/2008/06/rumor_amazon_hit_with_denialof.php*.

Replacing the Established Model of Network Zones and Tiers with Domains

The established isolation model of network zones and tiers no longer exists in the public IaaS and PaaS clouds. For years, network security has relied on zones, such as intranet versus extranet and development versus production, to segregate network traffic for improved security. This model was based on exclusion—only individuals and systems in specific roles have access to specific zones. Similarly, systems within a specific tier often have only specific access within or across a specific tier. For example, systems within a presentation tier are not allowed to communicate directly with systems in the database tier, but can communicate only with an authorized system within the application zone. SaaS clouds built on public IaaS or PaaS clouds have similar characteristics. However, a public SaaS built on a private IaaS (e.g., Salesforce.com) may follow the traditional isolation model, but that topology information is not typically shared with customers.

The traditional model of network zones and tiers has been replaced in public cloud computing with "security groups," "security domains," or "virtual data centers" that have logical separation between tiers but are less precise and afford less protection than the formerly established model. For example, the security groups feature in AWS allows your virtual machines (VMs) to access each other using a virtual firewall that has the ability to filter traffic based on IP address (a specific address or a subnet), packet types (TCP, UDP, or ICMP), and ports (or a range of ports). Domain names are used in various networking contexts and application-specific naming and addressing purposes, based on DNS. For example, Google's App Engine provides a logical grouping of applications based on domain names such as *mytestapp.test.mydomain.com* and *myprodapp.prod.mydomain.com*.

In the established model of network zones and tiers, not only were development systems logically separated from production systems at the network level, but these two groups of systems were also physically separated at the host level (i.e., they ran on physically separated servers in logically separated network zones). With cloud computing, however, this separation no longer exists. The cloud computing model of separation by domains provides logical separation for addressing purposes only. There is no longer any "required" physical separation, as a test domain and a production domain may very well be on the same physical server. Furthermore, the former logical network separation no longer exists; logical separation now is at the host level with both domains running on the same physical server and being separated only logically by VM monitors (hypervisors).

Network-Level Mitigation

Given the factors discussed in the preceding sections, what can you do to mitigate these increased risk factors? First, note that network-level risks exist regardless of what aspects of "cloud computing" services are being used (e.g., software-as-a-service, platform-as-a-service, or infrastructure-as-a-service). The primary determination of risk level is therefore not which *aaS is being used, but rather whether your organization intends to use or is using a public, private, or hybrid cloud. Although some IaaS clouds offer virtual network zoning, they may not match an internal private cloud environment that performs stateful inspection and other network security measures.

If your organization is large enough to afford the resources of a private cloud, your risks will decrease—assuming you have a true private cloud that is internal to your network. In some cases, a private cloud located at a cloud provider's facility can help meet your security requirements but will depend on the provider capabilities and maturity.

You can reduce your confidentiality risks by using encryption; specifically by using validated implementations of cryptography for data-in-transit. Secure digital signatures make it much more difficult, if not impossible, for someone to tamper with your data, and this ensures data integrity.

Availability problems at the network level are far more difficult to mitigate with cloud computing—unless your organization is using a private cloud that is internal to your network topology. Even if your private cloud is a private (i.e., non-shared) external network at a cloud provider's facility, you will face increased risk at the network level. A public cloud faces even greater risk. But let's keep some perspective here—greater than what?

Even large enterprises with significant resources face considerable challenges at the network level of infrastructure security. Are the risks associated with cloud computing actually higher than the risks enterprises are facing today? Consider existing private and public extranets, and take into account partner connections when making such a comparison. For large enterprises without significant resources, or for small to medium-size businesses (SMBs), is the risk of using public clouds (assuming that such enterprises lack the resources necessary for private clouds) really higher than the risks inherent in their current infrastructures? In many cases, the answer is probably no—there is *not* a higher level of risk.

Table 3-1 lists security controls at the network level.

TABLE 3-1. Security controls at the network level

Threat outlook	Low (with the exception of DoS attacks)
Preventive controls	Network access control supplied by provider (e.g., firewall), encryption of data in transit (e.g., SSL, IPSec)
Detective controls	Provider-managed aggregation of security event logs (security incident and event management, or SIEM), network-based intrusion detection system/intrusion prevention system (IDS/IPS)

NOTE
Since detective capabilities will vary from provider to provider, customers should assess providers for the equipped capabilities.

Infrastructure Security: The Host Level

When reviewing host security and assessing risks, you should consider the context of cloud services delivery models (SaaS, PaaS, and IaaS) and deployment models (public, private, and hybrid). Although there are no known new threats to hosts that are specific to cloud computing, some virtualization security threats—such as VM escape, system configuration drift, and insider threats by way of weak access control to the hypervisor—carry into the public cloud computing environment. The dynamic nature (elasticity) of cloud computing can bring new operational challenges from a security management perspective. The operational model motivates rapid provisioning and fleeting instances of VMs. Managing vulnerabilities and patches is therefore much harder than just running a scan, as the rate of change is much higher than in a traditional data center.

In addition, the fact that the clouds harness the power of thousands of compute nodes, combined with the homogeneity of the operating system employed by hosts, means the threats can be amplified quickly and easily—call it the "velocity of attack" factor in the cloud. More importantly, you should understand the trust boundary and the responsibilities that fall on your shoulders to secure the host infrastructure that you manage. And you should compare the same with providers' responsibilities in securing the part of the host infrastructure the CSP manages.

SaaS and PaaS Host Security

In general, CSPs do not publicly share information related to their host platforms, host operating systems, and the processes that are in place to secure the hosts, since hackers can exploit that information when they are trying to intrude into the cloud service. Hence, in the context of SaaS (e.g., Salesforce.com, Workday.com) or PaaS (e.g., Google App Engine, Salesforce.com's Force.com) cloud services, host security is opaque to customers and the responsibility of securing the hosts is relegated to the CSP. To get assurance from the CSP on the security hygiene of its hosts, you should ask the vendor to share information under a non-disclosure agreement (NDA) or simply demand that the CSP share the information via a controls assessment framework such as SysTrust or ISO 27002. From a controls assurance perspective, the CSP has to ensure that appropriate preventive and detective controls are in place and will have to ensure the same via a third-party assessment or ISO 27002 type assessment framework.

Since virtualization is a key enabling technology that improves host hardware utilization, among other benefits, it is common for CSPs to employ virtualization platforms, including Xen and VMware hypervisors, in their host computing platform architecture. You should understand how the provider is using virtualization technology and the provider's process for securing the virtualization layer.

Both the PaaS and SaaS platforms abstract and hide the host operating system from end users with a host abstraction layer. One key difference between PaaS and SaaS is the accessibility of the abstraction layer that hides the operating system services the applications consume. In the case of SaaS, the abstraction layer is not visible to users and is available only to the developers and the CSP's operations staff, where PaaS users are given indirect access to the host abstraction layer in the form of a PaaS application programming interface (API) that in turn interacts with the host abstraction layer. In short, if you are a SaaS or a PaaS customer, you are relying on the CSP to provide a secure host platform on which the SaaS or PaaS application is developed and deployed by the CSP and you, respectively.

In summary, host security responsibilities in SaaS and PaaS services are transferred to the CSP. The fact that you do not have to worry about protecting hosts from host-based security threats is a major benefit from a security management and cost standpoint. However, as a customer, you still own the risk of managing information hosted in the cloud services. It's your responsibility to get the appropriate level of assurance regarding how the CSP manages host security hygiene.

IaaS Host Security

Unlike PaaS and SaaS, IaaS customers are primarily responsible for securing the hosts provisioned in the cloud. Given that almost all IaaS services available today employ virtualization at the host layer, host security in IaaS should be categorized as follows:

Virtualization software security
>   The software layer that sits on top of bare metal and provides customers the ability to create and destroy virtual instances. Virtualization at the host level can be accomplished using any of the virtualization models, including OS-level virtualization (Solaris containers, BSD jails, Linux-VServer), paravirtualization (a combination of the hardware version and versions of Xen and VMware), or hardware-based virtualization (Xen, VMware, Microsoft Hyper-V). It is important to secure this layer of software that sits between the hardware and the virtual servers. In a public IaaS service, customers do not have access to this software layer; it is managed by the CSP only.

Customer guest OS or virtual server security
>   The virtual instance of an operating system that is provisioned on top of the virtualization layer and is visible to customers from the Internet; e.g., various flavors of Linux, Microsoft, and Solaris. Customers have full access to virtual servers.

Virtualization Software Security

Since the CSP manages the virtualization software that sits on top of the hardware, customers will have neither visibility nor access to this software. Hardware or OS virtualization enables the sharing of hardware resources across multiple guest VMs without interfering with each other so that you can safely run several operating systems and applications at the same time on a single computer. For the purpose of simplicity, we made an assumption that IaaS services are using "bare metal hypervisor" technologies (also known as type 1 hypervisors), such as VMware ESX, Xen, Oracle VM, and Microsoft's Hyper-V. These hypervisors support a variety of guest OSs, including Microsoft Windows, various Linux "flavors," and Sun's OpenSolaris.

Given that hypervisor virtualization is the essential ingredient that guarantees compartmentalization and isolation of customer VMs from each other in a multitenant environment, it is very important to protect the hypervisors from unauthorized users. A new arms race between hacker and defender (CSP) in the realm of virtualization security is already underway. Since virtualization is very critical to the IaaS cloud architecture, any attack that could compromise the integrity of the compartments will be catastrophic to the entire customer base on that cloud. A recent incident at a tiny UK-based company called Vaserv.com exemplifies the threat to hypervisor security. By exploiting a zero-day vulnerability in HyperVM (*http://wiki.whmcs.com/HyperVM*), a virtualization application made by a company called Lxlabs, hackers destroyed 100,000 websites hosted by Vaserv.com. The zero-day vulnerability gave the attackers the ability to execute sensitive Unix commands on the system, including `rm -rf`, which forces a recursive delete of all files. Evidently, just days before the intrusion, an anonymous user posted on a hacker website called milw0rm (*http://www.milw0rm .com/exploits/8880*) a long list of yet-unpatched vulnerabilities in Kloxo, a hosting control panel that integrates into HyperVM. The situation was worse for approximately 50% of Vaserv's customers who signed up for unmanaged service, which doesn't include data backup. It remains unclear whether those website owners will ever be able to retrieve their lost data.

CSPs should institute the necessary security controls, including restricting physical and logical access to hypervisor and other forms of employed virtualization layers. IaaS customers should understand the technology and security process controls instituted by the CSP to protect the hypervisor. This will help you to understand the compliance and gaps with reference to your host security standard, policies, and regulatory compliances. However, in general, CSPs lack transparency in this area and you may have no option but to take a leap of faith and trust CSPs to provide an "isolated and secured virtualized guest OS."

Threats to the hypervisor

The integrity and availability of the hypervisor are of utmost importance and are key to guaranteeing the integrity and availability of a public cloud built on a virtualized environment.

A vulnerable hypervisor could expose all user domains to malicious insiders. Furthermore, hypervisors are potentially susceptible to subversion attacks. To illustrate the vulnerability of the virtualization layer, some members of the security research community demonstrated a "Blue Pill" attack on a hypervisor. During Black Hat 2008 and Black Hat DC 2009[||] Joanna Rutkowska, Alexander Tereshkin, and Rafal Wojtczuk from Invisible Things Lab demonstrated

---

[||] Black Hat DC 2009 (*http://srmsblog.burtongroup.com/2009/02/still-cant-win-the-core-wars-a-report-from-black -hat.html*).

a number of ways to compromise Xen's virtualization.# Although Rutkowska and her team have identified problems with Xen implementations, generally they seem quite positive about the Xen approach. But their demonstration does illustrate the complexity of securing virtualized systems and the need for new approaches to protect hypervisors from such attacks.

Since virtualization layers within public clouds for the most part are proprietary and closed source (although some may employ a derivative of open source virtualization software such as Xen), the source code of software used by CSPs is not available for scrutiny by the security research community.

Virtual Server Security

Customers of IaaS have full access to the virtualized guest VMs that are hosted and isolated from each other by hypervisor technology. Hence customers are responsible for securing and ongoing security management of the guest VM.

A public IaaS, such as Amazon's Elastic Compute Cloud (EC2), offers a web services API to perform management functions such as provisioning, decommissioning, and replication of virtual servers on the IaaS platform. These system management functions, when orchestrated appropriately, can provide elasticity for resources to grow or shrink in line with workload demand. The dynamic life cycle of virtual servers can result in complexity if the process to manage the virtual servers is not automated with proper procedures. From an attack surface perspective, the virtual server (Windows, Solaris, or Linux) may be accessible to anyone on the Internet, so sufficient network access mitigation steps should be taken to restrict access to virtual instances. Typically, the CSP blocks all port access to virtual servers and recommends that customers use port 22 (Secure Shell or SSH) to administer virtual server instances. The cloud management API adds another layer of attack surface and must be included in the scope of securing virtual servers in the public cloud. Some of the new host security threats in the public IaaS include:

- Stealing keys used to access and manage hosts (e.g., SSH private keys)
- Attacking unpatched, vulnerable services listening on standard ports (e.g., FTP, NetBIOS, SSH)
- Hijacking accounts that are not properly secured (i.e., weak or no passwords for standard accounts)
- Attacking systems that are not properly secured by host firewalls
- Deploying Trojans embedded in the software component in the VM or within the VM image (the OS) itself

See *http://theinvisiblethings.blogspot.com/2008/08/our-xen-0wning-trilogy-highlights.html.*

Securing virtual servers

The simplicity of self-provisioning new virtual servers on an IaaS platform creates a risk that insecure virtual servers will be created. Secure-by-default configuration needs to be ensured by following or exceeding available industry baselines.

Securing the virtual server in the cloud requires strong operational security procedures coupled with automation of procedures. Here are some recommendations:

- Use a secure-by-default configuration. Harden your image and use a standard hardened image for instantiating VMs (the guest OS) in a public cloud. A best practice for cloud-based applications is to build custom VM images that have only the capabilities and services necessary to support the application stack. Limiting the capabilities of the underlying application stack not only limits the host's overall attack surface, but also greatly reduces the number of patches needed to keep that application stack secure.

- Track the inventory of VM images and OS versions that are prepared for cloud hosting. The IaaS provider provides some of these VM images. When a virtual image from the IaaS provider is used it should undergo the same level of security verification and hardening for hosts within the enterprise. The best alternative is to provide your own image that conforms to the same security standards as internal trusted hosts.

- Protect the integrity of the hardened image from unauthorized access.

- Safeguard the private keys required to access hosts in the public cloud.

- In general, isolate the decryption keys from the cloud where the data is hosted—unless they are necessary for decryption, and then only for the duration of an actual decryption activity. If your application requires a key to encrypt and decrypt for continuous data processing, it may not be possible to protect the key since it will be collocated with the application.

- Include no authentication credentials in your virtualized images except for a key to decrypt the filesystem key.

- Do not allow password-based authentication for shell access.

- Require passwords for sudo* or role-based access (e.g., Solaris, SELinux).

- Run a host firewall and open only the minimum ports necessary to support the services on an instance.

- Run only the required services and turn off the unused services (e.g., turn off FTP, print services, network file services, and database services if they are not required).

- Install a host-based IDS such as OSSEC or Samhain.

- Enable system auditing and event logging, and log the security events to a dedicated log server. Isolate the log server with higher security protection, including accessing controls.

* See *http://en.wikipedia.org/wiki/Sudo*.

- If you suspect a compromise, shut down the instance, snapshot your block volumes, and back up the root filesystem. You can perform forensics on an uncompromised system later.

- Institute a process for patching the images in the cloud—both offline and instantiated images.

- Periodically review logs for suspicious activities.

Table 3-2 lists security controls at the host level.

TABLE 3-2. Security controls at the host level

Threat outlook	High
Preventive controls	Host firewall, access control, patching, hardening of system, strong authentication
Detective controls	Security event logs, host-based IDS/IPS

Infrastructure Security: The Application Level

Application or software security should be a critical element of your security program. Most enterprises with information security programs have yet to institute an application security program to address this realm. Designing and implementing applications targeted for deployment on a cloud platform will require that existing application security programs reevaluate current practices and standards. The application security spectrum ranges from standalone single-user applications to sophisticated multiuser e-commerce applications used by millions of users. Web applications such as content management systems (CMSs), wikis, portals, bulletin boards, and discussion forums are used by small and large organizations. A large number of organizations also develop and maintain custom-built web applications for their businesses using various web frameworks (PHP,[†] .NET,[‡] J2EE,[§] Ruby on Rails, Python, etc.). According to SANS, until 2007 few criminals attacked vulnerable websites because other attack vectors were more likely to lead to an advantage in unauthorized economic or information access. Increasingly, however, advances in cross-site scripting (XSS) and other attacks have demonstrated that criminals looking for financial gain can exploit vulnerabilities resulting from web programming errors as new ways to penetrate important organizations. In this section, we will limit our discussion to web application security: web applications in the cloud accessed by users with standard Internet browsers, such as Firefox, Internet Explorer, or Safari, from any computer connected to the Internet.

† See *http://en.wikipedia.org/wiki/PHP*.

‡ See *http://msdn.microsoft.com/netframework/*.

§ See *http://en.wikipedia.org/wiki/J2EE*.

Since the browser has emerged as the end user client for accessing in-cloud applications, it is important for application security programs to include browser security into the scope of application security. Together they determine the strength of end-to-end cloud security that helps protect the confidentiality, integrity, and availability of the information processed by cloud services.

Application-Level Security Threats

According to SANS,[||] web application vulnerabilities in open source as well as custom-built applications accounted for almost half the total number of vulnerabilities discovered between November 2006 and October 2007.[#] The existing threats exploit well-known application vulnerabilities (e.g., the OWASP Top 10; see *http://www.owasp.org/index.php/Top_10_2007*), including cross-site scripting (XSS), SQL injection, malicious file execution, and other vulnerabilities resulting from programming errors and design flaws. Armed with knowledge and tools, hackers are constantly scanning web applications (accessible from the Internet) for application vulnerabilities. They are then exploiting the vulnerabilities they discover for various illegal activities including financial fraud, intellectual property theft, converting trusted websites into malicious servers serving client-side exploits, and phishing scams. All web frameworks and all types of web applications are at risk of web application security defects, ranging from insufficient validation to application logic errors.

It has been a common practice to use a combination of perimeter security controls and network- and host-based access controls to protect web applications deployed in a tightly controlled environment, including corporate intranets and private clouds, from external hackers. Web applications built and deployed in a public cloud platform will be subjected to a high threat level, attacked, and potentially exploited by hackers to support fraudulent and illegal activities. In that threat model, web applications deployed in a public cloud (the SPI model) must be designed for an Internet threat model, and security must be embedded into the Software Development Life Cycle (SDLC); see Figure 3-2.

|| See *http://www.sans.org/about/sans.php*.

See *http://www.sans.org/top20/*.

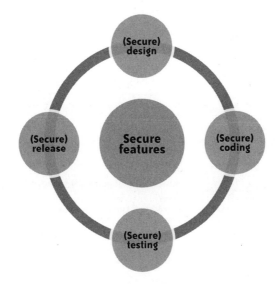

FIGURE 3-2. The SDLC

DoS and EDoS

Additionally, you should be cognizant of application-level DoS and DDoS attacks that can potentially disrupt cloud services for an extended time. These attacks typically originate from compromised computer systems attached to the Internet (routinely, hackers hijack and control computers infected by way of viruses/worms/malware and, in some cases, powerful unprotected servers). Application-level DoS attacks could manifest themselves as high-volume web page reloads, XML* web services requests (over HTTP or HTTPS), or protocol-specific requests supported by a cloud service. Since these malicious requests blend with the legitimate traffic, it is extremely difficult to selectively filter the malicious traffic without impacting the service as a whole. For example, a DDoS attack on Twitter on August 6, 2009, brought the service down for several hours (see Figure 3-3).

---

* XML stands for eXtensible Markup Language; see *http://en.wikipedia.org/wiki/XML*.

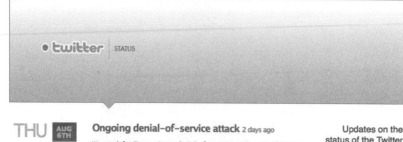

THU AUG 6TH **Ongoing denial–of–service attack** 2 days ago

We are defending against a denial–of–service attack, and will update status again shortly.

Update: the site is back up, but we are continuing to defend against and recover from this attack.

Update (9:46a): As we recover, users will experience some longer load times and slowness. This includes timeouts to API clients. We're working to get back to 100% as quickly as we can.

Update (4:14p): Site latency has continued to improve, however some web requests continue to fail. This means that some people may be unable to post or follow from the website.

Updates on the status of the Twitter service.

Related Links
Pingdom Uptime Report

Official Company Blog

Official Help Documents

FIGURE 3-3. DDoS attack on Twitter

Apart from disrupting cloud services, resulting in poor user experience and service-level impacts, DoS attacks can quickly drain your company's cloud services budget. DoS attacks on pay-as-you-go cloud applications will result in a dramatic increase in your cloud utility bill: you'll see increased use of network bandwidth, CPU, and storage consumption. This type of attack is also being characterized as *economic denial of sustainability* (EDoS).†

The low barriers for small and medium-size enterprises to adopt cloud computing for legitimate use are also leveling the field for hackers. Using hijacked or exploited cloud accounts, hackers will be able to link together computing resources to achieve massive amounts of computing without any of the capital infrastructure costs. In the not-so-distant future, you might witness DoS attacks launched from IaaS or PaaS clouds against other cloud services (such hostile and offensive cloud models are being characterized as *dark clouds*).

End User Security

You, as a customer of a cloud service, are responsible for end user security tasks—security procedures to protect your Internet-connected PC—and for practicing "safe surfing." Protection measures include use of security software, such as anti-malware, antivirus, personal firewalls, security patches, and IPS-type software on your Internet-connected computer. The new mantra of "the browser is your operating system" appropriately conveys the message that

† See, for example, *http://rationalsecurity.typepad.com/blog/2009/01/a-couple-of-followups-on-my-edos-economic -denial-of-sustainability-concept.html*.

browsers have become the ubiquitous "operating systems" for consuming cloud services. All Internet browsers routinely suffer from software vulnerabilities that make them vulnerable to end user security attacks. Hence, our recommendation is that cloud customers take appropriate steps to protect browsers from attacks. To achieve end-to-end security in a cloud, it is essential for customers to maintain good browser hygiene. The means keeping the browser (e.g., Internet Explorer, Firefox, Safari) patched and updated to mitigate threats related to browser vulnerabilities. Currently, although browser security add-ons are not commercially available, users are encouraged to frequently check their browser vendor's website for security updates, use the auto-update feature, and install patches on a timely basis to maintain end user security.‡

Who Is Responsible for Web Application Security in the Cloud?

Depending on the cloud services delivery model (SPI) and service-level agreement (SLA), the scope of security responsibilities will fall on the shoulders of both the customer and the cloud provider. The key is to understand what your security responsibilities are versus those of the CSP. In that context, recent security surveys have highlighted the fact that lack of transparency in security controls and practices employed by CSPs is a barrier to cloud adoption.

To start with, cloud customers do not have the transparency required in the area of software vulnerabilities in cloud services. This prevents customers from managing the operational risk that might come with the vulnerabilities. Furthermore, by treating their software as proprietary, CSPs are impeding security researchers from analyzing the software for security flaws and bugs. (The exception is cloud providers that are operating on open source software.) Due to this lack of transparency, customers are left with no choice but to trust their CSPs to disclose any new vulnerability that may affect the confidentiality, integrity, or availability of their application. For example, as of March 2009, no prominent IaaS, PaaS, or SaaS vendors are participating in the Common Vulnerability and Exposures (CVE) project. Case in point: AWS took 7.5 months to fix a vulnerability that Colin Percival reported in May 2007.§ This vulnerability was a cryptographic weakness in Amazon's request signing code that affected its database API (SimpleDB) and EC2 API services, and it was not made public until after it was fixed in December 2008. (Colin does acknowledge that Amazon took this issue seriously at all times, and the lengthy timeline was simply due to the large amount of work involved in rolling out a patch to the affected services.)

Enterprise customers should understand the vulnerability disclosure policy of cloud services and factor that into the CSP risk assessment. The following sections discuss the web application security in the context of the SPI cloud service delivery model.

---

‡ A good reference for browser security is Google's Browser Security Handbook (*http://code.google.com/p/browsersec/wiki/Main*).

§ See *http://www.daemonology.net/blog/2008-12-18-AWS-signature-version-1-is-insecure.html*.

SaaS Application Security

The SaaS model dictates that the provider manages the entire suite of applications delivered to users. Therefore, SaaS providers are largely responsible for securing the applications and components they offer to customers. Customers are usually responsible for operational security functions, including user and access management as supported by the provider. It is a common practice for prospective customers, usually under an NDA, to request information related to the provider's security practices. This information should encompass design, architecture, development, black- and white-box application security testing, and release management. Some customers go to the extent of hiring independent security vendors to perform penetration testing (black-box security testing) of SaaS applications (with consent from the provider) to gain assurance independently. However, penetration testing can be costly and not all providers agree to this type of verification.

Extra attention needs to be paid to the authentication and access control features offered by SaaS CSPs. Usually that is the only security control available to manage risk to information. Most services, including those from Salesforce.com and Google, offer a web-based administration user interface tool to manage authentication and access control of the application. Some SaaS applications, such as Google Apps, have built-in features that end users can invoke to assign read and write privileges to other users. However, the privilege management features may not be advanced, fine-grained access and could have weaknesses that may not conform to your organization's access control standard. One example that captures this issue is the mechanism that Google Docs employs in handling images embedded in documents, as well as access privileges to older versions of a document. Evidently, embedded images stored in Google Docs are not protected in the same way that a document is protected with sharing controls. That means if you have shared a document containing embedded images, the other person will always be able to view those images even after you've stopped sharing the document. A blogger[||] discovered this access control quirk and brought it to Google's attention. Although Google has acknowledged the issue, its response conveys that it believes[#] those concerns do not pose a significant security risk to its users.

Another incident related to Google Docs was a privacy glitch[*] that inappropriately shared access to a small fraction (Google claims 0.05% of the documents were affected) of word processing and presentation documents stored on its Google Apps cloud service. Though the documents were shared only with people whom the Google Docs users had already shared documents, rather than with the world at large, the problem illustrates the need to evaluate and understand cloud-specific access control mechanisms.

[||] Google Docs access control issue: *http://peekay.org/2009/03/26/security-issues-with-google-docs/*.

[#] Google Docs access control response to a weakness issue: *http://googledocs.blogspot.com/2009/03/just-to-clarify.html*.

[*] Google Docs privacy glitch: *http://www.techcrunch.com/2009/03/07/huge-google-privacy-blunder-shares-your-docs-without-permission/*.

Cloud customers should try to understand cloud-specific access control mechanisms—including support for strong authentication and privilege management based on user roles and functions—and take the steps necessary to protect information hosted in the cloud. Additional controls should be implemented to manage privileged access to the SaaS administration tool, and enforce segregation of duties to protect the application from insider threats. In line with security standard practices, customers should implement a strong password policy—one that forces users to choose strong passwords when authenticating to an application.[†]

It is a common practice for SaaS providers to commingle their customer data (structured and unstructured) in a single virtual data store and rely on data tagging to enforce isolation between customer data. In that multitenant data store model, where encryption may not be feasible due to key management and other design barriers, data is tagged and stored with a unique customer identifier. This unique data tag makes it possible for the business logic embedded in the application layer to enforce isolation between customers when the data is processed. It is conceivable that the application layer enforcing this isolation could become vulnerable during software upgrades by the CSP. Hence, customers should understand the virtual data store architecture and the preventive mechanisms the SaaS providers use to guarantee the compartmentalization and isolation required in a virtual multitenant environment.

Established SaaS providers, such as Salesforce.com, Microsoft, and Google, are known to invest in software security and practice security assurance as part of their SDLC. However, given that there is no industry standard to assess software security, it is almost impossible to benchmark providers against a baseline.[‡]

Table 3-3 lists security controls at the application level.

TABLE 3-3. Security controls at the application level

Threat outlook	Medium
Preventive controls	Identity management, access control assessment, browser hardened with latest patches, multifactor authentication via delegated authentication, endpoint security measures including antivirus and IPS
Detective controls	Login history and available reports from SaaS vendors

[†] See Chapter 5 for ways to strengthen authentication, including delegated authentication and access management.

[‡] The Payment Application Data Security Standard (PA-DSS) is applicable only to organizations that store, process, or transmit cardholder data—with guidance for software developers and manufacturers of applications and devices used in those transactions.

PaaS Application Security

PaaS vendors broadly fall into the following two major categories:

- Software vendors (e.g., Bungee, Etelos, GigaSpaces, Eucalyptus)
- CSPs (e.g., Google App Engine, Salesforce.com's Force.com, Microsoft Azure, Intuit QuickBase)

Organizations evaluating a private cloud may utilize PaaS software to build a solution for internal consumption. Currently, no major public clouds are known to be using commercial off-the-shelf or open source PaaS software such as Eucalyptus (Eucalyptus does offer a limited experimental pilot cloud for developers at Eucalyptus.com,§ however). Therefore, given the nascent stage of PaaS deployment, we will not discuss software security of standalone PaaS software in this chapter. Nonetheless, it is recommended that organizations evaluating PaaS software perform a risk assessment and apply the software security standard similar to acquiring any enterprise software.

By definition, a PaaS cloud (public or private) offers an integrated environment to design, develop, test, deploy, and support custom applications developed in the language the platform supports. PaaS application security encompasses two software layers:

- Security of the PaaS platform itself (i.e., runtime engine)
- Security of customer applications deployed on a PaaS platform

Generally speaking, PaaS CSPs (e.g., Google, Microsoft, and Force.com) are responsible for securing the platform software stack that includes the runtime engine that runs the customer applications. Since PaaS applications may use third-party applications, components, or web services, the third-party application provider may be responsible for securing their services. Hence, customers should understand the dependency of their application on all services and assess risks pertaining to third-party service providers. Until now, CSPs have been reluctant to share information pertaining to platform security using the argument that such security information could provide an advantage for hackers. However, enterprise customers should demand transparency from CSPs and seek information necessary to perform risk assessment and ongoing security management.

PaaS application container

In the multitenant PaaS service delivery model, the core security tenets are containment and isolation of multitenant applications from each other. In that model, access to your data should be restricted to your enterprise users and to applications that you own and manage. The security model of the PaaS platform runtime engine is the CSP's intellectual property, and it is essential to delivering the "sandbox" architecture in a multitenant computing model. Hence, the sandbox characteristic of the platform runtime engine is central in maintaining the

§ See *http://open.eucalyptus.com/wiki/EucalyptusPublicCloud*.

confidentiality and integrity of your application deployed in the PaaS. CSPs are responsible for monitoring new bugs and vulnerabilities that may be used to exploit the PaaS platform and break out of the sandbox architecture. This type of situation is the worst case scenario for a PaaS service; the privacy implications for customer-sensitive information are undesirable and could be very damaging to your business. Hence, enterprise customers should seek information from the CSP on the containment and isolation architecture of the PaaS service.

Network and host security monitoring outside the PaaS platform is also the responsibility of the PaaS cloud provider (i.e., monitoring of a shared network and system infrastructure hosting customer applications). PaaS customers should understand how PaaS CSPs are managing their platform, including updating of the runtime engine and change, release, and patch management.

Customer-Deployed Application Security

PaaS developers need to get familiar with specific APIs to deploy and manage software modules that enforce security controls. Furthermore, given that the API is unique to a PaaS cloud service, developers are required to become familiar with platform-specific security features— available to them in the form of security objects and web services for configuring authentication and authorization controls within the application. When it comes to PaaS API design, currently no standard is available, nor is there any concerted effort by CSPs to develop a ubiquitous and consistent API across clouds—and that makes porting of an application across PaaS clouds a monumental task. Currently, the Google App Engine supports only Python and Java, and Salesforce.com's Force.com supports only a proprietary language called Apex. (Apex differs from languages such as C++, Java, and .NET. Unlike those languages, Apex is much more limited in scope and is specific to building business applications on the Force.com platform.) In this regard, cloud services have the potential to retain customers more forcefully than traditional software licensing. The lack of an API standard has ramifications for both security management and portability of applications across the cloud.

Developers should expect CSPs to offer a set of security features, including user authentication, single sign-on (SSO) using federation, authorization (privilege management), and SSL or TLS support, made available via the API. Currently, there is no PaaS security management standard: CSPs have unique security models, and security features will vary from provider to provider. In the case of the Google App Engine, a developer using Python or Java objects can configure the user profile and select HTTPS as a transport protocol. Similarly, Force.com offers an Apex API to configure security parameters, manipulate various runtime configurations, and assign certain TCP ports for application-to-application connection-type interactions using Apex objects.[‖]

‖ For example, see *http://www.salesforce.com/us/developer/docs/api/Content/sforce_api_concepts_security.htm*.

Based on our assessment of major PaaS CSPs, the security features available to PaaS applications are limited to basic security configuration—SSL configuration, basic privilege management, and user authentication using the provider's identity store. In only a few cases, user federation is supported using the Security Assertion Markup Language (SAML).

Table 3-4 lists security controls applicable to PaaS applications.

TABLE 3-4. Security controls applicable to PaaS applications

Threat outlook	Medium
Preventive controls	User authentication, account management, browser hardened with latest patches, endpoint security measures including antivirus and IPS
Detective controls	Application vulnerability scanning

IaaS Application Security

IaaS cloud providers (e.g., Amazon EC2, GoGrid, and Joyent) treat the applications on customer virtual instances as a black box, and therefore are completely agnostic to the operations and management of the customer's applications. The entire stack—customer applications, runtime application platform (Java, .NET, PHP, Ruby on Rails, etc.), and so on—runs on the customer's virtual servers and is deployed and managed by customers. To that end, customers have full responsibility for securing their applications deployed in the IaaS cloud. Hence, customers should not expect any application security assistance from CSPs other than basic guidance and features related to firewall policy that may affect the application's communications with other applications, users, or services within or outside the cloud.

Web applications deployed in a public cloud must be designed for an Internet threat model, embedded with standard security countermeasures against common web vulnerabilities (e.g., the OWASP Top 10). In adherence with common security development practices, they should also be periodically tested for vulnerabilities, and most importantly, security should be embedded into the SDLC. Customers are solely responsible for keeping their applications and runtime platform patched to protect the system from malware and hackers scanning for vulnerabilities to gain unauthorized access to their data in the cloud. It is highly recommended that you design and implement applications with a "least-privileged" runtime model (e.g., configure the application to run using a lower privileged account).

Developers writing applications for IaaS clouds must implement their own features to handle authentication and authorization. In line with enterprise identity management practices, cloud applications should be designed to leverage delegated authentication service features supported by an enterprise Identity Provider (e.g., OpenSSO, Oracle IAM, IBM, CA) or third-party identity service provider (e.g., Ping Identity, Symplified, TriCipher). Any custom implementations of Authentication, Authorization, and Accounting (AAA) features can become a weak link if they are not properly implemented, and you should avoid them when possible.

In summary, the architecture for IaaS hosted applications closely resembles enterprise web applications with an *n*-tier distributed architecture. In an enterprise, distributed applications run with many controls in place to secure the host and the network connecting the distributed hosts. Comparable controls do not exist by default in an IaaS platform and must be added through a network, user access, or as application-level controls. Customers of IaaS clouds are responsible for all aspects of their application security and should take the steps necessary to protect their application to address application-level threats in a multitenant and hostile Internet environment.

Table 3-5 lists security controls applicable to IaaS applications.

TABLE 3-5. Security controls applicable to IaaS applications

Threat outlook	High
Preventive controls	Application developed using security-embedded SDLC process, least-privileged configuration, timely patching of application, user authentication, access control, account management, browser hardened with latest patches, endpoint security measures including antivirus, IPS, host-based IDS, host firewall, and virtual private network (VPN) for administration
Detective controls	Logging, event correlation, application vulnerability scanning and monitoring

Public Cloud Security Limitations

Customers evaluating the public cloud should keep in mind that there are limitations to the public cloud when it comes to support for custom security features. Security requirements such as an application firewall, SSL accelerator, cryptography, or rights management using a device that supports PKCS 12 are not supported in a public SaaS, PaaS, or IaaS cloud. In the future, IaaS and PaaS providers may offer some of these more sophisticated security features, depending on customer demand. In general, any mitigation controls that require deployment of an appliance or locally attached peripheral devices in the public IaaS/PaaS cloud are not feasible at this time.

Summary

In this chapter, we looked at network-, host-, and application-level security and the issues surrounding each level with specific regard to cloud computing. At the network level, although there are definitely security challenges with cloud computing, none of those challenges are caused specifically by cloud computing. All of the network-level security challenges associated with cloud computing are instead exacerbated by cloud computing—not specifically caused by it. Likewise, security issues at the host level, such as an increased need for host perimeter security (as opposed to organizational entity perimeter security) and secured virtualized environments, are exacerbated by cloud computing but not specifically caused by it. And the same holds true for the application level. Certainly, there is an increased need for secure software development life cycles due to the public-facing nature of (public) cloud applications, and the need to ensure that APIs have been thoroughly tested for security, but those application-level security requirements are again exacerbated by cloud computing and are not specifically caused by it.

Therefore, the issues of infrastructure security and cloud computing are about understanding which party provides which aspects of security (i.e., does the customer provide them or does the CSP provide them)—in other words, defining trust boundaries.

The use of APIs to control how a cloud infrastructure is harnessed has a pitfall: unlike HTTP, cloud APIs are not yet standardized, so each cloud provider has its own specific APIs for managing its services. This is the typical state of an industry in its infancy, where each vendor has its own proprietary technology that tends to lock in customers to their services because proprietary APIs make it difficult to change providers. Look for providers that use standard APIs wherever possible (*http://www.cloud-standards.org* has pointers to emerging standards). Standard APIs can be used today for access to storage, e.g., WebDAV for file storage; APIs for deploying and scaling applications are likely to be standardized over time. Also look for cloud providers that understand their own market and provide, for example, ways to archive and deploy libraries of VM images and preconfigured appliances.

CHAPTER FOUR

Data Security and Storage

IN TODAY'S WORLD OF (NETWORK-, HOST-, AND APPLICATION-LEVEL) INFRASTRUCTURE security, data security becomes more important when using cloud computing at all "levels": infrastructure-as-a-service (IaaS), platform-as-a-service (PaaS), and software-as-a-service (SaaS). This chapter describes several aspects of data security, including:

- Data-in-transit
- Data-at-rest
- Processing of data, including multitenancy
- Data lineage
- Data provenance
- Data remanence

The objective of this chapter is to help users evaluate their data security scenarios and make informed judgments regarding risk for their organizations. As with other aspects of cloud computing and security, not all of these data security facets are of equal importance in all topologies (e.g., the use of a public cloud versus a private cloud, or non-sensitive data versus sensitive data).

Aspects of Data Security

With regard to data-in-transit, the primary risk is in not using a vetted encryption algorithm. Although this is obvious to information security professionals, it is not common for others to understand this requirement when using a public cloud, regardless of whether it is IaaS, PaaS, or SaaS. It is also important to ensure that a protocol provides confidentiality as well as integrity (e.g., FTP over SSL [FTPS], Hypertext Transfer Protocol Secure [HTTPS], and Secure Copy Program [SCP])—particularly if the protocol is used for transferring data across the Internet. Merely encrypting data and using a non-secured protocol (e.g., "vanilla" or "straight" FTP or HTTP) can provide confidentiality, but does not ensure the integrity of the data (e.g., with the use of symmetric streaming ciphers).

Although using encryption to protect data-at-rest might seem obvious, the reality is not that simple. If you are using an IaaS cloud service (public or private) for simple storage (e.g., Amazon's Simple Storage Service or S3), encrypting data-at-rest is possible—and is strongly suggested. However, encrypting data-at-rest that a PaaS or SaaS cloud-based application is using (e.g., Google Apps, Salesforce.com) as a compensating control is not always feasible. Data-at-rest used by a cloud-based application is generally not encrypted, because encryption would prevent indexing or searching of that data.

Generally speaking, with data-at-rest, the economics of cloud computing are such that PaaS-based applications and SaaS use a multitenancy architecture. In other words, data, when processed by a cloud-based application or stored for use by a cloud-based application, is commingled with other users' data (i.e., it is typically stored in a massive data store, such as Google's BigTable). Although applications are often designed with features such as data tagging (see "SaaS Application Security" on page 54 for further information) to prevent unauthorized access to commingled data, unauthorized access is still possible through some exploit of an application vulnerability (e.g., Google's unauthorized data sharing between users of Documents and Spreadsheets in March 2009). Although some cloud providers have their applications reviewed by third parties or verified with third-party application security tools, data is not on a platform dedicated solely to one organization.

Although an organization's data-in-transit might be encrypted during transfer to and from a cloud provider, and its data-at-rest might be encrypted if using simple storage (i.e., if it is not associated with a specification application), an organization's data is definitely not encrypted if it is processed in the cloud (public or private). For any application to process data, that data *must be* unencrypted. Until June 2009, there was no known method for fully processing encrypted data. Therefore, unless the data is in the cloud for only simple storage, the data will be unencrypted during at least part of its life cycle in the cloud—processing at a minimum.

In June 2009, IBM announced that one of its researchers, working with a graduate student from Stanford University, had developed a fully homomorphic encryption scheme which allows data to be processed *without being decrypted*.* This is a huge advance in cryptography, and it will have a significant positive impact on cloud computing as soon as it moves into

---

* For example, see "IBM Discovers Encryption Scheme That Could Improve Cloud Security, Spam Filtering," at *http://www.eweek.com/c/a/Security/IBM-Uncovers-Encryption-Scheme-That-Could-Improve-Cloud -Security-Spam-Filtering-135413/*.

deployment. Earlier work on fully homomorphic encryption (e.g., 2-DNF[†]) was also conducted at Stanford University, but IBM's announcement bettered even that promising work. Although the homomorphic scheme has broken the theoretical barrier to fully homomorphic encryption, it required immense computational effort. According to Ronald Rivest (MIT professor and coinventor of the famous RSA encryption scheme), the steps to make it practical won't be far behind. Other cryptographic research efforts are underway to limit the amount of data that would need to be decrypted for processing in the cloud, such as predicate encryption.[‡]

Whether the data an organization has put into the cloud is encrypted or not, it is useful and might be required (for audit or compliance purposes) to know exactly where and when the data was specifically located within the cloud. For example, the data might have been transferred to a cloud provider, such as Amazon Web Services (AWS), on date x_1 at time y_1 and stored in a bucket on Amazon's S3 in *example1.s3.amazonaws.com*, then processed on date x_2 at time y_2 on an instance being used by an organization on Amazon's Elastic Compute Cloud (EC2) in *ec2-67-202-51-223.compute-1.amazonaws.com*, then restored in another bucket, *example2.s3.amazonaws.com*, before being brought back into the organization for storage in an internal data warehouse belonging to the marketing operations group on date x_3 at time y_3. Following the path of data (mapping application data flows or data path visualization) is known as *data lineage*, and it is important for an auditor's assurance (internal, external, and regulatory). However, providing data lineage to auditors or management is time-consuming, even when the environment is completely under an organization's control. Trying to provide accurate reporting on data lineage for a public cloud service is really not possible. In the preceding example, on what physical system is that bucket on *example1.s3.amazonaws.com*, and specifically where is (or was) that system located? What was the state of that physical system then, and how would a customer or auditor verify that information?

Even if data lineage can be established in a public cloud, for some customers there is an even more challenging requirement and problem: proving data provenance—not just proving the integrity of the data, but the more specific provenance of the data. There is an important difference between the two terms. *Integrity of data* refers to data that has not been changed in an unauthorized manner or by an unauthorized person. *Provenance* means not only that the data has integrity, but also that it is computationally accurate; that is, the data was accurately calculated. For example, consider the following financial equation:

$$SUM((((2*3)*4)/6)-2) = \$2.00$$

[†] 2-DNF (disjunctive normal form) is an example of homomorphic encryption that enables "computing with encrypted data." See "Evaluating 2-DNF Formulas on Ciphertexts" by Dan Boneh, Eu-Jin Goh, and Kobbi Nissim, at *http://crypto.stanford.edu/~dabo/papers/2dnf.pdf*.

[‡] Predicate encryption is a form of asymmetric encryption whereby different individuals (or groups) can selectively decrypt encrypted data instead of decrypting all of it. See "Predicate Encryption Supporting Disjunctions, Polynomial Equations, and Inner Products" by Jonathan Katz, Amit Sahai, and Brent Waters, at *http://eprint.iacr.org/2007/404.pdf*.

With that equation, the expected answer is $2.00. If the answer were different, there would be an integrity problem. Of course, the assumption is that the $2.00 is in U.S. dollars, but the assumption could be incorrect if a different dollar is used with the following associated assumptions:

- The equation is specific to the Australian, Bahamian, Barbadian, Belize, Bermudian, Brunei, Canadian, Cayman Islands, Cook Islands, East Caribbean, Fijian, Guyanese, Hong Kong, Jamaican, Kiribati, Liberian, Namibian, New Zealand, Samoan, Singapore, Solomon Islands, Surinamese, New Taiwan, Trinidad and Tobago, Tuvaluan, or Zimbabwean dollar.

- The dollar is meant to be converted from another country's dollars into U.S. dollars.

- The correct exchange rate is used and the conversion is calculated correctly and can be proven.

In this example, if the equation satisfies those assumptions, the equation has integrity but not provenance. There are many real-world examples in which data integrity is insufficient and data provenance is also required. Financial and scientific calculations are two obvious examples. How do you prove data provenance in a cloud computing scenario when you are using shared resources? Those resources are not under your physical or even logical control, and you probably have no ability to track the systems used or their state at the times you used them—even if you know some identifying information about the systems (e.g., their IP addresses) and the "general" location (e.g., a country, and not even a specific data center).

A final aspect of data security is *data remanence*. "Data remanence is the residual representation of data that has been in some way nominally erased or removed. This residue may be due to data being left intact by a nominal delete operation, or through physical properties of the storage medium. Data remanence may make inadvertent disclosure of sensitive information possible, should the storage media be released into an uncontrolled environment (e.g., thrown in the trash, or given to a third party)."§

The risk posed by data remanence in cloud services is that an organization's data can be inadvertently exposed to an unauthorized party—regardless of which cloud service you are using (SaaS, PaaS, or IaaS). When using SaaS or PaaS, the risk is almost certainly unintentional or inadvertent exposure. However, that is not reassuring after an unauthorized disclosure, and potential customers should question what third-party tools or reviews are used to help validate the security of the provider's applications or platform.

In spite of the increased importance of data security, the attention that cloud service providers (CSPs) pay to data remanence is strikingly low. Many do not even mention data remanence in their services. And if the subject of data security is broached, many CSPs rather glibly refer to compliance with U.S. Department of Defense (DoD) 5220.22-M (the National Industrial Security Program Operating Manual). We say "glibly" because it appears that providers (and other information technology vendors) have not actually read this manual. DoD 5220.22-M

§ See the Wikipedia definition of data remanence at *http://en.wikipedia.org/wiki/Data_remanence*.

states the two approved methods of data (destruction) security, but does not provide any specific requirements for how these two methods are to be achieved, nor does it provide any standards for how these methods are to be accomplished. Relevant information in DoD 5220.22-M regarding data remanence in this 141-page manual|| is limited to three paragraphs:

"8-301. Clearing and Sanitization"

> Instructions on clearing, sanitization, and release of information systems (IS) media shall be issued by the accrediting Cognizant Security Agency (CSA).

"a. Clearing"

> Clearing is the process of eradicating the data on media before reusing the media in an environment that provides an acceptable level of protection for the data that was on the media before clearing. All internal memory, buffer, or other reusable memory shall be cleared to effectively deny access to previously stored information.

"b. Sanitization"

> Sanitization is the process of removing the data from media before reusing the media in an environment that does not provide an acceptable level of protection for the data that was on the media before sanitizing. IS resources shall be sanitized before they are released from classified information controls or released for use at a lower classification level.

For specific information about *how* data security should be achieved, providers should refer to the National Institute of Standards and Technology (NIST) Special Publication, 800-88, "Guidelines for Media Sanitization."# Although this NIST publication provides guidelines only, and is officially meant for federal civilian departments and agencies only, many companies, especially those in regulated industries, voluntarily adhere to NIST guidelines and standards. In the absence of any other industry standard for data remanence, adherence to these NIST guidelines is important.

Data Security Mitigation

If prospective customers of cloud computing services expect that data security will serve as compensating controls for possibly weakened infrastructure security, since part of a customer's infrastructure security moves beyond its control and a provider's infrastructure security may (for many enterprises) or may not (for small to medium-size businesses, or SMBs) be less robust than expectations, you will be disappointed. Although data-in-transit can and should be encrypted, any use of that data in the cloud, beyond simple storage, requires that it be decrypted. Therefore, it is almost certain that in the cloud, data will be unencrypted. And if you are using a PaaS-based application or SaaS, customer-unencrypted data will also almost certainly be hosted in a multitenancy environment (in public clouds). Add to that exposure the difficulties in determining the data's lineage, data provenance—where necessary—and

---

|| DoD 5220.22-M, National Industrial Security Program Operating Manual, dated February 28, 2006.

Published in September 2006; see *http://csrc.nist.gov/publications/nistpubs/800-88/NISTSP800-88_rev1.pdf*.

even many providers' failure to adequately address such a basic security concern as data remanence, and the risks of data security for customers are significantly increased.

So, what should you do to mitigate these risks to data security? The only viable option for mitigation is to ensure that any sensitive or regulated data is not placed into a public cloud (or that you encrypt data placed into the cloud for simple storage only). Given the economic considerations of cloud computing today, as well as the present limits of cryptography, CSPs are not offering robust enough controls around data security. It may be that those economics change and that providers offer their current services, as well as a "regulatory cloud environment" (i.e., an environment where customers are willing to pay more for enhanced security controls to properly handle sensitive and regulated data). Currently, the only viable option for mitigation is to ensure that any sensitive or regulated data is not put into a public cloud.

Provider Data and Its Security

In addition to the security of your own customer data, customers should also be concerned about what data the provider collects and how the CSP protects that data. Specifically with regard to your customer data, what metadata does the provider have about your data, how is it secured, and what access do you, the customer, have to that metadata? As your volume of data with a particular provider increases, so does the value of that metadata.

Additionally, your provider collects and must protect a huge amount of security-related data. For example, at the network level, your provider should be collecting, monitoring, and protecting firewall, intrusion prevention system (IPS), security incident and event management (SIEM), and router flow data. At the host level your provider should be collecting system logfiles, and at the application level SaaS providers should be collecting application log data, including authentication and authorization information.

What data your CSP collects and how it monitors and protects that data is important to the provider for its own audit purposes (e.g., SAS 70, as discussed in Chapter 8). Additionally, this information is important to both providers and customers in case it is needed for incident response and any digital forensics required for incident analysis.

Storage

For data stored in the cloud (i.e., storage-as-a-service), we are referring to IaaS and not data associated with an application running in the cloud on PaaS or SaaS. The same three information security concerns are associated with this data stored in the cloud (e.g., Amazon's S3) as with data stored elsewhere: confidentiality, integrity, and availability.

Confidentiality

When it comes to the confidentiality of data stored in a public cloud, you have two potential concerns. First, what access control exists to protect the data? Access control consists of both authentication and authorization. As we will discuss further in Chapter 5, CSPs generally use weak authentication mechanisms (e.g., username + password), and the authorization ("access") controls available to users tend to be quite coarse and not very granular. For large organizations, this coarse authorization presents significant security concerns unto itself. Often, the only authorization levels cloud vendors provide are administrator authorization (i.e., the owner of the account itself) and user authorization (i.e., all other authorized users)—with no levels in between (e.g., business unit administrators, who are authorized to approve access for their own business unit personnel). Again, these access control issues are not unique to CSPs, and we discuss them in much greater detail in the following chapter.

What is definitely relevant to this section, however, is the second potential concern: how is the data that is stored in the cloud actually protected? For all practical purposes, protection of data stored in the cloud involves the use of encryption.

> **NOTE**
>
> There has been some discussion in recent years about alternative data protection techniques; for example, in connection with the Data Accountability and Trust Act, reported in May 2006. These alternative techniques included indexing, masking, redaction, and truncation. However, there are no accepted standards for indexing, masking, redaction, or truncation—or any other data protection technique. The only data protection technique for which there are recognized standards is encryption, such as the NIST Federal Information Processing Standards (FIPS); see *http://www.itl.nist.gov/fipspubs/*.

So, is a customer's data actually encrypted when it is stored in the cloud? And if so, with what encryption algorithm, and with what key strength? It depends, and specifically, it depends on which CSP you are using. For example, EMC's MozyEnterprise (*http://mozy.com/enterprise/?code =V5VT86*) does encrypt a customer's data. However, AWS S3 does *not* encrypt a customer's data. Customers are able to encrypt their own data themselves prior to uploading, but S3 does not provide encryption.

If a CSP does encrypt a customer's data, the next consideration concerns what encryption algorithm it uses. Not all encryption algorithms are created equal. Cryptographically, many algorithms provide insufficient security. Only algorithms that have been publicly vetted by a formal standards body (e.g., NIST) or at least informally by the cryptographic community should be used. Any algorithm that is proprietary should absolutely be avoided. Note that we are talking about symmetric encryption algorithms here. Symmetric encryption (see Figure 4-1) involves the use of a single secret key for both the encryption and decryption of data. Only symmetric encryption has the speed and computational efficiency to handle encryption of large volumes of data. It would be highly unusual to use an asymmetric algorithm for this encryption use case. (See Figure 4-2.)

Although the example in Figure 4-1 is related to email, the same concept (i.e., a single shared, secret key) is used in data storage encryption.

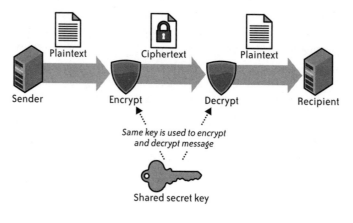

FIGURE 4-1. Symmetric encryption

Although the example in Figure 4-2 is related to email, the same concept (i.e., a public key and a private key) is *not* used in data storage encryption.

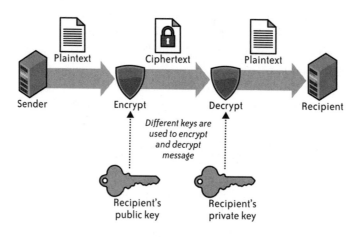

FIGURE 4-2. Asymmetric encryption

The next consideration for you is what key length is used. With symmetric encryption, the longer the key length (i.e., the greater number of bits in the key), the stronger the encryption. Although long key lengths provide more protection, they are also more computationally intensive, and may strain the capabilities of computer processors. What can be said is that key lengths should be a minimum of 112 bits for Triple DES (Data Encryption Standard) and 128-bits for AES (Advanced Encryption Standard)—both NIST-approved algorithms. For further information on key lengths, see NIST's "Special Publication 800-57, Recommendation for Key Management—Part 1: General (Revised)," dated March 2007, at *http://csrc.nist.gov/publications/ nistpubs/800-57/sp800-57-Part1-revised2_Mar08-2007.pdf*.

Another confidentiality consideration for encryption is key management. How are the encryption keys that are used going to be managed—and by whom? Are you going to manage your own keys? Hopefully, the answer is yes, and hopefully you have the expertise to manage your own keys. It is not recommended that you entrust a cloud provider to manage your keys—at least not the same provider that is handling your data. This means additional resources and capabilities are necessary. That being said, proper key management is a complex and difficult task. At a minimum, a customer should consult all three parts of NIST's 800-57, "Recommendation for Key Management":

- "Part 1: General"
- "Part 2: Best Practices for Key Management Organization"
- "Part 3: Application-Specific Key Management Guidance (Draft)"

Because key management is complex and difficult for a single customer, it is even more complex and difficult for CSPs to try to properly manage multiple customers' keys. For that reason, several CSPs do not do a good job of managing customers' keys. For example, it is common for a provider to encrypt all of a customer's data with a single key. Even worse, we are aware of one cloud storage provider that uses a single encryption key for all of its customers! The Organization for the Advancement of Structured Information Standards (OASIS) Key Management Interoperability Protocol (KMIP) is trying to address such issues; see *http://www .oasis-open.org/committees/tc_home.php?wg_abbrev=kmip*.

Integrity

In addition to the confidentiality of your data, you also need to worry about the integrity of your data. Confidentiality does not imply integrity; data can be encrypted for confidentiality purposes, and yet you might not have a way to verify the integrity of that data. Encryption alone is sufficient for confidentiality, but integrity also requires the use of message authentication codes (MACs). The simplest way to use MACs on encrypted data is to use a block symmetric algorithm (as opposed to a streaming symmetric algorithm) in cipher block chaining (CBC) mode, and to include a one-way hash function. This is not for the cryptographically uninitiated—and it is one reason why effective key management is difficult. At the very least, cloud customers should be asking providers about these matters. Not only is this important for the integrity of a customer's data, but it will also serve to provide insight on how sophisticated a provider's security program is—or is not. Remember, however, that not all providers encrypt customer data, especially for PaaS and SaaS services.

Another aspect of data integrity is important, especially with bulk storage using IaaS. Once a customer has several gigabytes (or more) of its data up in the cloud for storage, how does the customer check on the integrity of the data stored there? There are IaaS transfer costs associated with moving data into and back down from the cloud,* as well as network utilization (bandwidth) considerations for the customer's own network. What a customer really wants to do is to validate the integrity of its data while that data remains in the cloud—without having to download and reupload that data.

This task is even more difficult because it must be done in the cloud without explicit knowledge of the whole data set. Customers generally do not know on which physical machines their data is stored, or where those systems are located. Additionally, that data set is probably dynamic and changing frequently. Those frequent changes obviate the effectiveness of traditional integrity insurance techniques.

What is needed instead is a proof of retrievability—that is, a mathematical way to verify the integrity of the data as it is dynamically stored in the cloud.†

Availability

Assuming that a customer's data has maintained its confidentiality and integrity, you must also be concerned about the availability of your data. There are currently three major threats in this regard—none of which are new to computing, but all of which take on increased importance in cloud computing because of increased risk.

The first threat to availability is network-based attacks, which we discussed in Chapter 3 under "Infrastructure Security: The Network Level" on page 36.

The second threat to availability is the CSP's own availability. No CSPs offer the sought-after "five 9s" (i.e., 99.999%) of uptime. A customer would be lucky to get "three 9s" of uptime. As Table 4-1 shows, there is a considerable difference between five 9s and three 9s.

TABLE 4-1. Percentage of uptime

Availability	Total downtime (HH:MM:SS)		
	Per day	Per month	Per year
99.999%	00:00:00.4	00:00:26	00:05:15
99.99%	00:00:08	00:04:22	00:52:35
99.9%	00:01:26	00:43:49	08:45:56
99%	00:14:23	07:18:17	87:39:29

* For example, as of April 2009, AWS S3 charges $0.100 per gigabyte for all data transferred in, and $0.170 per gigabyte (for the first 10 TB) per month for all data transferred out.

† For more information on proofs of retrievability, see the academic paper "Ensuring Data Storage Security in Cloud Computing" by Cong Wang, Qian Wang, Kui Ren, and Wenjing Lou, published in 2009.

A number of high-profile cloud provider outages have occurred. For example, Amazon's S3 suffered a 2.5-hour outage in February 2008 and an eight-hour outage in July 2008. AWS is one of the more mature cloud providers, so imagine the difficulties that other, smaller or less mature cloud providers are having. These Amazon outages were all the more apparent because of the relatively large number of customers that the S3 service supports—and whom are highly (if not totally) reliant on S3's availability for their own operations.

In addition to service outages, in some cases data stored in the cloud has actually been lost. For example, in March 2009, "cloud-based storage service provider Carbonite Inc. filed a lawsuit charging that faulty equipment from two hardware providers caused backup failures that resulted in the company losing data for 7,500 customers two years ago."[‡]

A larger question for cloud customers to consider is whether cloud storage providers will even be in business in the future. In February 2009, cloud provider Coghead suddenly shut down, giving its customers fewer than 90 days (nine weeks) to get their data off its servers—or lose it altogether.

Finally, prospective cloud storage customers must be certain to ascertain just what services their provider is actually offering. Cloud storage does not mean the stored data is actually backed up. Some cloud storage providers do back up customer data, in addition to providing storage. However, many cloud storage providers do not back up customer data, or do so only as an additional service for an additional cost. For example, "data stored in Amazon S3, Amazon SimpleDB, or Amazon Elastic Block Store is redundantly stored in multiple physical locations as a normal part of those services and at no additional charge." However, "data that is maintained within running instances on Amazon EC2, or within Amazon S3 and Amazon SimpleDB, is all customer data and therefore AWS does not perform backups."[§] For availability, this is a seemingly simple yet critical question that customers should be asking of cloud storage providers.

All three of these considerations (confidentiality, integrity, and availability) should be encapsulated in a CSP's service-level agreement (SLA) to its customers. However, at this time, CSP SLAs are extremely weak—in fact, for all practical purposes, they are essentially worthless. Even where a CSP appears to have at least a partially sufficient SLA, how that SLA actually gets measured is problematic. For all of these reasons, data security considerations and how data is actually stored in the cloud should merit considerable attention by customers.

Summary

In this chapter we looked at aspects of customer data security, including the security of the customer data itself, as well as metadata about that data. As noted, in addition to being

---

‡ See "Latest cloud storage hiccups prompt data security questions," *ComputerWorld*, March 27, 2009.

§ "Amazon Web Services: Overview of Security Processes," September 2008, page 3.

concerned about your own customer data, customers also need to take interest in providers' data collection efforts, the monitoring of that data, and its security. Much provider data would be necessary for incident response and digital forensic analysis in the event of an incident (e.g., a possible compromise) involving a customer's own data.

The primary means of data security mitigation at this time is encryption—when it is used. Until the June 2009 announcement of a fully homomorphic encryption scheme, it was necessary to decrypt data for processing (except for relatively simple operations, such as supporting addition operation and one multiplication operation). With fully homomorphic encryption (it may take a few years to make this practical for commercial use), decrypting data for processing no longer is an issue unto itself, but another related concern still persists: key management.

As we discussed, key management is a significant problem today for enterprises, and even more of a problem for CSPs. Scalability is an issue, as well as the complexity of managing a huge number of keys for a large number of customers. Of course, some CSPs will take a far simpler approach to key management—and one that potentially puts your data at greater risk. Remember, you could end up effectively destroying your own data if you have a key management failure (e.g., you lose your keys).

Talk of alternative methods of data protection, such as redaction, truncations, obfuscation, and others, should be viewed with great concern. Not only are there no accepted standards for these alternative methods, but also there are no programs to validate the implementations of whatever could possibly be developed.

Do these concerns about data security negate the value of storage-as-a-service in the cloud? No, but they do mean that customers need to pay close attention to the security of their data. Is that data encrypted? If so, by whom? And who is responsible for key management, and how will that be accomplished specifically?

Given the large number of issues concerning data security, customers concerned about the security afforded by infrastructure security and who are counting on data security to provide compensating controls will almost certainly be disappointed. Data security is a significant task, with a lot of complexity, and it is just as important for customers to evaluate this thoroughly as the more traditional aspects of infrastructure security. It's your data and you should make significant efforts to protect it, as well as ensuring that your provider is protecting your data as well as its own data.

CHAPTER FIVE

Identity and Access Management

THIS CHAPTER PRESENTS THE CURRENT STATE OF THE PRACTICE OF IDENTITY AND ACCESS management (IAM) and support for IAM features that aid in Authentication, Authorization, and Auditing (AAA) of users accessing cloud services.

Trust Boundaries and IAM

In a typical organization where applications are deployed within the organization's perimeter the "trust boundary" is mostly static and is monitored and controlled by the IT department. In that traditional model, the trust boundary encompasses the network, systems, and applications hosted in a private data center managed by the IT department (sometimes third-party providers under IT supervision). And access to the network, systems, and applications is secured via network security controls including virtual private networks (VPNs), intrusion detection systems (IDSs), intrusion prevention systems (IPSs), and multifactor authentication.

With the adoption of cloud services, the organization's trust boundary will become dynamic and will move beyond the control of IT. With cloud computing, the network, system, and application boundary of an organization will extend into the service provider domain. (This may already be the case for most large enterprises engaged in e-commerce, supply chain management, outsourcing, and collaboration with partners and communities.) This loss of control continues to challenge the established trusted governance and control model (including the trusted source of information for employees and contractors), and, if not managed properly, will impede cloud service adoption within an organization.

To compensate for the loss of network control and to strengthen risk assurance, organizations will be forced to rely on other higher-level software controls, such as application security and user access controls. These controls manifest as strong authentication, authorization based on role or claims, trusted sources with accurate attributes, identity federation, single sign-on (SSO), user activity monitoring, and auditing. In particular, organizations need to pay attention to the identity federation architecture and processes, as they can strengthen the controls and trust between organizations and cloud service providers (CSPs).

Identity federation is an emerging industry best practice for dealing with the heterogeneous, dynamic, loosely coupled trust relationships that characterize an organization's external and internal supply chains and collaboration model. Federation enables the interaction of systems and applications separated by an organization's trust boundary, e.g., a sales person interacting with Salesforce.com from a corporate network. Since federation coupled with good IAM practice can enable strong authentication by way of delegation, web single sign-on, and entitlement management via centralized access control services, it will play a central role in accelerating cloud computing adoption within organizations.

In some cases, the practice of IAM within an organization may suffer due to a lack of central governance and identity information architecture. More often than not, identity storage is managed via manual entry by multiple administrators, and user provisioning processes are not well orchestrated. This process is not only inefficient, but it will also propagate existing bad practice to the cloud services. In such cases, the weak access model will extend excess privileges for unauthorized users to cloud services.

IAM is a two-way street. CSPs need to support IAM standards (e.g., SAML) and practices such as federation for customers to take advantage of and extend their practice to maintain compliance with internal policies and standards. Cloud services that support IAM features such as federation will accelerate the migration of traditional IT applications from trusted corporate networks into a trusted cloud service model. For customers, well-implemented user IAM practices and processes will help protect the confidentiality and integrity and manage compliance of the information stored in the cloud. Cloud services that support IAM standards such as SAML can accelerate the adoption of new cloud services and migration of IT applications from trusted corporate networks into a trusted cloud service model.

Why IAM?

Traditionally, organizations invest in IAM practices to improve operational efficiency and to comply with regulatory, privacy, and data protection requirements:

Improve operational efficiency
> Properly architected IAM technology and processes can improve efficiency by automating user on-boarding and other repetitive tasks (e.g., self-service for users requesting password resets that otherwise will require the intervention of system administrators using a help desk ticketing system).

Regulatory compliance management

To protect systems, applications, and information from internal and external threats (e.g., disgruntled employees deleting sensitive files) and to comply with various regulatory, privacy, and data protection requirements (e.g., HIPAA, SOX), organizations implement an "IT general and application-level controls" framework derived from industry standard frameworks such as ISO 27002 and Information Technology Infrastructure Library (ITIL). IAM processes and practices can help organizations meet objectives in the area of access control and operational security (e.g., enforcement of compliance requirements such as "segregation of duties" and assignment of limited privileges for staff members to perform their duties). Auditors routinely map internal controls to IT controls as they support management of regulatory compliance processes including Payment Card Industry (PCI) Data Security Standards (DSSs) and the Sarbanes-Oxley Act of 2003 (SOX).

In addition to improving operational efficiencies and effective compliance management, IAM can enable new IT delivery and deployment models (i.e., cloud services). For example, federated identity, a key IAM component, enables the linking and portability of identity information across trust boundaries. As such, it enables enterprises and cloud service providers to bridge security domains through web single sign-on and federated user provisioning.

Some of the cloud use cases that require IAM support from the CSP include:

- Employees and on-site contractors of an organization accessing a SaaS service using identity federation (e.g., sales and support staff members accessing Salesforce.com with corporate identities and credentials)
- IT administrators accessing the CSP management console to provision resources and access for users using a corporate identity (e.g., IT administrators of Newco.com provisioning virtual machines or VMs in Amazon's EC2 service, configured with identities, entitlements, and credentials for operating the VMs [i.e., start, stop, suspend, and delete VMs])
- Developers creating accounts for partner users in a PaaS platform (e.g., developers from Newco.com provisioning accounts in Force.com for Partnerco.com employees contracted to perform business process tasks for Newco.com)
- End users accessing storage service in the cloud (e.g., Amazon S3) and sharing files and objects with users, within and outside a domain using access policy management features
- An application residing in a cloud service provider (e.g., Amazon EC2) accessing storage from another cloud service (e.g., Mosso)

Since IAM features such as SSO allow applications to externalize authentication features, businesses can rapidly adopt *aaS services (an example is Salesforce.com) by reducing the time required to integrate with service providers. IAM capabilities can also help a business outsource a process or service to partners with a reduced impact to the business's privacy and security; for example, employees of an order fulfillment partner of a merchant can use their federated identities to access real-time information stored in a merchant application to manage the product fulfillment process. In short, extending your IAM strategy, practice, and architecture allows your organization to extend your user access management practices and processes to the cloud. Hence, organizations with established IAM practices can rapidly adopt cloud services while maintaining the efficiency and efficacy of their security controls.

IAM Challenges

One critical challenge of IAM concerns managing access for diverse user populations (employees, contractors, partners, etc.) accessing internal and externally hosted services. IT is constantly challenged to rapidly provision appropriate access to the users whose roles and responsibilities often change for business reasons. Another issue is the turnover of users within the organization. Turnover varies by industry and function—seasonal staffing fluctuations in finance departments, for example—and can also arise from changes in the business, such as mergers and acquisitions, new product and service releases, business process outsourcing, and changing responsibilities. As a result, sustaining IAM processes can turn into a persistent challenge.

Access policies for information are seldom centrally and consistently applied. Organizations can contain disparate directories, creating complex webs of user identities, access rights, and procedures. This has led to inefficiencies in user and access management processes while exposing these organizations to significant security, regulatory compliance, and reputation risks.

To address these challenges and risks, many companies have sought technology solutions to enable centralized and automated user access management. Many of these initiatives are entered into with high expectations, which is not surprising given that the problem is often large and complex. Most often those initiatives to improve IAM can span several years and incur considerable cost. Hence, organizations should approach their IAM strategy and architecture with both business and IT drivers that address the core inefficiency issues while preserving the control's efficacy (related to access control). Only then will the organizations have a higher likelihood of success and return on investment.

IAM Definitions

To start, we'll present the basic concepts and definitions of IAM functions for any service:

Authentication

Authentication is the process of verifying the identity of a user or system (e.g., Lightweight Directory Access Protocol [LDAP] verifying the credentials presented by the user, where the identifier is the corporate user ID that is unique and assigned to an employee or contractor). Authentication usually connotes a more robust form of identification. In some use cases, such as service-to-service interaction, authentication involves verifying the network service requesting access to information served by another service (e.g., a travel web service that is connecting to a credit card gateway to verify the credit card on behalf of the user).

Authorization
Authorization is the process of determining the privileges the user or system is entitled to once the identity is established. In the context of digital services, authorization usually follows the authentication step and is used to determine whether the user or service has the necessary privileges to perform certain operations—in other words, authorization is the process of enforcing policies.

Auditing
In the context of IAM, auditing entails the process of review and examination of authentication, authorization records, and activities to determine the adequacy of IAM system controls, to verify compliance with established security policies and procedures (e.g., separation of duties), to detect breaches in security services (e.g., privilege escalation), and to recommend any changes that are indicated for countermeasures.

IAM Architecture and Practice

IAM is not a monolithic solution that can be easily deployed to gain capabilities immediately. It is as much an aspect of architecture (see Figure 5-1) as it is a collection of technology components, processes, and standard practices. Standard enterprise IAM architecture encompasses several layers of technology, services, and processes. At the core of the deployment architecture is a directory service (such as LDAP or Active Directory) that acts as a repository for the identity, credential, and user attributes of the organization's user pool. The directory interacts with IAM technology components such as authentication, user management, provisioning, and federation services that support the standard IAM practice and processes within the organization. It is not uncommon for organizations to use several directories that were deployed for environment-specific reasons (e.g., Windows systems using Active Directory, Unix systems using LDAP) or that were integrated into the environment by way of business mergers and acquisitions.

The IAM processes to support the business can be broadly categorized as follows:

User management
Activities for the effective governance and management of identity life cycles

Authentication management
Activities for the effective governance and management of the process for determining that an entity is who or what it claims to be

Authorization management
Activities for the effective governance and management of the process for determining entitlement rights that decide what resources an entity is permitted to access in accordance with the organization's policies

Access management

> Enforcement of policies for access control in response to a request from an entity (user, services) wanting to access an IT resource within the organization

Data management and provisioning

> Propagation of identity and data for authorization to IT resources via automated or manual processes

Monitoring and auditing

> Monitoring, auditing, and reporting compliance by users regarding access to resources within the organization based on the defined policies

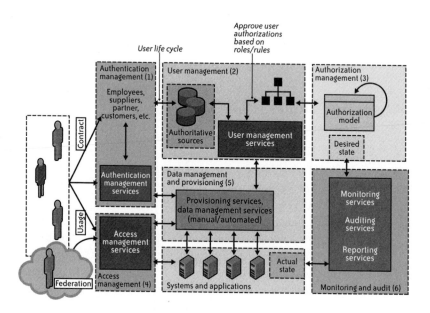

FIGURE 5-1. Enterprise IAM functional architecture

IAM processes support the following operational activities:

Provisioning

> This is the process of on-boarding users to systems and applications. These processes provide users with necessary access to data and technology resources. The term typically is used in reference to enterprise-level resource management. Provisioning can be thought of as a combination of the duties of the human resources and IT departments, where users are given access to data repositories or systems, applications, and databases based on a unique user identity. Deprovisioning works in the opposite manner, resulting in the deletion or deactivation of an identity or of privileges assigned to the user identity.

Credential and attribute management

These processes are designed to manage the life cycle of credentials and user attributes—create, issue, manage, revoke—to minimize the business risk associated with identity impersonation and inappropriate account use. Credentials are usually bound to an individual and are verified during the authentication process. The processes include provisioning of attributes, static (e.g., standard text password) and dynamic (e.g., one-time password) credentials that comply with a password standard (e.g., passwords resistant to dictionary attacks), handling password expiration, encryption management of credentials during transit and at rest, and access policies of user attributes (privacy and handling of attributes for various regulatory reasons).

Entitlement management

Entitlements are also referred to as *authorization policies*. The processes in this domain address the provisioning and deprovisioning of privileges needed for the user to access resources including systems, applications, and databases. Proper entitlement management ensures that users are assigned only the required privileges (least privileges) that match with their job functions. Entitlement management can be used to strengthen the security of web services, web applications, legacy applications, documents and files, and physical security systems.

Compliance management

This process implies that access rights and privileges are monitored and tracked to ensure the security of an enterprise's resources. The process also helps auditors verify compliance to various internal access control policies, and standards that include practices such as segregation of duties, access monitoring, periodic auditing, and reporting. An example is a user certification process that allows application owners to certify that only authorized users have the privileges necessary to access business-sensitive information.

Identity federation management

Federation is the process of managing the trust relationships established beyond the internal network boundaries or administrative domain boundaries among distinct organizations. A federation is an association of organizations that come together to exchange information about their users and resources to enable collaborations and transactions (e.g., sharing user information with the organizations' benefits systems managed by a third-party provider). Federation of identities to service providers will support SSO to cloud services.

Centralization of authentication (authN) and authorization (authZ)

A central authentication and authorization infrastructure alleviates the need for application developers to build custom authentication and authorization features into their applications. Furthermore, it promotes a loose coupling architecture where applications become agnostic to the authentication methods and policies. This approach is also called an "externalization of authN and authZ" from applications.

Figure 5-2 illustrates the identity life cycle management phases.

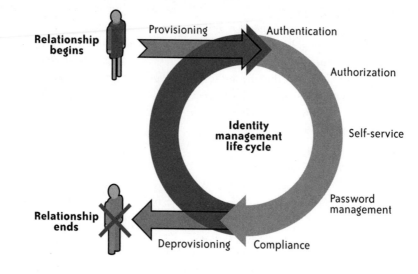

FIGURE 5-2. Identity life cycle

Getting Ready for the Cloud

As a first step, organizations planning for cloud services must plan for basic user management functions such as user account provisioning and ongoing user account management, including timely deprovisioning of users when they no longer need access to the cloud service. Organizations that have invested in identity and access management practices should be able to leverage their existing infrastructure and architecture to get ahead. Enterprises that haven't established procedures for identity and access management can use cloud-based solutions from a number of vendors that offer identity management services (examples include Symplified, Ping Identity, Conformity, and TriCipher). Because there are many IAM standards in varying states of maturity and adoption, it is likely that multiprotocol gateways provided by vendors such as Symplified and Vordel will be widely used for some time to come. These vendor-based solutions provide federation-enabling gateways to cloud services. We will discuss emerging cloud-based identity solutions in "Identity management-as-a-service" on page 96.

Organizations should start with an IAM strategy and architecture and invest in foundational technology elements that support user management and federation. In addition to providing a consistent user experience, federation can help to mitigate risks to organizations since it supports the SSO user experience: users will not be required to sign in multiple times, nor will they have to remember cloud-service-specific user authentication information (e.g., one user ID/password pair per provider).

Architecting an identity federation model will help organizations gain capabilities to support an identity provider (IdP), also known as an *SSO provider* (using an existing directory service or cloud-based identity management service). In that architecture, enterprise can share identities with trusted CSPs without sharing user credentials or private user attributes. Management of identity attributes also plays a role in federation; the definition, descriptions, and management of mandatory, non-mandatory, and key attributes are necessary steps to prepare for federation. This approach can help organizations extend IAM processes and practices, and implement a standardized federation model to *federate identities* and support single or reduced sign-on to cloud services.

Federation technology is typically built on a centralized identity management architecture leveraging industry-standard identity management protocols, such as Security Assertion Markup Language (SAML), WS Federation (WS-*), or Liberty Alliance. Of the three major protocol families associated with federation, SAML seems to be recognized as the de facto standard for enterprise-controlled federation.

These federation standards combined their work in enhancing SAML 1.0 to create SAML 2.0, which is the culmination of work stemming from the Organization for the Advancement of Structured Information Standards (OASIS), the Liberty Alliance, and the Shibboleth Project. In March 2005, SAML 2.0 was ratified as an official OASIS industry standard and is now backed by vendors and organizations around the world as the de facto industry standard for deploying and managing open identity-based applications. SAML is required for the U.S. Federal E-Authentication profile, the Liberty eGov profile (internationally adopted), the higher-education Shibboleth and Eduserv federations, as well as many other industry federations. SAML can be leveraged in a private community* cloud where federation among community members will be essential in sharing information in a secure way. Gartner, an industry analyst firm, further validated this in 2007 by declaring SAML 2.0 "the de facto federation standard across industries."

To establish a user federation model for their users, organizations must follow the necessary technology architecture steps: establishing an authoritative source for the identity, identifying the necessary user profile attributes, and planning and implementing an IdP that supports an SSO service and is accessible by CSPs; in other words, implementing an Internet-facing IdP. Internet-facing IdPs can be deployed using federation technology components that interact with your directory. In an enterprise architecture, the core access management capabilities are built around a directory, such as LDAP or Active Directory. Organizations that have directories accessible via a DMZ network, either by design or by replication, may be able to accelerate federation deployment. Similarly, in organizations with a federation-friendly architecture where directories may be accessible to approved third-party providers via network access controls (e.g., firewalls, site-to-site VPNs) or proxies, federation can be accomplished with

---

* According to the National Institute of Standards and Technology (NIST), a private community cloud infrastructure is shared by several organizations and supports a specific community that has shared concerns (e.g., mission, security requirements, policy, and compliance considerations). It may be managed by the organizations or by a third party and may exist on or off the premises. More details are available at *http://csrc.nist.gov/groups/SNS/cloud-computing/index.html*.

minor investments. Organizations usually deploy an identity federation product that seamlessly integrates with their directory service to enable delegated authentication or the SSO feature (examples include Sun's OpenSSO, Oracle's Federation Manager, and CA's Federation Manager).

Relevant IAM Standards and Protocols for Cloud Services

In the previous sections, we established the requirements and benefits of applying standard IAM principles and practices to cloud services. In this section, we will discuss the relevant IAM standards that act as catalysts for organizations adopting cloud services. Organizations that are currently evaluating cloud services based on business and operational criteria should also take into consideration the CSP's commitment to and support for IAM standards.

IAM Standards and Specifications for Organizations

The following IAM standards and specifications will help organizations implement effective and efficient user access management practices and processes in the cloud. These sections are ordered by four major challenges in user and access management faced by cloud users:

1. How can I avoid duplication of identity, attributes, and credentials and provide a single sign-on user experience for my users? SAML.

2. How can I automatically provision user accounts with cloud services and automate the process of provisoning and deprovisioning? SPML.

3. How can I provision user accounts with appropriate privileges and manage entitlements for my users? XACML.

4. How can I authorize cloud service X to access my data in cloud service Y without disclosing credentials? OAuth.

Security Assertion Markup Language (SAML)

SAML is the most mature, detailed, and widely adopted specifications family for browser-based federated sign-on for cloud users. Once the user authenticates to the identity service, she can freely access provisioned cloud services that fall within the trusted domain, thereby sidestepping the cloud-specific sign-on process. Since SAML enables delegation (SSO), by using risk-based authentication policies customers can elect to employ strong authentication (multifactor authentication) for certain cloud services. This can be easily achieved by using the organization's IdP, which supports strong authentication and delegated authentication. By employing strong authentication techniques such as dual-factor authentication, users are less vulnerable to phishing attacks that have been growing steadily on the Internet. Strong authentication to cloud services is also advisable to protect user credentials from man-in-the-middle attacks—i.e., when computers or browsers fall victim to trojans and botnet attacks. By supporting a SAML standard that enables a delegated authentication model for cloud customers, the CSP can delegate the authentication policies to the customer organization. In short, SAML helps CSPs to become agnostic to customer authentication requirements.

Figure 5-3 illustrates an SSO into Google Apps from the browser. The figure illustrates the following steps involved in the SSO process of a user who is federated to Google:

1. The user from your organization attempts to reach a hosted Google application, such as Gmail, Start Pages, or another Google service.

2. Google generates a SAML authentication request. The SAML request is encoded and embedded into the URL for your organization's IdP supporting the SSO service. The Relay State parameter containing the encoded URL of the Google application that the user is trying to reach is also embedded in the SSO URL. This Relay State parameter is meant to be an opaque identifier that is passed back without any modification or inspection.

3. Google sends a redirect to the user's browser. The redirect URL includes the encoded SAML authentication request that should be submitted to your organization's IdP service.

4. Your IdP decodes the SAML request and extracts the URL for both Google's Assertion Consumer Service (ACS) and the user's destination URL (the Relay State parameter). Your IdP then authenticates the user. Your IdP could authenticate the user by either asking for valid login credentials or checking for valid session cookies.

5. Your IdP generates a SAML response that contains the authenticated user's username. In accordance with the SAML 2.0 specification, this response is digitally signed with the partner's public and private DSA/RSA keys.

6. Your IdP encodes the SAML response and the Relay State parameter and returns that information to the user's browser. Your IdP provides a mechanism so that the browser can forward that information to Google's ACS. For example, your IdP could embed the SAML response and destination URL in a form and provide a button that the user can click to submit the form to Google. Your IdP could also include JavaScript on the page that automatically submits the form to Google.

7. Google's ACS verifies the SAML response using your IdP's public key. If the response is successfully verified, ACS redirects the user to the destination URL.

8. The user has been redirected to the destination URL and is logged in to Google Apps.

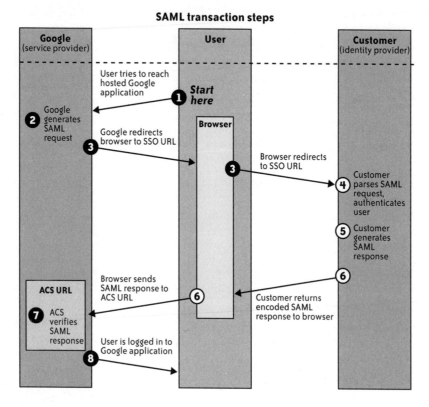

SAML transaction steps

FIGURE 5-3. SSO transaction steps using SAML

Service Provisioning Markup Language (SPML)

SPML is an XML-based framework being developed by OASIS for exchanging user, resource, and service provisioning information among cooperating organizations. SPML is an emerging standard that can help organizations automate provisioning of user identities for cloud services (e.g., an application or service running at a customer site requesting Salesforce.com for new accounts). When SPML is available, organizations should use it to provision user accounts and profiles with the cloud service. If SPML is supported, software-as-a-service (SaaS) providers can enable "just-in-time provisioning" to create accounts for new users in real time (as opposed to preregistering users). In that model, the CSP extracts attributes from the SAML token of a new user, creates an SPML message on the fly, and hands the request to a provisioning service which in turn adds the user identity to the cloud user database.

Adoption of SPML can lead to standardization and automation of user or system access and entitlement rights to cloud services so that customers are not locked into proprietary solutions.

Figure 5-4 illustrates an SPML use case in which an HR system is requesting a provisioning system in the cloud with the SPML request. In the figure, HR System of Record (requesting authority) is an SPML web services client interacting with the SPML provisioning service provider at the cloud service provider, which is responsible for provisioning user accounts on the cloud services (provisioning service target).

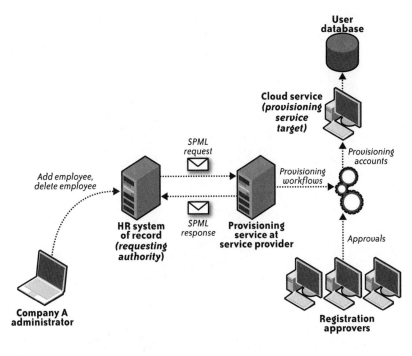

FIGURE 5-4. SPML use case

eXensible Access Control Markup Language (XACML)

XACML is an OASIS-ratified, general-purpose, XML-based access control language for policy management and access decisions. It provides an XML schema for a general policy language which is used to protect any kind of resource and make access decisions over these resources. The XACML standard not only gives the model of the policy language, but also proposes a processing environment model to manage the policies and to conclude the access decisions. The XACML context also specifies the request/response protocol that the application environment can use to communicate with the decision point. The response to an access request is also specified using XML.

Most applications (web or otherwise) have a built-in authorization module that grants or denies access to certain application functions or resources based on entitlements assigned to the user. In a centrally managed IAM architecture, application-specific authorization models (silos) make it difficult to state the access rights of individual users across all applications. Hence, the goal of XACML is to provide a standardized language, a method of access control, and policy enforcement across all applications that implement a common authorization standard. These authorization decisions are based on various authorization policies and rules centered on the user role and job function. In short, XACML allows for unified authorization policies (i.e., the use of one consistent XACML policy for multiple services).

Figure 5-5 illustrates the interaction among various health care participants with unique roles (authorization privileges) accessing sensitive patient records stored in a health care application.

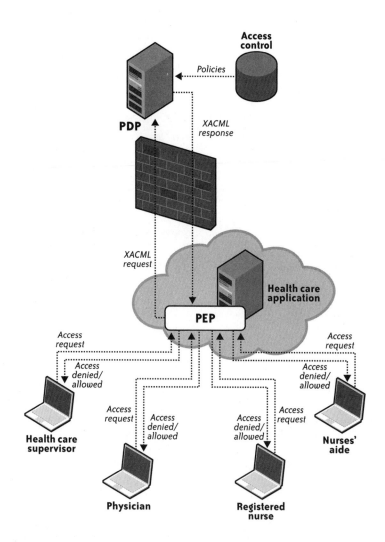

FIGURE 5-5. XACML use case

The figure illustrates the following steps involved in the XACML process:

1. The health care application manages various hospital associates (the physician, registered nurse, nurses' aide, and health care supervisor) accessing various elements of the patient record. This application relies on the policy enforcement point (PEP) and forwards the request to the PEP.

2. The PEP is actually the interface of the application environment. It receives the access requests and evaluates them with the help of the policy decision point (PDP). It then permits or denies access to the resource (the health care record).

3. The PEP then sends the request to the PDP. The PDP is the main decision point for access requests. It collects all the necessary information from available information sources and concludes with a decision on what access to grant. The PDP should be located in a trusted network with strong access control policies, e.g., in a corporate trusted network protected by a corporate firewall.

4. After evaluation, the PDP sends the XACML response to the PEP.

5. The PEP fulfills the obligations by enforcing the PDP's authorization decision.

The interaction takes place using a request-response protocol with the XACML message as the payload. In this way, XACML is used to convey the evaluation of policies against access decision requests.

Open Authentication (OAuth)

OAuth is an emerging authentication standard that allows consumers to share their private resources (e.g., photos, videos, contact lists, bank accounts) stored on one CSP with another CSP without having to disclose the authentication information (e.g., username and password). OAuth is an open protocol and it was created with the goal of enabling authorization via a secure application programming interface (API)—a simple and standard method for desktop, mobile, and web applications. For application developers, OAuth is a method for publishing and interacting with protected data. For CSPs, OAuth provides a way for users to access their data hosted by another provider while protecting their account credentials.

Within an enterprise, OAuth may play a role to enable SSO with a trusted service provider by employing a web services SSO model. OAuth facilitates authorization of a pair of services to interact without requiring an explicit federation architecture. Much like OpenID, OAuth started in the consumer-centric world to help consumer services access customer data hosted across providers. Recently, Google released a hybrid version of an OpenID and OAuth protocol that combines the authorization and authentication flow in fewer steps to enhance usability. Google's GData API recently announced support for OAuth. (GData also supports SAML for browser SSO.)

Figure 5-6 illustrates the sequence of interactions between customer or partner web application, Google services, and end user:

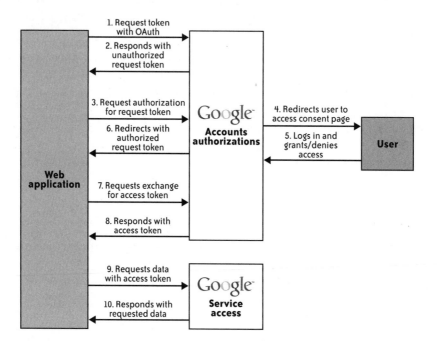

FIGURE 5-6. OAuth use case

1. Customer web application contacts the Google Authorization service, asking for a request token for one or more Google service.

2. Google verifies that the web application is registered and responds with an unauthorized request token.

3. The web application directs the end user to a Google authorization page, referencing the request token.

4. On the Google authorization page, the user is prompted to log into his account (for verification) and then either grant or deny limited access to his Google service data by the web application.

5. The user decides whether to grant or deny access to the web application. If the user denies access, he is directed to a Google page and not back to the web application.

6. If the user grants access, the Authorization service redirects him back to a page designated with the web application that was registered with Google. The redirect includes the now-authorized request token.

7. The web application sends a request to the Google Authorization service to exchange the authorized request token for an access token.

8. Google verifies the request and returns a valid access token.

9. The web application sends a request to the Google service in question. The request is signed and includes the access token.

10. If the Google service recognizes the token, it supplies the requested data.

IAM Standards, Protocols, and Specifications for Consumers

The following protocols and specifications are oriented toward consumer cloud services, and are not relevant from an enterprise cloud computing standpoint.

OpenID

OpenID is an open, decentralized standard for user authentication and access control, allowing users to log on to many services with the same digital identity—i.e., a single sign-on user experience with services supporting OpenID. As such, it replaces the common logon process that uses a logon username and password, by allowing a user to log on once and gain access to the resources of multiple software systems. OpenID is primarily targeted for consumer services offered by Internet companies including Google, eBay, Yahoo!, Microsoft, AOL, BBC, PayPal, and so on. OpenID adoption for enterprise use (e.g., non-consumer use) is almost non-existent due to trust issues; some researchers have revealed that OpenID could accelerate phishing attacks that can result in compromising user credentials.

Information cards

Information cards are another open standard for identity on the Web. The standard itself is directed by the Information Card Foundation, whose steering members include representatives from Google, Microsoft, PayPal, Oracle Novell, and Equifax. The Foundations states that its mission is "to reduce the instance of identity theft by securing digital identities in place of traditional logons and passwords." The goal of this standard is to provide users with a safe, consistent, phishing-resistant user interface that doesn't require a username and password. People can use an information card digital identity across multiple sites for convenience without compromising their login information (similar to using an OpenID identity across multiple sites). The Information Cards Protocol is designed for use in high-value scenarios, such as banking, where phishing resistance and support for secure authentication mechanisms such as smart cards are critical business requirements.

Any service provider can implement, issue, or accept information cards (also called i-cards). Information cards are composed using WS-* specifications instead of HTTP redirect, so the specifications are significantly more complicated than OpenID. Even though this system offers great protection against identity theft and phishing, it still has a few issues that prevent it from achieving its mission. The greatest problem with the system is that it only works if the website used by the consumer is participating and accepts information cards. If this affiliation is not present, the information card is useless. As more and more websites accept information cards, the system will become more and more useful, but until that time, they have limited use. For example, one can use a managed information card issued by Microsoft Windows Live ID to provide single sign-on to most of Microsoft's sites, including MSDN, TechNet, Live, and Connect.

Open Authentication (OATH)

OATH is a collaborative effort of IT industry leaders aimed at providing an architecture reference for universal, strong authentication across all users and all devices over all networks. The goal of this initiative is to address the three major authentication methods:

- Subscriber Identity Module (SIM)-based authentication (using a Global System for Mobile Communications/General Packet Radio Service [GSM/GPRS] SIM)
- Public Key Infrastructure (PKI)-based authentication (using an X.509v3 certificate)
- One-Time Password (OTP)-based authentication

This authentication protocol leverages well-established infrastructure components, such as a directory server and a Remote Authentication Dial-In User Service (RADIUS) server, and also leverages federated identity protocols.

Open Authentication API (OpenAuth)

OpenAuth is an AOL-proprietary API that enables third-party websites and applications to authenticate AOL and AOL Instant Messenger (AIM) users through their websites and applications. Using this authentication method, an AIM- or AOL-registered user can log on to a third-party website or application and access AOL services or new services built on top of AOL services. According to AOL, the OpenAuth API provides the following features:

- A secure method to sign in. User credentials are never exposed to the websites or applications the user signs into.
- A secure method to control which sites are allowed to read private or protected content.
- Automatic granting of permissions only if the user selects Allow Always on the Consent page.
- A prompt for user consent when the website or application attempts to read any private or protected content (e.g., separate consent requests to allow Buddy List information, to send IMs, to read albums).
- Access to other non-AOL websites without the need to create a new user account at each site that supports AOL OpenAuth APIs.

Given the proprietary nature of the protocol, the cloud computing community does not regard OpenAuth as an open standard, and OpenAuth is not adopted outside the AOL network.

Comparison of Enterprise and Consumer Authentication Standards and Protocols

Given that various "Open*" acronyms are being circulated in the context of authentication, authorization, and federation protocols and standards, Table 5-1 is an attempt to compare them from the point of open standards support and their relevance in enterprise and consumer cloud services.

TABLE 5-1. Comparison of IAM standards and protocols

IAM protocols and standards	Enabling vendors	Enterprise cloud customer requirements	CSP requirements
SAML	IdM software vendors such as Sun, Oracle, CA, IBM, and Novell, and identity management service providers such as Microsoft Azure, Symplified, TriCipher, and Ping Identity	Support strong authentication and web SSO, avoid duplication of identity, and share only selected attributes to protect user privacy	Enable customers to delegate authentication and choose authentication methods (e.g., dual-factor authentication using corporate identity) that enable adoption of the cloud service
XACML	Supported by Sun, CA, IBM, Jericho Systems, Oracle, Red Hat, Securent (Cisco), and Oracle	A standard way to express authorization policies across a diverse set of cloud services and externalize authorization and enforcement from the application	Support authorization that can represent complex policies required by enterprise-scale applications and administrators
OAuth	Supported via an API by service providers including Google, Twitter, Facebook, and Plaxo	Publish and interact with protected data stored on one CSP and accessed from another CSP using a standard API and without disclosing credentials	Enable users to access their data hosted by another service provider while protecting their account and credential information
OpenID	Supported by many service providers including Google, IBM, Microsoft, Yahoo!, Orange, PayPal, VeriSign, Yandex, AOL, and USTREAM	Not adopted due to trust issues	Support SSO for consumers participating in this federated identity service
OATH	Supported by many authentication hardware and software vendors including	Not relevant	Not relevant

IAM protocols and standards	Enabling vendors	Enterprise cloud customer requirements	CSP requirements
	VeriSign, SanDisk, Gemalto, and Entrust		
OpenAuth	Supported by AOL only for users accessing partner services	Not relevant	Support AOL users accessing partner applications using AOL or AIM user IDs

IAM Practices in the Cloud

When compared to the traditional applications deployment model within the enterprise, IAM practices in the cloud are still evolving.

In the current state of IAM technology, standards support by CSPs (SaaS, PaaS, and IaaS) is not consistent across providers. Although large providers such as Google, Microsoft, and Salesforce.com seem to demonstrate basic IAM capabilities, our assessment is that they still fall short of enterprise IAM requirements for managing regulatory, privacy, and data protection requirements. Table 5-2 illustrates the current maturity model, based on the authors' assessment, generalized across SPI service delivery models.

TABLE 5-2. Comparison of SPI maturity models in the context of IAM

Level	SaaS	PaaS	IaaS
User Management, New Users	Capable	Immature	Aware
User Management, User Modifications	Capable	Immature	Immature
Authentication Management	Capable	Aware	Capable
Authorization Management	Aware	Immature	Immature

The maturity model takes into account the dynamic nature of IAM users, systems, and applications in the cloud and addresses the four key components of the IAM automation process:

- User Management, New Users
- User Management, User Modifications
- Authentication Management
- Authorization Management

Table 5-3 defines the maturity levels as they relate to the four key components.

TABLE 5-3. Comparison of maturity levels for IAM components

Level	Immature	Aware	Capable	Mature	Industry-leading
User Management, New Users	Manual, ad hoc, with no formal process	Manual, ad hoc, following established processes	Automated where appropriate Disparate processes	Automated using more than one process	Automated using a single provisioning process
User Management, User Modifications	Manual, ad hoc, per application	Manual, ad hoc, per application group	Manual or automated per application group	Automated per class of application and resource	Automated across the application space
Authentication Management	Manual, ad hoc No common security policy	Addressed per application No common authorization mechanism	Common authentication mechanism No common authentication module	Common authentication module Minimal credentials Common security policy	Common authentication mechanism as a component service to applications Common security policy
Authorization Management	Manual, ad hoc No rule- or role-based authorization	Addressed per application No common authorization mechanism	Common service No common module	Common module Application-specific attributes disparately maintained	Common mechanism Centrally managed attributes Support role Rule-based

By matching the model's descriptions of various maturity levels with the cloud services delivery model's (SaaS, PaaS, IaaS) current state of IAM, a clear picture emerges of IAM maturity across the four IAM components. If, for example, the service delivery model (SPI) is "immature" in one area but "capable" or "aware" in all others, the IAM maturity model can help focus attention on the area most in need of attention.

Although the principles and purported benefits of established enterprise IAM practices and processes are applicable to cloud services, they need to be adjusted to the cloud environment. Broadly speaking, user management functions in the cloud can be categorized as follows:

- Cloud identity administration
- Federation or SSO
- Authorization management
- Compliance management

We will now discuss each of the aforementioned practices in detail.

Cloud Identity Administration

Cloud identity administrative functions should focus on life cycle management of user identities in the cloud—provisioning, deprovisioning, identity federation, SSO, password or credentials management, profile management, and administrative management. Organizations that are not capable of supporting federation should explore cloud-based identity management services. This new breed of services usually synchronizes an organization's internal directories with its directory (usually multitenant) and acts as a proxy IdP for the organization.

By federating identities using either an internal Internet-facing IdP or a cloud identity management service provider, organizations can avoid duplicating identities and attributes and storing them with the CSP. Given the inconsistent and sparse support for identity standards among CSPs, customers may have to devise custom methods to address user management functions in the cloud. Provisioning users when federation is not supported can be complex and laborious. It is not unusual for organizations to employ manual processes, web-based administration, outsourced (delegated) administration that involves uploading of spreadsheets, and execution of custom scripts at both the customer and CSP locations. The latter model is not desirable as it is not scalable across multiple CSPs and will be costly to manage in the long run.

Federated Identity (SSO)

Organizations planning to implement identity federation that enables SSO for users can take one of the following two paths (architectures):

- Implement an enterprise IdP within an organization perimeter.
- Integrate with a trusted cloud-based identity management service provider.

Both architectures have pros and cons.

Enterprise identity provider

In this architecture, cloud services will delegate authentication to an organization's IdP. In this delegated authentication architecture, the organization federates identities within a trusted circle of CSP domains. A circle of trust can be created with all the domains that are authorized to delegate authentication to the IdP. In this deployment architecture, where the organization will provide and support an IdP, greater control can be exercised over user identities, attributes, credentials, and policies for authenticating and authorizing users to a cloud service. Figure 5-7 illustrates the IdP deployment architecture.

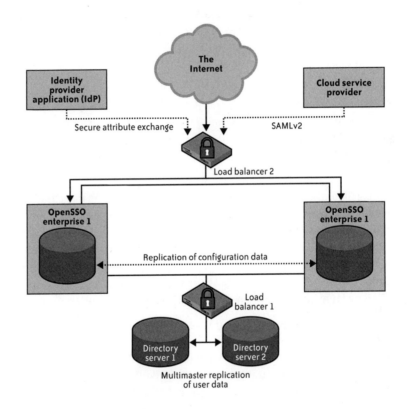

FIGURE 5-7. Identity provider deployment architecture

Here are the specific pros and cons of this approach:

Pros

Organizations can leverage the existing investment in their IAM infrastructure and extend the practices to the cloud. For example, organizations that have implemented SSO for applications within their data center exhibit the following benefits:

- They are consistent with internal policies, processes, and access management frameworks.

- They have direct oversight of the service-level agreement (SLA) and security of the IdP.

- They have an incremental investment in enhancing the existing identity architecture to support federation.

Cons

By not changing the infrastructure to support federation, new inefficiencies can result due to the addition of life cycle management for non-employees such as customers.

Most organizations will likely continue to manage employee and long-term contractor identities using organically developed IAM infrastructures and practices. But they seem to prefer to outsource the management of partner and consumer identities to a trusted cloud-based identity provider as a service partner.

Identity management-as-a-service

In this architecture, cloud services can delegate authentication to an identity management-as-a-service (IDaaS) provider. In this model, organizations outsource the federated identity management technology and user management processes to a third-party service provider, such as Ping Identity, TriCipher's Myonelogin.com, or Symplified.com.

When federating identities to the cloud, organizations may need to manage the identity life cycle using their IAM system and processes. However, the organization might benefit from an outsourced multiprotocol federation gateway (identity federation service) if it has to interface with many different partners and cloud service federation schemes. For example, as of this writing, Salesforce.com supports SAML 1.1 and Google Apps supports SAML 2.0. Enterprises accessing Google Apps and Salesforce.com may benefit from a multiprotocol federation gateway hosted by an identity management CSP such as Symplified or TriCipher.

In cases where credentialing is difficult and costly, an enterprise might also outsource credential issuance (and background investigations) to a service provider, such as the GSA Managed Service Organization (MSO) that issues personal identity verification (PIV) cards and, optionally, the certificates on the cards. The GSA MSO[†] is offering the USAccess management end-to-end solution as a shared service to federal civilian agencies.

In essence, this is a SaaS model for identity management, where the SaaS IdP stores identities in a "trusted identity store" and acts as a proxy for the organization's users accessing cloud services, as illustrated in Figure 5-8.

† For more information on this, see *http://www.fedidcard.gov/overview.aspx*.

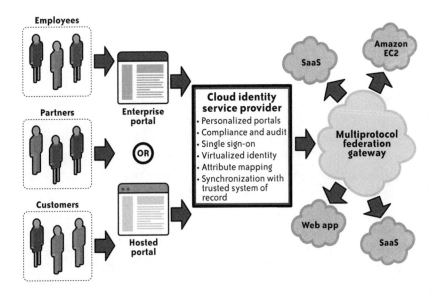

FIGURE 5-8. Identity management-as-a-service (IDaaS)

The identity store in the cloud is kept in sync with the corporate directory through a provider-proprietary scheme (e.g., agents running on the customer's premises synchronizing a subset of an organization's identity store to the identity store in the cloud using SSL VPNs).

Once the IdP is established in the cloud, the organization should work with the CSP to delegate authentication to the cloud identity service provider. The cloud IdP will authenticate the cloud users prior to them accessing any cloud services (this is done via browser SSO techniques that involve standard HTTP redirection techniques).

Here are the specific pros and cons of this approach:

Pros

> Delegating certain authentication use cases to the cloud identity management service hides the complexity of integrating with various CSPs supporting different federation standards. Case in point: Salesforce.com and Google support delegated authentication using SAML. However, as of this writing, they support two different versions of SAML: Google Apps supports only SAML 2.0, and Salesforce.com supports only SAML 1.1. Cloud-based identity management services that support both SAML standards (multiprotocol federation gateways) can hide this integration complexity from organizations adopting cloud services.

> Another benefit is that there is little need for architectural changes to support this model. Once identity synchronization between the organization directory or trusted system of record and the identity service directory in the cloud is set up, users can sign on to cloud

services using corporate identity, credentials (both static and dynamic), and authentication policies.

Cons

When you rely on a third party for an identity management service, you may have less visibility into the service, including implementation and architecture details. Hence, the availability and authentication performance of cloud applications hinges on the identity management service provider's SLA, performance management, and availability. It is important to understand the provider's service level, architecture, service redundancy, and performance guarantees of the identity management service provider.

Another drawback to this approach is that it may not be able to generate custom reports to meet internal compliance requirements.

In addition, identity attribute management can also become complex when identity attributes are not properly defined and associated with identities (e.g., definitions of attributes, both mandatory and optional). New governance processes may be required to authorize various operations (add/modify/remove attributes) to govern user attributes that move outside the organization's trust boundary. Identity attributes will change through the life cycle of the identity itself and may get out of sync.

Although both approaches enable the identification and authentication of users to cloud services, various features and integration nuances are specific to the service delivery model—SaaS, PaaS, and IaaS—as we will discuss in the next section.

Cloud Authorization Management

Medium-size and large organizations usually have specific requirements for authorization features for their cloud users (i.e., assignment of privileges, or entitlements, to users based on their job functions). In some cases, a business application may require role-based access control (RBAC), in which case authorization is structured to suit the organization's functional role requirements. As of this writing, cloud service authorization enforcement and management capabilities are weak, and when they are available they are very coarse-grained. The services available may not meet your enterprise requirements.

Most cloud services support at least dual roles (privileges): administrator and end user. It is a normal practice among CSPs to provision the administrator role with administrative privileges. These privileges allow administrators to provision and deprovision identities, basic attribute profiles, and, in some cases, to set access control policies such as password strength and trusted networks from which connections are accepted.

As we mentioned earlier, XACML is the preferred standard for expressing and enforcing authorization and user authentication policies. As of this writing, we are not aware of any cloud services supporting XACML to express authorization policies for users.

IAM Support for Compliance Management

As much as cloud IAM architecture and practices impact the efficiency of internal IT processes, they also play a major role in managing compliance within the enterprise. Properly implemented IAM practices and processes can help improve the effectiveness of the controls identified by compliance frameworks. For example, by automating the timely provisioning and deprovisioning of users and entitlements, organizations can reduce the risk of unauthorized users accessing cloud services and meet your privacy and compliance requirements. In addition, identity and attribute management will be key areas of compliance focus for regulatory and privacy issues—proper IAM governance processes should be instituted to address these issues.

IAM practices and processes offer a centralized view of business operations and an automated process that can stop insider threats before they occur. However, given the sparse support for IAM standards such as SAML (federation), SPML (provisioning), and XACML (authorization) by the CSP, you should assess the CSP capabilities on a case-by-case basis and institute processes for managing compliance related to identity (including attribute) and access management. Refer to Chapter 8 for information on compliance management in the cloud.

Cloud Service Provider IAM Practice

From the CSP's (SaaS, PaaS, or IaaS) perspective, IAM features should be included in the cloud service's design criteria, with the goal of delegating user authentication and authorization to the customer using user management and federation standards. Support for IAM features has integration implications for both customers (e.g., single sign-on, user provisioning) and CSPs (e.g., billing, accounting resource utilization). For both the customer and CSP, IAM integration considerations at the early stage of service design will help avoid costly retrofits. Hence, cloud service architects and platform application developers should be embedding IAM features at various stages of the product life cycle—architecture, design, and implementation (e.g., externalize the authentication from the application using the federation feature).

From a cloud customer perspective, the application's IAM capabilities (or lack thereof), such as identity federation, will impact the cloud service governance, integration, and user experience (e.g., barriers to adopt the cloud service). Hence, architects, designers, and developers of cloud applications should understand the IAM requirements of cloud applications and bake the features into the RFP or CSP evaluation criteria.

Enterprise IAM requirements include:

- Provisioning of cloud service accounts to users, including administrators.
- Provisioning of cloud services for service-to-service integration (e.g., private [internal] cloud integration with a public cloud).
- SSO support for users based on federation standards (e.g., SAML support).

- Support for internal- and regulatory-policy compliance requirements, including segregation of duties using RBAC, rules, or claims-based authentication methodology. RBAC features promote a least-privilege-based access model where a user is granted the right number of privileges required to perform the job. Claims-based methodology enables some important privacy use cases because it allows for only the user's entitlements, not her actual identity, to flow with messages, which allows for fine-grained authorization without the requirement to actually embed the user's identity into messages.

- User activity monitoring, logging, and reporting dictated by internal policies and regulatory compliance, such as SOX, PCI, and HIPAA.

SaaS

One of the primary concerns of IT and business decision makers regarding software-as-a-service applications is security management.

Although most SaaS vendors have been able to demonstrate that their cloud-based applications are secure from an operational point of view, there are still access control issues that organizations need to address to ensure that their corporate data is fully secure from a corporate policies and procedures standpoint.

It is becoming particularly important to address these issues because SaaS applications are gaining popularity due to their low barrier to adoption and their pay-as-you-go service model. In some cases, business units are sidestepping IT and directly engaging with SaaS vendors, which can lead to additional IT headaches. IT must manage risks that may come out of this loss of visibility and control, and be able to ensure that the right users have the right level of access to information hosted by SaaS vendors.

Organizations considering integrating into SaaS services should consider two major challenges for identity management:

- Is the organization ready to provision and manage the user life cycle by extending its established IAM practice to the SaaS service?

- Are the SaaS provider capabilities sufficient to automate user provisioning and life cycle management without implementing a custom solution for the SaaS service?

Customer responsibilities

In SaaS services, customers have limited responsibility and available controls to secure information. In general, SaaS solutions are multitenant and are delivered to the customer via a web browser. The only controls that are available to the customer are IAM controls such as identity provisioning, authentication policies (e.g., password strength), profile configuration, and basic authorization policies that manifest as user profiles. The following are the responsibilities of customers from an IAM perspective:

User provisioning

User provisioning methods are typically unique to the SaaS provider. Customers need to understand the preferred method, lag time to activate users, and user attributes that are supported by the SaaS service. Most often the provisioning process is manual and may involve uploading spreadsheets or documents in XML format. Almost all SaaS providers support bulk upload of user identities, as that's the most common use case for provisioning users. Some SaaS providers may support just-in-time provisioning where user identities are created on the fly using a provisioning request (sometimes SPML-employed) that is usually triggered by user activity such as the user clicking on a hyperlink that is unique to the user identity.

Profile management

As part of the provisioning process, customers may have the ability to create user profiles that play a role in user authorization. User profiles such as *user* and *manager* are an approach to assigning entitlements to users within the SaaS application. Admittedly, these are not sophisticated features and will require customers to understand the flexibility and management of the profiles.

SaaS IAM capability evaluation

Customers are responsible for evaluating the support for IAM features such as SSO (using identity federation) by CSPs. SAML is the de facto standard for federating identities and is now supported by large SaaS providers (among them Google and Salesforce.com). However, not all providers are supporting SAML 2.0, and some may support only SAML 1.1. For example, Salesforce.com supports SAML 1.1 while Google Apps supports SAML 2.0. Hence, it is important to understand what federation protocols are supported by which providers and the integration requirements to federate and support SSO.

Investigation support

Logs and audit trails are also often needed to investigate incidents. For example, PCI DSS requires the provider to "provide for timely forensic investigation" if the service provider suffers a breach. Since the SaaS provider's logs are internal and are not necessarily accessible externally or by customers, monitoring (let alone investigation) is difficult. Since access to logs is required for PCI compliance and may be requested by auditors and regulators, make sure to negotiate access to the provider's logs as part of any service agreement.

Compliance management

Although the same security concerns companies already have within their own networks—securing the network, hardware, applications, and data—apply for companies outsourcing their data with SaaS, trust and transparency exacerbate the situation in cloud computing. When compliance with government regulations such as SOX, the Gramm-Leach-Bliley Act (GLBA), and HIPAA and with industry standards such as PCI DSS come into the scope of the data hosted in SaaS, it could be challenging to meet those demands. In general, customers of SaaS services are responsible for compliance management, although the provider hosts the data. Make an effort to understand the access control, logging, reporting, and auditing capabilities offered by SaaS providers and assess whether those controls are adequate to meet compliance management requirements.

CSP responsibilities

With regard to IAM, some responsibilities belong to the CSP and some belong to the customer. Here are CSP responsibilities:

Authentication services

Unless the SaaS provider supports delegated authentication via federation, it typically authenticates the SaaS users—usually via a web form delivered over HTTPS—using a user identifier and static password. Since users can be accessing the service from anywhere on the Internet, it is up to the SaaS provider to authenticate users based on the network trust level. For example, some CSPs can preregister the IP address or IP range of a user's location (home, office, etc.) to protect data from hackers who are stealing the user's identity and credentials using keystroke loggers (potentially installed on the user's computer in a stealthy manner). Given that authentication activity is a precursor to the actual use of the SaaS service, it is critical for the CSP to deliver and maintain a continuously available authentication service.

Account management policies

CSPs should communicate the account management policies including account lock-outs (after many login failures), account provisioning methods, and privilege account management roles.

Federation

CSPs supporting identity federation using standards such as SAML should publish the information necessary for customers to take advantage of this feature and enable SSO for their users. Such information includes the version (SAML 1.1, SAML 2.0), a use case implementation example, and implementation details of the federation using the API (e.g., support for SAML using REST and SOAP).

PaaS

Organizations considering extending their established IAM practices to PaaS cloud providers have few options at their disposal. PaaS CSPs typically delegate authentication functions using federation to the PaaS provider's IdP (e.g., the Google App Engine delegates authentication to Google's authentication service). In some cases, such as Salesforce.com's Force.com, there is limited support for delegated authentication and it is usually performed without the aid of SAML assertions (e.g., it is proprietary to each PaaS provider implementation). CSPs also supply software components that can be invoked using programming languages (usually PaaS-specific) to perform authentication and limited authorization.

Microsoft recently introduced the "Geneva" Claims-Based Access Platform that is SAML 2.0 compliant (and is still in beta as of this writing). The project's goal is to help developers externalize authentication, authorization, and personalization from .NET applications, and help organizations federate users using Microsoft's federation offering, Security Token Service (STS). Microsoft developers could potentially utilize STS deployed in an enterprise, and interoperate with applications that are deployed on an Azure platform. This solution is specifically targeted toward Microsoft customers who are interested in extending their Active Directory directory into a cloud by way of federation. Therefore, it is not apparent whether the Geneva Claims-Based Access Platform will interoperate with existing SaaS and PaaS providers who are SAML 2.0 compliant.

IaaS

As of this writing, enterprises considering extending their established IAM practices to IaaS cloud providers (computing and storage) have limited or no options. Because IaaS providers provide computing or storage-as-a-service, they do not have visibility to applications that are hosted on the IaaS platform. Almost all IaaS providers use Secure Shell (SSH) to log on and administer users and credentials; few providers, such as Amazon Web Services (AWS) EC2, offer a web console to provision users, manage user keys, and assign users to security groups that relate to the administrative functions of IaaS.

Some of the responsibilities and challenges in managing users in IaaS services are:

User provisioning
> Provisioning of users (developers, administrators) on IaaS systems that are dynamic in nature. Given that hundreds of systems are provisioned for workload management, user provisioning will have to be automated at the time of image creation and should be policy-based. Ideally, systems should rely on corporate directories (LDAP, Active Directory) for user management to avoid duplication of identities on systems. However, the virtual network topology in cloud and network security policies may interfere with directory-based authentication schemes and should be assessed on a per-CSP basis.

Privileged user management
> Managing private keys of system administrators and protecting the keys when system administrators leave the company (e.g., SSH host keys).

Customer key assignment
> Assigning IDs and keys required to access the service. These keys are used for managing access to customer accounts for billing reasons, as well as for authenticating customers to their services. For example, Amazon assigns an Access Key ID, a Secret Access Key, an X.509 certificate, and a corresponding private key to every EC2 customer. You authenticate to an AWS request using either the Access Key ID and Secret Access Key or the X.509 certificate and private key. Hence, customers are responsible for provisioning and safeguarding these keys.

Developer user management
> Provisioning of developers and testers to IaaS instances, and deprovisioning the same when access is no longer required.

End user management
> Provisioning users who need access to applications hosted on IaaS.

Currently, there is no automated way to synchronize an organizational LDAP or Active Directory directory with IaaS providers to avoid a redundant user database at each of the IaaS clouds. Some third-party identity management service providers claim to have developed adapters for EC2 user provisioning and management, however.

Guidance

Handling identity and access management in the cloud remains one of the major hurdles for enterprise adoption of cloud services. IAM support for business needs ranges from secure collaboration with global partners to secure access for global employees who are consuming sensitive information from any location and any device at any time.

Although the basic technology building blocks (trusted identity stores, provisioning processes, authorization and authentication methods, federation) for IAM exist today, migrating or extending those technologies into cloud services, in their current form, will not yield the purported IAM benefits of efficiency, efficacy, and business agility. The sheer volume of dynamic cloud compute resources (compute nodes, storage, network policies) combined with the magnitude of users and services accessing those resources will challenge the scalability and automation of processes, to manage users in a dynamic environment—both users and applications in the cloud.

The legacy IAM solutions deployed in the enterprise will exacerbate the problem. IAM architecture and solutions in their current form are complex, require extensive customization, and are expensive to extend to cloud services. Trusted sources of identities in the cloud are still an issue and need to be addressed. On the other hand, the support for IAM practices and standards by CSPs is sparse and is not adequate for most enterprises. Although large SaaS cloud services are showing signs of support for federation standards such as SAML, they are largely absent from PaaS and IaaS services.

A small set of CSPs (mostly large SaaS providers, such as Salesforce.com, Google, and Microsoft) are beginning to pay attention to enterprise IAM requirements, including support for standards such as SAML that facilitate SSO using identity federation techniques. However, given the early adoption cycle by large enterprises, from an enterprise perspective the IAM capabilities are primitive at best. Customers should continue to demand that their CSPs provide IAM features, including SAML support, user provisioning using SPML, XACML support for authorization, and an open API to support various user and access automation processes.

This IAM capability chasm has given birth to a new breed of cloud-based identity management services that move your identity trust boundary out of your perimeter and into the cloud. Identity services and frameworks such as Microsoft's Azure STS support federation from Active Directory to Microsoft's cloud services and facilitate user SSO from an on-premises Active Directory to Microsoft's cloud services. In addition, start-ups such as Symplified, Ping Identity, and TriCipher are offering varying approaches to SSO access control, usage tracking, and centralized management of multiple SaaS applications. Although these cloud-based identity management services are lowering the barriers to entry for small and medium-size businesses (SMBs), they may be deemed inadequate by some enterprises to meet stringent requirements in the areas of custom reporting and compliance management.

Trusting cloud service provider and user data management are other barriers to entry, since most enterprises are not willing to store their trusted sources for identity outside controlled enterprise boundaries. This issue is further exacerbated by use cases in which attribute data associated with identities is either copied or stored in the cloud service. Synchronizing multiple identity repositories remains a key challenge for enterprises. Working with cloud-based services and addressing synchronization issues by way of federation, virtual directories, and an open API will reduce these barriers.

To avoid costly retrofits and integration with after-market products, organizations looking to adopt cloud-based services should embed the IAM strategy into their cloud services strategy road map. Organizations that have been investing in directories, IAM capabilities, and IAM practices should therefore stand to gain by leveraging an optimized internal IAM strategy and practice in the cloud. The most important success factor for an enterprise to effectively manage identities and access control in the cloud is the presence of a robust directory and federated identity management capability within the organization (internal or cloud-based identity management service): architecture and systems, user and access life cycle management processes, and audit and compliance capabilities.

When it comes to authenticating users and services to the cloud, organizations need to pay attention to simplicity and ease of use in addition to risk-based authentication methods (e.g., log when sensitive data is accessed). Another premise to keep in mind is that all clouds are not created equal, so enterprises need to have a strategy for employing risk-based IAM methods including strong authentication, automated provisioning, deprovisioning, auditing, and monitoring to address risks specific to a CSP.

Although identification and authentication challenges can be overcome (when the CSP makes those capabilities available) with a well-architected IAM infrastructure and IT processes, authorization services in the cloud are very basic and evolving.

Organizations using cloud services should be aware that granular application authorization is immature at this point. Where it does exist, it is usually implemented using the CSP's proprietary profiles and primitive roles—often CSPs offer primitive roles such as "user" and "administrator." As a long-term strategy, customers should be advocating for greater support of XACML-compliant entitlement management on the part of cloud providers, even if XACML has not been implemented internally. XACML provides a standardized language and method of access control and policy enforcement across all applications that enforce a common authorization standard. At the very least, chief information security officers (CISOs) should be thinking about authorization standards and avoid any temptation to customize solutions based on their provider's capability.

Business and IT stakeholders should also be advocating standardization of enterprise roles within the enterprise at a coarse granular level; roles that are mapped to higher-level business functions (e.g., accounts payable manager, HR manager, or purchase order approver). Limited use of the role attribute can be useful for access control in some organizations, but is not viable for others. However, rule-based access control (leveraging multiple attributes, groups, etc.) is more flexible as it allows you to respond to business changes quickly.

In the future, well-defined enterprise roles should be mapped to the cloud service roles or profiles supported by the CSPs. We believe SPML and XACML will play a role in that regard. Currently, we are not aware of any effort to standardize the naming conventions of enterprise roles.

IT architects should be advocating externalization of authentication and authorization components from applications (loosely coupled) as this can aid in the rapid adoption of cloud-based services including cloud identity management services, policy-based authentication, centralized logging, and auditing. For example, Sun Microsystems' OpenSSO and Microsoft's Geneva claims-based authentication framework can help externalize authentication.

Organizations that have less mature IAM infrastructure, capabilities, and processes should strive to standardize IAM features across their applications, cloud or otherwise. A major benefit of centralized management should be easier management, allowing for faster cloud adoption by enterprises. In addition, self-service capabilities, password management, and auditing and reporting features can help improve the efficiency and response efficacy to compliance demands. Standard identity repositories for cloud applications can make use of attributes more quickly and with standard security models.

Organizations evaluating cloud services, in addition to core CSP service capabilities, should include CSP support for identity and access management, including support for federation, in the evaluation criteria. Today, support for IAM features including identity federation and SSO is sparse and is not consistent across CSPs. Customers will have to assess identity integration with CSPs on a case-by-case basis. If possible, customers should avoid any temptations to customize their user access management solution to suit a specific CSP as this will reduce IAM process efficiency and increase management costs in the long run. Standardization of IAM processes across CSPs (multiple clouds) will provide the benefit of centralized user and access management and will mitigate risks related to unauthorized access of cloud services.

Summary

Customers considering cloud services (IaaS, PaaS, or SaaS) should consider their organization's operational, security, privacy, and compliance requirements; CSP support for IAM practices (e.g., federation) and standards (e.g., SAML, OAuth); and the ongoing operational requirements to provision and manage the user identity life cycle. Organizations that either suffer from weak IAM practices or lack a federated architecture may benefit from identity management-as-a-service when interfacing with many different partners and cloud service federation schemes. To save costly integration and avoid retrofitting of features, enterprises should prepare with an IAM strategy and architecture that allows them to extend their IAM practice using standard protocols, such as SAML, SPML, and XACML, to manage user account provisioning, authentication, and authorization in the cloud.

CHAPTER SIX

Security Management in the Cloud

WITH THE ADOPTION OF PUBLIC CLOUD SERVICES, A LARGE PART OF YOUR NETWORK, system, applications, and data will move under third-party provider control. The cloud services delivery model will create islands (clouds) of virtual perimeters as well as a security model with responsibilities shared between the customer and the cloud service provider (CSP). This shared responsibility model will bring new security management challenges to the organization's IT operations staff. With that in mind, the first question a chief information security officer (CISO) must answer is whether she has adequate transparency from cloud services to manage the governance (shared responsibilities) and implementation of security management processes (preventive and detective controls) to assure the business that the data in the cloud is appropriately protected. The answer to this question has two parts: what security controls must the customer provide over and above the controls inherent in the cloud platform, and how must an enterprise's security management tools and processes adapt to manage security in the cloud. Both answers must be continually reevaluated based on the sensitivity of the data and the service-level changes over time.

As a customer of the cloud, you should start with the exercise of understanding the trust boundary of your services in the cloud. You should understand all the layers you own, touch, or interface with in the cloud service—network, host, application, database, storage, and web services including identity services (see Figure 6-1). You also need to understand the scope of IT system management and monitoring responsibilities that fall on your shoulders, including access, change, configuration, patch, and vulnerability management.

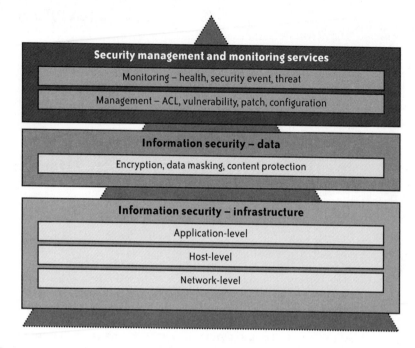

FIGURE 6-1. Security management and monitoring scope

Although you may be transferring some of the operational responsibilities to the provider, the level of responsibilities will vary and will depend on a variety of factors, including the service delivery model (SPI), provider service-level agreement (SLA), and provider-specific capabilities to support the extension of your internal security management processes and tools.

Mature IT organizations are known to employ security management frameworks, such as ISO/ IEC 27000 and the Information Technology Infrastructure Library (ITIL) service management framework. These industry standard management frameworks provide guidance for planning and implementing a governance program with sustaining management processes that protect information assets. For example, ITIL gives a detailed description of a number of important IT practices with comprehensive checklists, tasks, and procedures that can be tailored to any IT organization. A key tenet of ITIL, and one that is applicable to cloud computing, is that organizations (people, processes) and information systems are constantly changing. Hence, management frameworks such as ITIL will help with the continuous service improvement that is necessary to align and realign IT services to changing business needs. Continuous service improvement means identifying and implementing improvements to the IT services that support business processes such as sales force automation using a cloud service provider. Given the dynamic characteristics of cloud computing services, the activities present within the security management processes must be continually revised to remain current and effective.

In short, security management is a constant process and will be very relevant to cloud security management.

The goal of the ITIL Security Management framework is divided into two parts:

Realization of security requirements
> Security requirements are usually defined in the SLA as well as in other external requirements, which are specified in underpinning contracts, legislation, and internally or externally imposed policies.

Realization of a basic level of security
> This is necessary to guarantee the security and continuity of the organization and to reach simplified service-level management for information security management.

Well-established security management processes are also aligned with an organization's IT policies and standards, with the goal of protecting the confidentiality, integrity, and availability of information. Figure 6-2 illustrates the ITIL life cycle in a enterprise. Security management disciplines are represented by relevant ISO and ITIL functions.

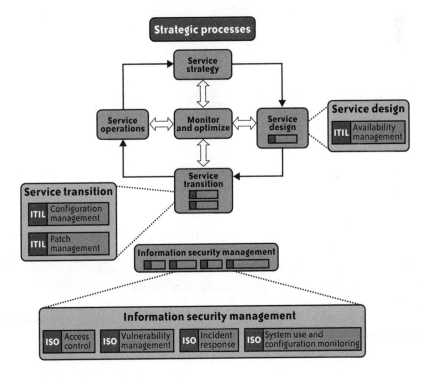

FIGURE 6-2. The ITIL life cycle in a enterprise

So, how does security management manifest in cloud services? What security management functions can customers expect from CSPs? This chapter discusses the current state, your responsibility scope, and guidance for security management in public clouds in the context of the SPI (SaaS, PaaS, IaaS) service delivery model.

Security Management Standards

Based on the authors' assessment, the standards that are relevant to security management practices in the cloud are ITIL and ISO/IEC 27001 and 27002.

ITIL

The Information Technology Infrastructure Library (ITIL) is a set of best practices and guidelines that define an integrated, process-based approach for managing information technology services. ITIL can be applied across almost every type of IT environment including cloud operating environment. ITIL seeks to ensure that effective information security measures are taken at strategic, tactical, and operational levels. Information security is considered an iterative process that must be controlled, planned, implemented, evaluated, and maintained.

ITIL breaks information security down into:

Policies
> The overall objectives an organization is attempting to achieve

Processes
> What has to happen to achieve the objectives

Procedures
> Who does what and when to achieve the objectives

Work instructions
> Instructions for taking specific actions

The ITIL-process security management is based on the code of practice for information security management also known as ISO/IEC 17799:2005. The ITIL security management process has relationships with almost all other ITIL processes. However, the most obvious relationships will be to the service-level management process, incident management process, and change management process, since they greatly influence the state of security in the system (server, network, or application). ITIL also is related to ISO/IEC 20000 as that's the first international standard for IT Service Management (ITSM). It is based on and is intended to supersede the earlier British standard, BS 15000.

Organizations and management systems cannot be certified as "ITIL-compliant." An organization that has implemented ITIL guidance in ITSM can, however, achieve compliance with and seek certification under ISO/IEC 20000.

ISO 27001/27002

ISO/IEC 27001 formally defines the mandatory requirements for an Information Security Management System (ISMS). It is also a certification standard and uses ISO/IEC 27002 to indicate suitable information security controls within the ISMS. However, since ISO/IEC 27002 is merely a code of practice/guideline rather than a certification standard, organizations are free to select and implement controls as they see fit.

Given the current trend of organizations moving toward ISO/IEC 27001 for information security management, there is a general consensus among information security practitioners to revise the ITIL security management best practices with the goal of strengthening the application and logical security in the Information and Communication Technology (ICT) infrastructure domain.

Essentially, the ITIL, ISO/IEC 20000, and ISO/IEC 27001/27002 frameworks help IT organizations internalize and respond to basic questions such as:

- How do I ensure that the current security levels are appropriate for your needs?
- How do I apply a security baseline throughout your operation?

To that end, they help you to respond to the question: how do I ensure that my services are secure?

Security Management in the Cloud

After analyzing the management process disciplines across the ITIL and ISO frameworks, we (the authors) identified the following relevant processes as the recommended security management focus areas for securing services in the cloud:

- Availability management (ITIL)
- Access control (ISO/IEC 27002, ITIL)
- Vulnerability management (ISO/IEC 27002)
- Patch management (ITIL)
- Configuration management (ITIL)
- Incident response (ISO/IEC 27002)
- System use and access monitoring (ISO/IEC 27002)

We selected these security management processes based on the cloud security considerations discussed in Chapters 2, 3, and 5 and the impact they will have in minimizing the overall risk to the organization. Other ITIL management domains, such as problem management and service continuity management, may be more relevant to your business in the context of security management, but the focus of this chapter is limited to the subset of domains with the highest impact to organizations in managing security and operational risk. In subsequent sections, we will discuss the security management processes that are relevant to cloud services. We have also attempted to highlight the current state of cloud service support for security management processes in the context of the SPI delivery model and deployment models (private, public, and hybrid). Clearly, this is an evolving area, and we recommend that you periodically reexamine cloud service capabilities and fine-tune your security management processes accordingly.

Table 6-1 highlights the relevance of various security management functions available to you for each of the SPI cloud delivery models in the context of deployment models (private and public). As you can see from the table, security management practice cuts across the delivery and deployment models. These functions need to be factored into your cloud security operations model.

TABLE 6-1. *Relevant security management functions for SPI cloud delivery models in the context of deployment models (private, public)*

Cloud deployment/SPI	Public clouds	Private clouds
Software-as-a-service (SaaS)	• Access control (partial) • Monitoring system use and access (partial) • Incident response	The following functions typically managed by your IT department or managed services: • Availability management • Access control • Vulnerability management • Patch management • Configuration management • Incident response • Monitoring system use and access
Platform-as-a-service (PaaS)	The following are limited to customer applications deployed in PaaS (CSP is responsible for the PaaS platform): • Availability management • Access control • Vulnerability management • Patch management • Configuration management • Incident response • Monitoring system use and access	
Infrastructure-as-a-service (IaaS)	• Availability management (virtual instances) • Access control (user and limited network) • Vulnerability management (operating system and applications) • Patch management (operating system and applications)	

Cloud deployment/SPI	Public clouds	Private clouds
	• Configuration management (operating system and applications) • Incident response • Monitoring system use and access (operating system and applications)	

Hence, organizations looking to augment the public cloud for certain use cases can leverage and extend their internal security management practices and processes developed for their internal private cloud services.

Availability Management

Cloud services are not immune to outages, and the severity and scope of impact to the customer can vary based on the outage situation. Similar to any internal IT-supported application, business impact due to a service outage will depend on the criticality of the cloud application and its relationship to internal business processes. In the case of business-critical applications where businesses rely on the continuous availability of service, even a few minutes of service outage can have a serious impact on your organization's productivity, revenue, customer satisfaction, and service-level compliance.

According to the Cloud Computing Incidents Database (CCID), which tracks cloud service outages, major CSPs have suffered downtime ranging from a few minutes to a few hours. In one case, a service outage lasted more than 24 hours! Furthermore, depending on the severity of the incident and the scope of the affected infrastructure, outages may affect all or a subset of customers. During a cloud service disruption, affected customers will not be able to access the cloud service and in some cases may suffer degraded performance or user experience. For example, when a storage service is disrupted, it will affect the availability and performance of a computing service that depends on the storage service.

Figures 6-3* and 6-4 show some examples of recent outages.

In regard to Figure 6-4, web users across the globe were reporting outages on myriad Google services, including Gmail, Google News, Google Docs, Google Calendar, Google Analytics, Google Maps, Google AdSense, and Google Search. Google acknowledged the problem and says it has been solved, blaming the traffic slowdown on a routing mistake.

* Posted at *http://blogs.msdn.com/netservicesannounce/archive/2009/05/20/net-services-outage-notification-5-20 .aspx.*

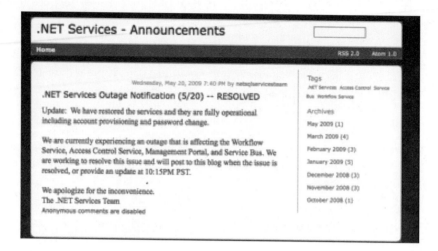

.NET Services - Announcements

Home   RSS 2.0   Atom 1.0

Wednesday, May 20, 2009 7:40 PM by netsqlservicesteam

.NET Services Outage Notification (5/20) -- RESOLVED

Update: We have restored the services and they are fully operational including account provisioning and password change.

We are currently experiencing an outage that is affecting the Workflow Service, Access Control Service, Management Portal, and Service Bus. We are working to resolve this issue and will post to this blog when the issue is resolved, or provide an update at 10:15PM PST.

We apologize for the inconvenience.
The .NET Services Team
Anonymous comments are disabled

Tags
.NET Services Access Control Service
Bus Workflow Service

Archives
May 2009 (1)
March 2009 (4)
February 2009 (3)
January 2009 (5)
December 2008 (3)
November 2008 (3)
October 2008 (1)

FIGURE 6-3. Microsoft Azure .NET Services Outage Notification (5/20) – RESOLVED

The Official **Google** Blog   Insights from Googlers into our products, technology, and the Google culture.

This is your pilot speaking. Now, about that holding pattern...

5/14/2009 12:15:00 PM

Imagine if you were trying to fly from New York to San Francisco, but your plane was routed through an airport in Asia. And a bunch of other planes were sent that way too, so your flight was backed up and your journey took much longer than expected. That's basically what happened to some of our users today for about an hour, starting at 7:48 am Pacific time.

An error in one of our systems caused us to direct some of our web traffic through Asia, which created a traffic jam. As a result, about 14% of our users experienced slow services or even interruptions. We've been working hard to make our services ultrafast and "always on," so it's especially embarrassing when a glitch like this one happens. We're very sorry that it happened, and you can be sure that we'll be working even harder to make sure that a similar problem won't happen again. All planes are back on schedule now.

Posted by Urs Hoelzle, SVP, Operations

FIGURE 6-4. Google outage, May 14, 2009

In another example, on December 20, 2005 Salesforce.com (the on-demand customer relationship management service) said it suffered from a system outage that prevented users from accessing the system during business hours. Users "experienced intermittent access" from 9:30 a.m. to 12:41 p.m. Eastern time and from 2:00 p.m. to 4:45 p.m. Eastern time because of a database cluster error in one of the company's four global network nodes, company officials said in a statement the day following the outage. The statement added that "Salesforce.com addressed the issue with the database vendor" so that service could be restored in the afternoon.

Factors Impacting Availability

The cloud service resiliency and availability depend on a few factors, including the CSP's data center architecture (load balancers, networks, systems), application architecture, hosting location redundancy, diversity of Internet service providers (ISPs), and data storage architecture. Following is a list of the major factors:

- SaaS and PaaS application architecture and redundancy.
- Cloud service data center architecture, and network and systems architecture, including geographically diverse and fault-tolerance architecture.
- Reliability and redundancy of Internet connectivity used by the customer and the CSP.
- Customer's ability to respond quickly and fall back on internal applications and other processes, including manual procedures.
- Customer's visibility of the fault. In some downtime events, if the impact affects a small subset of users, it may be difficult to get a full picture of the impact and can make it harder to troubleshoot the situation.
- Reliability of hardware and software components used in delivering the cloud service.
- Efficacy of the security and network infrastructure to withstand a distributed denial of service (DDoS) attack on the cloud service.
- Efficacy of security controls and processes that reduce human error and protect infrastructure from malicious internal and external threats, e.g., privileged users abusing privileges.

SaaS Availability Management

By virtue of the service delivery and business model, SaaS service providers are responsible for business continuity, application, and infrastructure security management processes. This means the tasks your IT organization once handled will now be handled by the CSP. Some mature organizations that are aligned with industry standards, such as ITIL, will be faced with new challenges of governance of SaaS services as they try to map internal service-level categories to a CSP. For example, if a marketing application is considered critical and has a high service-level requirement, how can the IT or business unit meet the internal marketing department's availability expectation based on the SaaS provider's SLA? In some cases, SaaS vendors may not offer SLAs and may simply address service terms via terms and conditions. For example, Salesforce.com does not offer a standardized SLA that describes and specifies performance criteria and service commitments. However, another CRM SaaS provider, NetSuite, offers the following SLA clauses:

> Uptime Goal—NetSuite commits to provide 99.5% uptime with respect to the NetSuite application, excluding regularly scheduled maintenance times.

> Scheduled and Unscheduled Maintenance—Regularly scheduled maintenance time does not count as downtime. Maintenance time is regularly scheduled if it is communicated at least two full business days in advance of the maintenance time. Regularly scheduled maintenance time typically is communicated at least a week in advance, scheduled to occur at night on the weekend, and takes less than 10–15 hours each quarter.

> NetSuite hereby provides notice that every Saturday night 10:00pm–10:20pm Pacific Time is reserved for routine scheduled maintenance for use as needed.

Here is another SLA example:

> During the Term of the applicable Google Apps Agreement, the Google Apps Covered Services web interface will be operational and available to Customer at least 99.9% of the time in any calendar month (the "Google Apps SLA"). If Google does not meet the Google Apps SLA, and if Customer meets its obligations under this Google Apps SLA, Customer will be eligible to receive the Service Credits described below. This Google Apps SLA states Customer's sole and exclusive remedy for any failure by Google to provide the Service.

Monthly Uptime Percentage	Days of Service added to the end of the Service term, at no charge to Customer
< 99.9% – ≥ 99.0%	3
< 99.0% – ≥ 95.0%	7
< 95.0%	15

> Customer Must Request Service Credit. In order to receive any of the Service Credits described above, Customer must notify Google within thirty days from the time Customer becomes eligible to receive a Service Credit. Failure to comply with this requirement will forfeit Customer's right to receive a Service Credit.

> Maximum Service Credit. The aggregate maximum number of Service Credits to be issued by Google to Customer for any and all Downtime Periods that occur in a single calendar month shall not exceed fifteen days of Service added to the end of Customer's term for the Service. Service Credits may not be exchanged for, or converted to, monetary amounts.

Google Apps SLA Exclusions. The Google Apps SLA does not apply to any services that expressly exclude this Google Apps SLA (as stated in the documentation for such services) or any performance issues: (i) caused by factors outside of Google's reasonable control; or (ii) that resulted from Customer's equipment or third party equipment, or both (not within the primary control of Google).

There is no such thing as standard SLA among cloud service providers. Uptime guarantee, service credits, and service exclusions clauses will vary from provider to provider.

Customer Responsibility

Customers should understand the SLA and communication methods (e.g., email, RSS feed, website URL with outage information) to stay informed on service outages. When possible, customers should use automated tools such as Nagios or Siteuptime.com to verify the availability of the SaaS service.

As of this writing, customers of a SaaS service have a limited number of options to support availability management. Hence, customers should seek to understand the availability management factors, including the SLA of the service, and clarify with the CSP any gaps in SLA exclusions and service credits when disruptions occur. In a recently published white paper by the U.S.-based Software & Information Industry Association (SIIA), the efficacy of SaaS SLAs was analyzed in the context of software vendors moving to a SaaS delivery model. The paper concluded that certain elements are necessary to make the SLA an effective document, and states that:

Communication and clear expectations are required from both the service provider and their customers to identify what is important and realistic with respect to standards and expectations.

Customers of cloud services should note that a multitenant service delivery model is usually designed with a "one size fits all" operating principle, which means CSPs typically offer a standard SLA for all customers. Thus, CSPs may not be amenable to providing custom SLAs if the standard SLA does not meet your service-level requirements. However, if you are a medium or large enterprise with a sizable budget, a custom SLA may still be feasible.

Since most SaaS providers use virtualization technologies to deliver a multitenant service, customers should also understand how resource democratization occurs within the CSP to best predict the likelihood of system availability and performance during business fluctuations. If the resources (network, CPU, memory, storage) are not allocated in a fair manner across the tenants to perform the workload, it is conceivable that a highly demanding tenant may starve other tenants, which can result in lower service levels or poor user experience.

SaaS Health Monitoring

The following options are available to customers to stay informed on the health of their service:

- Service health dashboard published by the CSP. Usually SaaS providers, such as Salesforce.com, publish the current state of the service, current outages that may impact customers, and upcoming scheduled maintenance services on their website (e.g., *http:// trust.salesforce.com/trust/status/*).

- The Cloud Computing Incidents Database (CCID). (This database is generally community-supported, and may not reflect all CSPs and all incidents that have occurred.)

- Customer mailing list that notifies customers of occurring and recently occurred outages.

- Internal or third-party-based service monitoring tools that periodically check SaaS provider health and alert customers when service becomes unavailable (e.g., Nagios monitoring tool).

- RSS feed hosted at the SaaS service provider.

PaaS Availability Management

In a typical PaaS service, customers (developers) build and deploy PaaS applications on top of the CSP-supplied PaaS platform. The PaaS platform is typically built on a CSP owned and managed network, servers, operating systems, storage infrastructure, and application components (web services). Given that the customer PaaS applications are assembled with CSP-supplied application components and, in some cases, third-party web services components (mash-up applications), availability management of the PaaS application can be complicated—for example, a social network application on the Google App Engine that depends on a Facebook application for a contact management service. In that mashed-up software deployment architecture the onus of availability management is shared between the customer and the CSP. The customer is responsible for managing the availability of the customer-developed application and third-party services, and the PaaS CSP is responsible for the PaaS platform and any other services supplied by the CSP. For example, Force.com is responsible for the management of the AppExchange platform, and customers are responsible for managing the applications developed and deployed on that platform.

By design, PaaS applications may rely on other third-party web services components that are not part of the PaaS service offerings; hence, understanding the dependency of your application on third-party services, including services supplied by the PaaS vendor, is essential (e.g., your web 2.0 application using Google Maps for geo mapping). PaaS providers may also offer a set of web services, including a message queue service, identity and authentication service, and database service, and your application may depend on the availability of those service components (an example is Google's BigTable). Hence, your PaaS application availability depends on the robustness of your application, the PaaS platform on which the application is built, and third-party web services components.

Customers are encouraged to read and understand the PaaS platform service levels (if available), including quota triggers that may limit resource availability for their application (usually outlined in the SLA, or in the terms and conditions of the PaaS service). In cases where the PaaS platform enforces quotas on compute resources (CPU, memory, network I/O), upon reaching the thresholds the application may not be able to respond within the normal latency expectations and could eventually become unavailable. For example, the Google App Engine has a quota system whereby each App Engine resource is measured against one of two kinds of quotas: a billable quota or a fixed quota.

Billable quotas are resource maximums set by you, the application's administrator, to prevent the cost of the application from exceeding your budget. Every application gets an amount of each billable quota for free. You can increase billable quotas for your application by enabling billing, setting a daily budget, and then allocating the budget to the quotas. You will be charged only for the resources your app actually uses, and only for the amount of resources used above the free quota thresholds.

Fixed quotas are resource maximums set by the App Engine to ensure the integrity of the system. These resources describe the boundaries of the architecture, and all applications are expected to run within the same limits. They ensure that another app that is consuming too many resources will not affect the performance of your app.

You can find details on App Engine quotas at *http://code.google.com/appengine/docs/quotas.html*.

Another example is Force.com's Apex governor feature. Because the Apex application runs in a multitenant environment, the Apex runtime engine strictly enforces a number of limits to ensure that runaway scripts do not monopolize shared resources. Governors track and enforce the limits based on a policy shared with customers. If a script ever exceeds a limit, the associated governor issues a runtime exception that cannot be handled.

Customer Responsibility

Considering all of the variable parameters in availability management, the PaaS application customer should carefully analyze the dependencies of the application on the third-party web services (components) and outline a holistic management strategy to manage and monitor all the dependencies.

The following considerations are for PaaS customers:

PaaS platform service levels
> Customers should carefully review the terms and conditions of the CSP's SLAs and understand the availability constraints.

Third-party web services provider service levels
> When your PaaS application depends on a third-party service, it is critical to understand the SLA of that service. For example, your PaaS application may rely on services such as

Google Maps and use the Google Maps API to embed maps in your own web pages with JavaScript.

Network connectivity parameters for the network (Internet)-connecting PaaS platform with third-party service providers

The parameters typically include bandwidth and latency factors.

PaaS Health Monitoring

In general, PaaS applications are always web-based applications hosted on the PaaS CSP platform (e.g., your Java or Python application hosted on the Google App Engine). Hence, most of the techniques and processes used for monitoring a SaaS application also apply to PaaS applications. Given the composition of PaaS applications, customers should monitor their application, as well as the third-party web component services. Configuring your management tools to monitor the health of web services will require the knowledge of the web services protocol (HTTP, HTTPS) and the required protocol parameters (e.g., URI) to verify the availability of the service.

When CSPs support monitoring via application programming interfaces (APIs), monitoring your application can involve a standard web services protocol, such as Representational State Transfer (REST), Simple Object Access Protocol (SOAP), eXtensible Markup Language/Hypertext Transfer Protocol (XML/HTTP), and in a few cases, proprietary protocols.

The following options are available to customers to monitor the health of their service:

- Service health dashboard published by the CSP (e.g., *http://status.zoho.com*)
- CCID (this database is generally community-supported, and may not reflect all CSPs and all incidents that have occurred)
- CSP customer mailing list that notifies customers of occurring and recently occurred outages
- RSS feed for RSS readers with availability and outage information
- Internal or third-party-based service monitoring tools that periodically check your PaaS application, as well as third-party web services that monitor your application (e.g., Nagios monitoring tool)

IaaS Availability Management

Availability considerations for the IaaS delivery model should include both a computing and storage (persistent and ephemeral) infrastructure in the cloud. IaaS providers may also offer other services such as account management, a message queue service, an identity and authentication service, a database service, a billing service, and monitoring services. Hence, availability management should take into consideration all the services that you depend on for your IT and business needs. Customers are responsible for all aspects of availability management since they are responsible for provisioning and managing the life cycle of virtual servers.

Managing your IaaS virtual infrastructure in the cloud depends on five factors:

- Availability of a CSP network, host, storage, and support application infrastructure. This factor depends on the following:
  - CSP data center architecture, including a geographically diverse and fault-tolerance architecture.
  - Reliability, diversity, and redundancy of Internet connectivity used by the customer and the CSP.
  - Reliability and redundancy architecture of the hardware and software components used for delivering compute and storage services.
  - Availability management process and procedures, including business continuity processes established by the CSP.
  - Web console or API service availability. The web console and API are required to manage the life cycle of the virtual servers. When those services become unavailable, customers are unable to provision, start, stop, and deprovision virtual servers.
  - SLA. Because this factor varies across CSPs, the SLA should be reviewed and reconciled, including exclusion clauses.
- Availability of your virtual servers and the attached storage (persistent and ephemeral) for compute services (e.g., Amazon Web Services' S3[†] and Amazon Elastic Block Store).
- Availability of virtual storage that your users and virtual server depend on for storage service. This includes both synchronous and asynchronous storage access use cases. Synchronous storage access use cases demand low data access latency and continuous availability, whereas asynchronous use cases are more tolerant to latency and availability. Examples for synchronous storage use cases include database transactions, video streaming, and user authentication. Inconsistency or disruptions to storage in synchronous storage has a higher impact on overall server and application availability. A common example of an asynchronous use case is a cloud-based storage service for backing up your computer over the Internet.
- Availability of your network connectivity to the Internet or virtual network connectivity to IaaS services. In some cases, this can involve virtual private network (VPN) connectivity between your internal private data center and the public IaaS cloud (e.g., hybrid clouds).
- Availability of network services, including a DNS, routing services, and authentication services required to connect to the IaaS service.

[†] Amazon Simple Storage Service (S3). See *http://aws.amazon.com/s3/* for more information.

IaaS Health Monitoring

The following options are available to IaaS customers for managing the health of their service:

- Service health dashboard published by the CSP.

- CCID (this database is generally community-supported, and may not reflect all CSPs and all incidents that have occurred).

- CSP customer mailing list that notifies customers of occurring and recently occurred outages.

- Internal or third-party-based service monitoring tools (e.g., Nagios) that periodically check the health of your IaaS virtual server. For example, Amazon Web Services (AWS) is offering a cloud monitoring service called CloudWatch. This web service provides monitoring for AWS cloud resources, including Amazon's Elastic Compute Cloud (EC2). It also provides customers with visibility into resource utilization, operational performance, and overall demand patterns, including metrics such as CPU utilization, disk reads and writes, and network traffic.

- Web console or API that publishes the current health status of your virtual servers and network.

Similar to SaaS service monitoring, customers who are hosting applications on an IaaS platform should take additional steps to monitor the health of the hosted application. For example, if you are hosting an e-commerce application on your Amazon EC2 virtual cloud, you should monitor the health of both the e-commerce application and the virtual server instances.

Access Control

Generally speaking, access control management is a broad function that encompasses access requirements for your users and system administrators (privileged users) who access network, system, and application resources. The access control management functions should address the following:

- Who should have access to what resource? (Assignment of entitlements to users)

- Why should the user have access to the resource? (Assignment of entitlements based on the user's job functions and responsibilities)

- How should you access the resource? (What authentication method and strength are required prior to granting access to the resource)

- Who has access to what resource? (Auditing and reporting to verify entitlement assignments)

The aforementioned aspects of the access control domain should be addressed by your organization's access policies and standards and aligned with the user's roles and responsibilities, including end users and privileged system administrators.

Access Control in the Cloud

In a cloud computing consumption model, where users are accessing cloud services from any Internet-connected host, network access control will play a diminishing role. The reason is that traditional network-based access controls are focused on protecting resources from unauthorized access based on host-based attributes, which in most cases is inadequate, is not unique across users, and can cause inaccurate accounting. In the cloud, network access control manifests as cloud firewall policies enforcing host-based access control at the ingress and egress points of entry to the cloud and logical grouping of instances within the cloud. This is usually achieved using policies (rules) using standard Transmission Control Protocol/Internet Protocol (TCP/IP) parameters, including source IP, source port, destination IP, and destination port.

In contrast to network-based access control, user access control should be strongly emphasized in the cloud, since it can strongly bind a user's identity to the resources in the cloud and will help with fine granular access control, user accounting, support for compliance, and data protection. User access management controls, including strong authentication, single sign-on (SSO), privilege management, and logging and monitoring of cloud resources, play a significant role in protecting the confidentiality and integrity of your information in the cloud.

ISO/IEC 27002 has defined six access control objectives that cover end user, privileged user, network, application, and information access control. Readers are encouraged to assess cloud services and understand the relevant ISO/IEC 27002 control objectives that mitigate the most risk for the business. The following user access management control statement from ISO 27002 is particularly relevant to cloud services:

> Objective: To ensure authorized user access and to prevent unauthorized access to information systems. Formal procedures should be in place to control the allocation of access rights to information systems and services. The procedures should cover all stages in the lifecycle of user access, from the initial registration of new users to the final de-registration of users who no longer require access to information systems and services. Special attention should be given, where appropriate, to the need to control the allocation of privileged access rights, which allow users to override system controls.

The following are the six control statements:

- Control access to information.
- Manage user access rights.
- Encourage good access practices.
- Control access to network services.
- Control access to operating systems.
- Control access to applications and systems.

Similar to ISO 27002, ITIL dictates an access management function that was added as a new process to ITIL v3. The decision to include this dedicated process was motivated by IT security reasons: from an IT security perspective, granting access to IT services and applications only to authorized users should be of high importance.

The objective of this function is to grant authorized users the right to use a service, while preventing access to non-authorized users. The access management processes essentially execute policies defined in IT security management.

Access Control: SaaS

In the SaaS delivery model, the CSP is responsible for managing all aspects of the network, server, and application infrastructure. In that model, since the application is delivered as a service to end users, usually via a web browser, network-based controls are becoming less relevant and are augmented or superseded by user access controls, e.g., authentication using a one-time password. Hence, customers should focus on user access controls (authentication, federation, privilege management, deprovisioning, etc.) to protect the information hosted by SaaS. Some SaaS services, such as Salesforce.com, augment network access control (e.g., source IP address/network-based control) to user access control in which case customers have the option to enforce access based on network and user policy parameters.

Support for user access control is not consistent across providers, and capabilities may vary. A small set of CSPs (mostly large SaaS providers, such as Salesforce.com, Google, and Microsoft) are beginning to pay attention to enterprise IAM requirements, including support for standards such as SAML that facilitate SSO using identity federation techniques. However, given the early adoption cycle by large enterprises, from an enterprise perspective the IAM capabilities are primitive at best. Customers should continue to demand that their CSPs provide IAM features, including SAML support, user provisioning using SPML, and an open API to support various user and access automation processes. Organizations should leverage their established identity management practices, processes, and architecture (e.g., IdP) to support user access management and federation. For details about identity and access management in a SaaS delivery model, refer to Chapter 5.

Access Control: PaaS

In the PaaS delivery model, the CSP is responsible for managing access control to the network, servers, and application platform infrastructure. However, the customer is responsible for access control to the applications deployed on a PaaS platform. Access control to applications manifests as end user access management, which includes provisioning and authentication of users.

Support for user access control is not consistent across providers, and capabilities may vary. As of this writing, major PaaS providers—with the exception of Force.com and Microsoft Azure (still in beta)—offer rudimentary user access management support. Enterprises that leverage their internal identity provider (IdP) will have to understand PaaS capabilities, including support for federation. It is conceivable for a PaaS CSP to offer a standard API such as OAuth to manage authentication and access control to applications. For example, Google supports a hybrid version of an OpenID and OAuth protocol that combines the authorization and authentication flow in fewer steps to enhance usability. You could also delegate authentication to your IdP if the CSP supports federation standards, such as the Security Assertion Markup Language (SAML). For details about identity and access management in a PaaS delivery model, see Chapter 5.

Access Control: IaaS

IaaS customers are entirely responsible for managing all aspects of access control to their resources in the cloud. Access to the virtual servers, virtual network, virtual storage, and applications hosted on an IaaS platform will have to be designed and managed by the customer. In an IaaS delivery model, access control management falls into one of the following two categories:

CSP infrastructure access control
> Access control management to the host, network, and management applications that are owned and managed by the CSP

Customer virtual infrastructure access control
> Access control management to your virtual server (virtual machines or VMs), virtual storage, virtual networks, and applications hosted on virtual servers

CSP infrastructure access control

The CSP is responsible for managing access control to the administrative network that is used to perform administrator functions. This includes access control to administrative processes, such as backups, host (hypervisor) and network maintenance, router and firewall policy management, and system monitoring and management. Access to administrative functions should be protected using strong authentication and role-based access control. Strong operational procedures should be implemented to support the provisioning and revocation of administrative privileges. Periodic access control audits and administrative user certifications should be implemented to validate least privileges and separation of duties. In this regard, the aforementioned AWS security white paper states that:

> Amazon.com's Information Security Policies, followed by AWS, are guided by the fundamental principle of least privilege. Least privilege protects customer information assets by requiring that no individual, program or system is granted more access privileges than are necessary to perform the task. Any employee found to have violated this policy may be subject to disciplinary action, including termination.

Customer virtual infrastructure access control

To start with, IaaS customers must understand the virtual resources (network, host, firewall, load balancers, management console, etc.) and the available protection mechanisms to restrict access to authorized users. It is not uncommon for CSPs to provide customers with full root access and administrative control over rented virtual servers. In addition, customers can be assigned privileges to manage network access policies for both the ingress and egress of their virtual network and virtual servers. Hence, the customer is responsible for taking the necessary steps to protect access to virtual resources.

> **N O T E**
>
> **It is a standard practice for IaaS CSPs to provide APIs (REST, SOAP, or HTTP with XML/JavaScript Object Notation [JSON]) to perform most management functions, such as access control from a remote location. Some providers also offer a web-based console from which access control features can be invoked. Organizations consuming IaaS services should design and implement access management processes with access request or approval and a gatekeeper, and maintain a catalog of privileged users who have access to IaaS resources.**

Consider the following areas when managing access control of your infrastructure in the cloud:

Network access control

Check with the provider on the default configuration of the network access that is typically enforced by a firewall managed by the CSP. It is customary for CSPs to deny all access to your virtual servers by default (factory settings), which automatically denies all inbound traffic to your virtual servers. This forces you to explicitly add new rules to allow access to your virtual servers in the cloud—for example, allow access to IP 10.0.0.1 from 192.168.0.1 to port 22 (Secure Shell or SSH), where 10.0.0.1 is the IP address of the virtual server and 192.168.0.1 is the trusted IP address from which 10.0.0.1 can be accessed using SSH. Amazon EC2 offers network group features that allow the creation of multiple security groups to enforce different ingress policies as needed. According to Amazon, a customer can control each security group with a PEM-encoded X.509 certificate and restrict traffic to each EC2 instance by protocol, service port, or source IP address.

Virtual server access control

Virtual servers running your preferred OS (Linux, Solaris, or Windows) should be protected with access controls, such as OS authentication mechanisms. It is a standard practice to configure Unix servers with SSH-based logins with strong authentication. Strong authentication protects against several security threats (e.g., IP spoofing, fake routes, man-in-the-middle, and DNS spoofing). The authentication methods include Rivest-Shamir-Adleman (RSA) encryption algorithm-based host authentication, pure RSA authentication, one-time passwords with S/Key, and authentication using Kerberos. When using RSA keys, it is recommended that the keys are stored in a secure form of media and that they are secured with a passphrase. These measures help to protect your keys from unauthorized users.

Cloud management station

Management of your virtual resources on the cloud is usually accomplished from a client system with applications that manipulate remote resources using a CSP-proprietary API (REST, SOAP, or HTTP with XML/JSON). A client management toolkit (supplied by the CSP) is installed on the management station, which interacts with the CSP management service via the published API. Because the station contains sensitive information, including host and user keys, and firewall policies, the cloud management station should be viewed as a command and control center for the cloud infrastructure. Hence, access to the management station should be protected with strong authentication and sound access provisioning procedures.

Web-based console

Some CSPs supplement the cloud management station with a web-based console feature by which customers can manage access to their virtual infrastructure in the cloud. The console offers an alternative means to the cloud management station for managing the cloud infrastructure. Similar to the management station, the console offers access to sensitive information, including access to your host keys and firewall policies with just a few mouse clicks; it acts as a management station for your cloud infrastructure. Because the web console is a powerful tool that can control your virtual network and virtual server instances, you should adequately protect console access. For example, the web console should be accessed only with HTTPS protocol.

Access Control Summary

Access control is a critical security management function in the SPI (SaaS, PaaS, and IaaS) cloud delivery model and across the standard deployment models (public, private, and hybrid). Access management is critical to protecting your information hosted in SPI clouds and may be the primary means of security control in the absence of encryption and other data controls. As of this writing, access management features in public clouds are not consistent and are still evolving. In their current form, access control capabilities offered by CSPs may not be adequate for enterprise customers, for the following reasons:

- Access control mechanisms, practices, and processes are not standardized across CSPs. To effectively manage access control to their virtual cloud infrastructure, customers have to make an extra effort to understand the CSP-specific access control features and customize them on a CSP basis.

- The lack of a standard API across CSPs makes it very difficult to manage access across multiple clouds. For example, SAML support is not available from any of the major CSPs, including AWS.

- User access controls to cloud resources are generally weak. Access controls from CSPs typically support granular network-level access management, but coarse user access management. User access controls mostly address the authentication aspects and are rudimentary at best for managing user authorization to the cloud infrastructure. CSPs should offer granular privilege access based on roles that support the principles of least privilege and separation of duties (e.g., console manager, network access manager, zone manager, host manager).

In summary, from an enterprise customer perspective, access management is an essential security process to protect the confidentiality, integrity, and availability (CIA) of information hosted in the cloud. A robust access management program should include procedures for provisioning, timely deprovisioning, flexible authentication, privilege management, accounting, auditing, and support for compliance management. Cloud customers should understand the CSP-specific access control features for networks, systems, and applications, and appropriately manage access.

Security Vulnerability, Patch, and Configuration Management

The ability for malware (or a cracker) to remotely exploit vulnerabilities of infrastructure components, network services, and applications remains a major threat to cloud services. It is an even greater risk for a public PaaS and IaaS delivery model where vulnerability, patch, and configuration management responsibilities remain with the customer. Customers should remember that in cloud computing environments, the lowest or highest common denominator of security is shared by all tenants in a multitenant virtual environment. Hence, the onus is with the customers to understand the scope of their security management responsibilities. Customers should demand that CSPs become more transparent about their cloud security operations to help customers understand and plan complementary security management functions.

By and large, CSPs are responsible for the vulnerability, patch, and configuration (VPC) management of the infrastructure (networks, hosts, applications, and storage) that is CSP-managed and operated, as well as third-party services that they may rely on. However, customers are not spared from their VPC duties and should understand the VPC aspects for which they are responsible. A VPC management scope should address end-to-end security and should include customer-managed systems and applications that interface with cloud services. As a standard practice, CSPs may have instituted these programs within their security management domain, but typically the process is internal to the CSP and is not apparent to customers. CSPs should assure their customers of their technical vulnerability management program using ISO/IEC 27002 type control and assurance frameworks.

What is your responsibility in managing vulnerabilities in the cloud? How does security patch management manifest in cloud services? Who is responsible for patch and security configuration of the cloud infrastructure? What options do you have to extend your current security management processes to cloud services?

The following sections discuss these VPC issues in the SPI delivery model context, and outline the VPC responsibilities for CSPs and their customers.

Security Vulnerability Management

Vulnerability management is an essential threat management element to help protect hosts, network devices, and applications from attacks against known vulnerabilities. Mature organizations have instituted a vulnerability management process that involves routine scanning of systems connected to their network, assessing the risks of vulnerabilities to the organization, and a remediation process (usually feeding into a patch management program) to address the risks. Organizations using ISO/IEC 27002 are known to address this program using a technical vulnerability management control objective, which states:

> Objective: To reduce risks resulting from exploitation of published technical vulnerabilities.
>
> Technical vulnerability management should be implemented in an effective, systematic, and repeatable way with measurements taken to confirm its effectiveness. These considerations should include operating systems, and any other applications in use.

Both the customer and the CSP are responsible for vulnerability management of the cloud infrastructure, depending on the SPI service in context.

Security Patch Management

Similar to vulnerability management, security patch management is a vital threat management element in protecting hosts, network devices, and applications from unauthorized users exploiting a known vulnerability. Patch management processes follow a change management framework and feeds directly from the actions directed by your vulnerability management program. Security patch management mitigates risk to your organization by way of insider and outsider threats. Hence, SaaS providers should be routinely assessing new vulnerabilities and patching the firmware and software on all systems that are involved in delivering the *aaS service to customers.

The scope of patch management responsibility for customers will have a low-to-high relevance in the order of SaaS, PaaS, and IaaS services—that is, customers are relieved from patch management duties in a SaaS environment, whereas they are responsible for managing patches for the whole stack of software (operating system, applications, and database) installed and operated on the IaaS platform. Customers are also responsible for patching their applications deployed on the PaaS platform.

Security Configuration Management

Security configuration management is another significant threat management practice to protect hosts and network devices from unauthorized users exploiting any configuration weakness. Security configuration management is closely related to the vulnerability management program and is a subset of overall IT configuration management. Protecting the configuration of the network, host, and application entails monitoring and access control to critical system and database configuration files, including OS configuration, firewall policies, network zone configuration, locally and remotely attached storage, and an access control management database.

In the SPI service delivery model, configuration management from a customer responsibility perspective has a low-to-high relevance in the order of SaaS, PaaS, and IaaS services—that is, SaaS and PaaS service providers are responsible for configuration management of their platform, whereas IaaS customers are responsible for configuration management of the operating system, application, and database hosted on the IaaS platform. Customers are also responsible for configuration management of their applications deployed on the PaaS platform.

SaaS VPC Management

SaaS VPC management focuses on managing vulnerabilities, security patching, and system configuration in the CSP-managed infrastructure, as well as the customer infrastructure interfacing with the SaaS service. Since the SaaS delivery model is anchored on the premise that the application service is delivered over the Internet to a web browser running on any computing device (personal computer, virtual desktop, or mobile device), it is important to secure the endpoints from which the cloud is accessed. Hence, a VPC management program should include endpoint VPC management requirements and should be tailored to the corporate environment. It is standard practice for most companies to institute a standard OS image for personal computers that include security tools such as antivirus, anti-malware, firewall, and automatic patch management from a central management station.

SaaS provider responsibilities

The following list represents SaaS VPC scope:

- Systems, networks, hosts, applications, and storage that are owned and operated by the CSP
- Systems, networks, hosts, applications, and storage that are managed by third parties
- Personal computers and smartphones owned by the SaaS employees and contractors

SaaS customer responsibilities

Because SaaS services are typically delivered to web browsers and, in some cases, are integrated with customer applications (via an XML interface), the customer has limited responsibilities for VPC management of the infrastructure in the cloud. However, SaaS customers are responsible for VPC management of their systems that interface with the SaaS service. The responsibilities include:

- Personal computers of a SaaS user.
- Applications or services that interface with the SaaS service.
- Security testing of the SaaS service. Although SaaS providers are responsible for vulnerability management of the software delivered as a service, some enterprise

customers can choose to independently assess the state of application security. Customers evaluating this independent verification option should gain the consent of the CSP, because SaaS security testing can be performed only with the permission and cooperation of the SaaS vendor. This type of application testing, usually performed by a third-party tester, may involve an active analysis of the application and a simulation of real attack scenarios with the objective of discovering vulnerabilities in the application. This is a qualitative method, and the scope of testing could vary based on the identified vulnerability. Hence, it is advisable to verify and agree on the scope prior to the exercise. This type of testing can reveal the top web application vulnerabilities that are categorized as OWASP Top 10 vulnerabilities. SQL injection, parameter manipulation, cookie poisoning, and cross-site scripting (XSS) are common types of vulnerabilities found during the application vulnerability testing cycle.

NOTE

The scope of the VPC management program should include browser security, systems, and applications (on both trusted and untrusted zones) located at a customer's premises interfacing with SaaS services.

PaaS VPC Management

PaaS VPC management focuses on VPC management in the CSP-managed infrastructure, as well as the customer infrastructure interfacing with the PaaS service. Since applications deployed on a PaaS platform are accessed from a web browser running on an endpoint device (personal computer, virtual desktop, or mobile device), the program should include endpoint VPC management scope.

PaaS provider responsibilities

Similar to a SaaS model, the PaaS CSP is responsible for VPC management of the infrastructure that is operated by the CSP, as well as third-party services that they may rely on. Refer to "SaaS provider responsibilities" on page 132 for responsibility items.

PaaS customer responsibilities

In addition to the responsibilities outlined in "SaaS customer responsibilities" on page 132, PaaS customers are responsible for VPC management of the applications implemented and deployed on the PaaS platform. Vulnerabilities or the configuration weakness of applications deployed on a PaaS platform should be treated similarly to a standard application operating in your data center (e.g., private cloud). Software vulnerabilities are introduced by design flaws or coding errors. Configuration weakness can be introduced by improper configuration of an application in the area of authentication and privilege management. In addition, PaaS applications that rely on third-party web services may simply become weak and vulnerable by way of vulnerabilities in the third-party service, and that is out of your control. Although you have the ability to fix vulnerabilities in the source code of your PaaS application, you must work with the PaaS vendor or third-party service providers to fix vulnerabilities or flaws in their services. Hence, customers should understand the vulnerability disclosure methods, SLAs, and PaaS policies of third-party service providers. PaaS customers should follow standard practices embedded in the Software Development Life Cycle (SDLC), which helps to reduce software application vulnerabilities. Following are some of the standard practices:

Application white-box testing

Analyze the source code for vulnerabilities using testing tools that look for vulnerabilities such as buffer overflows, e.g., Ounce Labs and Fortify source code analysis tools.

Application black-box testing

This type of testing (performed by testers) requires knowledge of the application's functionality. Source code access is generally not required. This type of testing can reveal OWASP Top 10 application vulnerabilities, including SQL injection, parameter manipulation, cookie poisoning, and XSS. For example, service providers such as Cigital and Veracode.

Application penetration testing

Although PaaS providers are responsible for vulnerability management of the software platform delivered as a service, some enterprise customers can choose to independently verify application platform security. Customers evaluating this independent verification option should check with their PaaS CSPs first, because platform testing can be performed only with the permission and cooperation of the PaaS vendor. This type of application testing, usually performed by a third-party tester, involves active analysis of the application and a simulation of real attack scenarios with the objective of discovering vulnerabilities in the application. This is a qualitative method, and the scope of testing could vary based on the identified vulnerability. Hence, it is advisable to verify and agree on the scope prior to the exercise. This type of testing can uncover OWASP Top 10 application vulnerabilities, including SQL injection, parameter manipulation, cookie poisoning, and XSS.

Vulnerability alerts

Customers should understand the means by which PaaS providers, companies, or communities supporting the PaaS programming language disseminate vulnerability-related information to customers. PaaS providers can choose email, RSS, or a web portal to communicate with their customers. Likewise, you should choose the appropriate methods to stay informed of any new vulnerability in the platform or the third-party service providers.

PaaS customers are also responsible for VPC management of their systems that interface with the PaaS service. These systems include:

- Personal computers of a PaaS user
- Browsers used for accessing the PaaS service
- Applications located at the customer's premises that interface with the PaaS service

IaaS VPC Management

IaaS VPC management focuses on the CSP-managed infrastructure, as well as the customer infrastructure interfacing with the IaaS service. IaaS VPC management diverges from SaaS and PaaS in that the infrastructure delineation, network boundary between customers, and CSP infrastructure are blurred. For each layer of infrastructure (network, host, storage), the customer and CSP have responsibilities in managing VPC in the respective layers from their perspective (i.e., the CSP is responsible for the common CSP infrastructure available to all customers, and the customer is responsible for the virtual infrastructure available to the customer for the duration of use). Hence, a VPC management program should address both the common and shared infrastructures.

IaaS provider responsibilities

In general, an IaaS CSP is responsible for VPC management of the infrastructure that is owned and operated by the CSP, as well as the third-party infrastructure and services they may rely on. The VPC management scope should include:

- Systems, networks, hosts (hypervisors), storage, and applications that are CSP-owned and operated
- Systems, networks, hosts, storage, and applications that are managed by third parties
- The web console or management station used by customers to manage their virtual infrastructure
- Personal computers owned by the IaaS employees and contractors

IaaS customer responsibilities

IaaS customers are responsible for VPC management of the virtual infrastructure allocated by an IaaS CSP for customer use. The VPC management scope should include:

Virtual servers

This includes VMs that are active or dormant. The VPC management process of VMs must consider the OSs of the virtual servers and customize the program accordingly (e.g., Fedora Linux, Solaris 10, Windows 2003). Customers are advised to follow the standard practice in managing VMs, which includes:

Image standardization via a security-by-default approach

Customers are advised to standardize the image after sufficiently hardening it using the security-by-default approach. Loss of security by default is more apparent in the early days of cloud services, until experience and best practices catch up. The security-by-default concept is the implicit security existing in day-to-day operations.

Configuration standards

The OS, applications server, database, and web server must be installed and configured in accordance with least-privilege and security hardening principles to reduce their overall attack surface. For example, the Center for Internet Security (*http://www.cisecurity.org/*) publishes *Internet security benchmarks* for major OS, databases, and application servers based on recognized best practices for deployment, configuration, and operation of networked systems. The center's security-enhancing benchmarks encompass all three factors in Internet-based attacks and disruptions: technology (software and hardware), process (system and network administration), and human (end user and management behavior).

Configuration management

This refers to centralized configuration management where the appropriate configuration information is necessary to manage a large number of nodes and zones in a public IaaS cloud. Numerous configuration management tools are available, including open source tools (e.g., Puppet) and tools from commercial vendors such as BMC, Configuresoft, HP, Microsoft, and IBM. However, configuration management of virtual servers hosted in the cloud will require customization per CSP, given the uniqueness of the CSP-specific management API.

Network access policies

Firewalling is heavily used to establish security zones for applications hosted in an IaaS cloud, and network zoning plays a large role in the security architecture. The configuration of network policies that permit traffic in and out of a customer infrastructure should be carefully managed to mitigate risk due to improper configuration. Improper configuration of network access policies can expose vulnerable services to crackers on the Internet. Policies are typically grouped into the following trust categories:

Internet policy

Allow traffic between customer virtual servers and hosts on the Internet (e.g., allow only ports 22, 80, and 443 to servers). Deny all outbound traffic initiated from customer virtual servers.

Zone policy

Allow traffic between virtual servers within the cloud (e.g., allow port 3306 [MySQL] from server zone A to server zone B).

IaaS administrators are also responsible for VPC management of their systems that interface
with an IaaS service. These systems include:

- Cloud management station, which is the host that the customer manages for managing
  the virtual infrastructure in an IaaS cloud
- Personal computers of IaaS administrators
- Browsers used for accessing the IaaS service

IaaS customers have options to leverage third-party services, such as RightScale, Enomaly,
Elastra, and 3tera, to manage the deployment of their public and private IaaS clouds. However,
the type of security management service will vary among providers, and you will have to work
with your provider to include security management functions in your SLA.

Intrusion Detection and Incident Response

The multitenant delivery model of a large-scale cloud provider providing SaaS, PaaS, and IaaS
services creates significant incident response and intrusion management challenges for both
customers and CSPs. Intrusion and incident management are key functions within a corporate
information security management domain to mange and mitigate risks, including loss of
intellectual property, regulatory non-compliance, brand erosion, and fraud. These critical
functions support security management and allow organizations to respond to intrusions and
data breaches. Furthermore, organizations are legally obligated to comply with privacy data
breaches. More than 44 U.S. states have adopted security breach disclosure laws that require
the custodian of personal and regulated data to notify individuals whose data might have been
compromised during a breach of security. Since public cloud computing by definition is
multitenant and delivered to customers using shared infrastructure resources and services,
both the customer and the CSP are responsible for managing intrusion and incident response.
Both parties will need to be prepared to respond to and manage security breaches.

ISO 27002 provides the following control guidance for incident response and notification:

> **13.1 Reporting information security events and weaknesses.**   Objective: To ensure
> information security events and weaknesses associated with information systems are
> communicated in a manner allowing timely corrective action to be taken.
>
> Formal event reporting and escalation procedures should be in place. All employees, contractors
> and third party users should be made aware of the procedures for reporting the different types

of event and weakness that might have an impact on the security of organizational assets. They should be required to report any information.

13.2 Management of information security incidents and improvements.   Objective: To ensure a consistent and effective approach is applied to the management of information security incidents.

Responsibilities and procedures should be in place to handle information security events and weaknesses effectively once they have been reported. A process of continual improvement should be applied to the response to, monitoring, evaluating, and overall management of information security incidents. Where evidence is required, it should be collected to ensure compliance with legal requirements.

Traditionally, medium and large enterprise customers managed security and incident monitoring processes either using an internal security operations center (SOC) or via a third-party managed service. A SOC today monitors events from firewalls and intrusion detection platforms and responds to incidents using a Computer Emergency Response Team (CERT) process. The cloud application deployment will challenge the traditional network security-monitoring model because those applications will no longer be protected by the monitored firewalls and IDS. The responsibility scope of intrusion monitoring and incident response in the cloud will depend on the SPI (SaaS, PaaS, IaaS) delivery model, CSP-specific SLA, incident disclosure policy, and data governance model within the CSP. Since the CSPs may host hundreds of thousands of virtual servers (IaaS), application instances (PaaS), and commingled customer data (SaaS), the scale of operation will challenge them in different ways. Can the CSP identify the scope of affected customers? And isolate security incidents to affected customers? And inform the affected customers within the time period dictated by the SLA or policy?

Incident notification in the cloud, however, is not as simple as current incident management processes followed by a SOC or CERT team. In the traditional model, those processes belong to a single governance and incident response model where one internal group handles the notification and remediation for all applications governed by the organization's IT department. In the case of a cloud where thousands of application owners have a stake, the notification process is more complex and will not follow traditional methods. New incident response tools may need to emerge to manage the complexity—e.g., an application registry implemented by the CSPs, with the contact details of the application owners and an automated notification system to handle a large number of customers (tenants).

Best practices from a privacy perspective dictate the isolation of application data. In the traditional architecture, the breach management process will focus on one entity and not several. Unfortunately, in the cloud, the data separation will blur quickly and an incident procedure will have to be very specific to handling a commingled data environment and identify the dependencies so that the incident notification can be delivered to all parties in a line of data custody.

Customer Versus CSP Responsibilities

Given the shared infrastructure and responsibilities, both the customer and CSP should have in place a security incident response plan to address any kind of security breach thoroughly and expeditiously. The team should promptly disclose to other tenants the existence of a vulnerability that affects its operation to prevent further ripple effects (e.g., cascading infections within or outside the cloud). The serviced customer may have to inform its own customers or employees of the occurrence of the breach. The cloud service provider may also have to inform its other tenants that the breach has occurred.

In the case of an IaaS or a PaaS environment, the system and application trust boundary interlaces both the CSP and customer environment, and as a result, both parties share responsibilities for security monitoring and incident response domains. Those responsibilities should be clearly identified and documented. For example, a PaaS CSP should be responsible for intrusion detection and incident response for the shared network and system infrastructure, for the PaaS platform runtime engine software, and for supported service components; the customer is responsible for their deployed applications and hosted data.

The provider collects and must protect a huge amount of security-related data. For example, at the network level, the provider should be collecting, monitoring, and protecting firewall, intrusion prevention system (IPS), security incident and event management (SIEM), and router flow data. At the host level, the provider should be collecting system logfiles, and at the application level, SaaS providers should be collecting application log data, including authentication and authorization information. They should have in place a security monitoring and incident response plan to address the security breach thoroughly and expeditiously.

What data the CSP collects and how it monitors and protects that data is important to the provider for its own audit purposes (e.g., SAS 70, as discussed in Chapter 8). Additionally, this information is important to both providers and customers in case it is needed for incident response and any digital forensics required for incident analysis.

Table 6-2 summarizes the responsibilities of customers and CSPs for both intrusion detection and incident response functions.

TABLE 6-2. Responsibilities of customers and CSPs for intrusion detection and incident response

Monitoring activities	IaaS	PaaS	SaaS
Intrusion detection	Customer responsible for: • Monitoring the network interfaces of their virtual instances • Monitoring security events from host	Customer responsible for: • Monitoring intrusions of applications deployed on a PaaS platform CSP responsible for:	Customer responsible for: • Monitoring network, system, application, and database intrusions

Monitoring activities	IaaS	PaaS	SaaS
	intrusion detections system such as OSSEC • Monitoring security events from VM, application, and database systems stored in system logs • Monitoring third-party services that you may rely on, e.g., data encryption CSP responsible for: • Monitoring intrusions of shared network/system/application infrastructure, including hypervisors; e.g., a DOS attack on their network	• Monitoring shared network/system/application/database infrastructure, including a PaaS platform runtime engine and supported services; e.g., a privilege escalation attack on a PaaS runtime engine	
Incident response (CERT)	Customer responsible for: • Responding to incidents and data breaches on their virtual servers • Informing the affected users (internal and external) of the systems and applications hosted on the compromised virtual servers	Customer responsible for: • Informing the affected users (internal and external) • Responding to the incident by performing forensics and remediating the application CSP responsible for: • Notifying the customer about intrusions specific to their applications and data or when their users are compromised	Customer responsible for: • Informing the affected users and working with the CSP in remediating the incident CSP responsible for: • Notifying the customer about intrusions specific to their data or when their users are compromised

Caveats

Prior to designing a VPC program, customers are advised to read and understand the terms and conditions and user agreements with their CSP, because there may be potential restrictions for scanning network services, brute force testing, and penetration testing of applications deployed on that CSP's *aaS platform. Furthermore, network port scanning, application security scanning, and active penetration testing can trigger a CSP's intrusion detection system/intrusion prevention system (IDS/IPS) alarms, which in turn can result in suspension or deactivation of your service temporarily or permanently. For example, Amazon AWS, as a matter of policy, prohibits port scanning of your virtual servers. According to the AWS security white paper,[‡] "Port scans by Amazon EC2 customers are a violation of the Amazon EC2 Acceptable Use Policy (AUP). Violations of the AUP are taken seriously, and every reported violation is investigated."

Summary

With the adoption of cloud services, a large part of your network, system, applications, and data will move to a third-party provider's control. The cloud services delivery model brings new challenges to the IT operations and management staff in the area of availability, access control, vulnerability, and security patch and configuration management. As a first step, cloud customers will have to understand the service delivery model (SPI) and the layers they own, touch, or interface with—network, host, application, database, storage, and web services, including identity services. To tackle these challenges, you will need to understand the scope of IT system management responsibilities, including your system management responsibilities for access, change, configuration, patch, and vulnerability management. Table 6-3 summarizes the security management responsibilities for customers of public cloud services.

TABLE 6-3. Security management for SPI services: customer responsibilities

Activities	IaaS	PaaS	SaaS
Availability management	• Manage VM availability with fault-tolerant architecture	• Manage this activity for applications deployed in the PaaS platform (the provider is responsible for their runtime engine and services)	• Provider responsibility
Patch and configuration management	• Manage VM image hardening	• Manage this activity for applications deployed in the PaaS platform	• Provider responsibility

‡ See *http://awsmedia.s3.amazonaws.com/pdf/AWS_Security_Whitepaper.pdf.*

Activities	IaaS	PaaS	SaaS
	• Harden your VMs, applications, and database using your established security hardening process • Manage activities for your VMs, database, and applications using your established security management process	• Test your application for OWASP Top 10 vulnerabilities	
Vulnerability management	• Manage OS, application, and database vulnerabilities leveraging your established vulnerability management process	• Manage this activity for applications deployed in the PaaS platform (the provider is responsible for their runtime engine and services)	• Provider responsibility
Access control management	• Manage network and user access control to VM, secure privilege access to management consoles, install host IDS, and manage host firewall policies	• Manage developer access provisioning • Restrict access using authentication methods (user- and network-based controls) • Federate identity and enable SSO if SAML is supported	• Manage user provisioning • Restrict access using authentication methods (user- and network-based controls) • Federate identity and enable SSO if SAML is supported

Although you may be transferring some of the operational responsibilities to the provider, you may still own some of the security management responsibilities; review the SLA and check with your CSP on the scope of your responsibilities. Major factors to consider are the SLA, monitoring, and provider-specific API and security management capabilities to support the extension of your internal operations management processes and tools.

Today, customers largely rely on CSPs for basic service instrumentation (i.e., primarily to measure and manage the availability of their services in the cloud). Most CSPs share the overall service metrics via a dashboard (e.g., Amazon's service health dashboard at *http://status.aws .amazon.com/*). Although a CSP may be publishing the most up-to-the-minute information of its overall system status across all customers, the onus is on you to keep abreast of the service status. To manage the availability of your application you will need to measure, monitor, and manage service levels from your perspective (i.e., for your virtual environment).

Unfortunately, the lack of standards and weak capabilities from CSPs to help customers place probes into their virtualized environment have exacerbated cloud service management. Hence, as a tenant of a *aaS service, you will have to understand what your service provider offers to help you manage service levels to your users. Table 6-4 summarizes the security monitoring responsibilities from a customer perspective.

TABLE 6-4. Security monitoring for SPI services: customer responsibilities

Monitoring activities	IaaS	PaaS	SaaS
Network monitoring	• Monitor the network interfaces of your virtual instances	• Provider responsibility (metrics not available to customers)	• Provider responsibility (metrics not available to customers)
Host monitoring	• Monitor security events from host IDSs such as OSSEC • Log events to a dedicated and persistent log server • Monitor security events from VMs stored in system logs	• Provider responsibility (metrics not available to customers)	• Provider responsibility (metrics not available to customers)
Database monitoring	• Install database security monitoring tool on VMs hosting database and log events to a dedicated and persistent log server	• Provider responsibility (metrics not available to customers)	• Provider responsibility (metrics not available to customers)
Application monitoring	• Monitor your application vulnerabilities (OWASP Top 10) and application event logs for intrusions	• Monitor your application logs for vulnerabilities (may be available via the PaaS platform)	• Provider responsibility

From a security management perspective, a key issue is the lack of enterprise-grade access management features. Since access control features will vary among service delivery models (SPI) and providers, customers will have to understand what access control features are available (strong authentication, user provisioning, federation, auditing, etc.) and what their responsibilities are in managing the life cycle of user access to the cloud service. Some service providers are making an effort to keep their customers informed of new threats and educating them on ways to protect the information hosted in their cloud (e.g., Salesforce.com publishing threat and security practice information via *http://trust.salesforce.com/*). However, for the most part it is still up to the customer to monitor and manage threats and risks to your services.

In a virtualized environment where infrastructure is shared across multiple tenants, your data is commingled with that of other customers at every phase of the life cycle—during transit, processing, and storage. Even if you are able to install monitoring probes at infrastructure layers available to you, the resource bottlenecks and security incidents that are visible to your instrumentation may not be able to give you the necessary information to manage security incidents or perform root-cause analysis (e.g., latency of packets between your system nodes in the cloud). Another dimension in cloud computing is the issue of monitoring and measuring disruptions across your users—depending on the cloud service architecture, failures of the infrastructure components may impact only a subset of the population and it would be hard to detect the service disruption unless the affected users report it (e.g., Google mail disruption events that impact only a subset of users). Hence, it is important to review and understand the location of the service, service-level guarantees such as internode communication, and storage access (read and write) latency.

In conclusion, the scope of security management of cloud services will vary with the service delivery model (SPI), provider capabilities, and maturity. Customers will have to make trade-offs with respect to the flexibility and control offered by the SPI services. The more flexible the service (i.e., the lower the service abstraction), the more control you can exercise on the service, and with that come additional security management responsibilities. Given that most cloud service offerings lack transparency in the area of SLAs, provider management capabilities, and security responsibilities, management functions will continue to challenge enterprises that have established IT governance, tools, and processes. Those frameworks, processes, and tools that address systemic qualities including reliability, availability, and security may not be extensible to the cloud service provider. If you have adopted standard IT frameworks including ITIL and ISO 27002 in your organization, they should be reviewed and continuously adjusted based on the cloud service capabilities, sensitivity of information, and SLAs that govern various management functions.

CHAPTER SEVEN

Privacy

> **"You can have security and not have privacy, but you cannot have privacy without security."**
>
> *—Tim Mather*

A **COMMON MISCONCEPTION IS THAT DATA PRIVACY IS A SUBSET OF INFORMATION SECURITY.** The two are indeed interrelated, but privacy brings a host of concerns all its own. In this chapter, we will discuss these components in the context of cloud computing, and analyze the differences and similarities with traditional computing models.

Particularly in less regulated industries (those other than health care and financial services) responsibility and accountability for privacy is often (erroneously) assigned to IT instead of the business unit that owns the data. In many cases, it is treated as a checkbox to verify among several other burdensome requirements.

As we have seen from our review, infrastructure and data security in public cloud computing is, for many organizations (e.g., large enterprises), likely to be less robust than their own current capabilities. With this likely less-secure, greater-risk security posture, it follows that the risk of a privacy breach is also increased. It should, however, be noted that many small and medium-size businesses (SMBs) have limited IT and dedicated information security resources, and as a result they place limited focus on this area. For these organizations, the security afforded by a public cloud service provider (CSP) can be greater.

Even a seemingly small data breach can have a considerable financial impact (e.g., cost of incident response and possible forensic investigation, restitution to victims of identity theft, punitive damages), as well as long-term consequences such as negative publicity and loss of customer confidence. Despite the all-too-familiar headlines, privacy considerations are often not proportional to the level of inherent risk.

What Is Privacy?

The concept of privacy varies widely among (and sometimes within) countries, cultures, and jurisdictions. It is shaped by public expectations and legal interpretations; as such, a concise definition is elusive if not impossible. Privacy rights or obligations are related to the collection, use, disclosure, storage, and destruction of personal data (or personally identifiable information—PII). At the end of the day, privacy is about the accountability of organizations to data subjects, as well as the transparency to an organization's practice around personal information.

Likewise, there is no universal consensus about what constitutes personal data. For the purposes of this discussion, we will use the definition adopted by the Organization for Economic Cooperation and Development (OECD): any information relating to an identified or identifiable individual (data subject).*

Another definition gaining popularity is the one provided by the American Institute of Certified Public Accountants (AICPA) and the Canadian Institute of Chartered Accountants (CICA) in the Generally Accepted Privacy Principles (GAPP) standard: "The rights and obligations of individuals and organizations with respect to the collection, use, retention, and disclosure of personal information."

What Is the Data Life Cycle?

Personal information should be managed as part of the data used by the organization. It should be managed from the time the information is conceived through to its final disposition.

Protection of personal information should consider the impact of the cloud on each of the following phases as detailed in Figure 7-1.

* See *http://www.oecd.org/document/18/0,3343,en_2649_34255_1815186_1_1_1_1,00.html.*

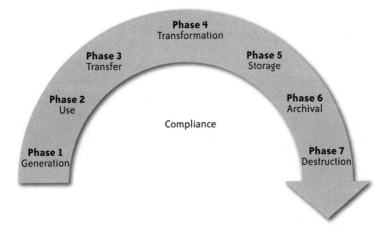

FIGURE 7-1. KPMG data life cycle

The components within each of these phases are:

Generation of the information

- *Ownership*: Who in the organization owns PII, and how is the ownership maintained if the organization uses cloud computing?
- *Classification*: How and when is PII classified? Are there limitations on the use of cloud computing for specific data classes?
- *Governance*: Is there a governance structure to ensure that PII is managed and protected through its life cycle, even when it is stored or processed in a cloud computing environment?

Use

- *Internal versus external*: Is PII used only within the collecting organization, or is it used outside the organization (e.g., in a public cloud)?
- *Third party*: Is the information shared with third parties (e.g., subcontractors or CSPs)?
- *Appropriateness*: Is the use of the information consistent with the purpose for which it was collected? Is the use within the cloud appropriate based on the commitments the organization made to the data subjects?
- *Discovery/subpoena*: Is the information managed in the cloud in a way that will enable the organization to comply with legal requirements in case of legal proceedings?

Transfer

- *Public versus private networks*: When information is transferred to a cloud is the organization using public networks, and is it protected appropriately? (PII should always be protected to address the risk level and legal requirements.)

- *Encryption requirements*: Is the PII encrypted? Some laws require that PII will be encrypted when transmitted via a public network (and this will be the case when the organization is using a public cloud).
- *Access control*: Are there appropriate access controls over PII when it is in the cloud?

Transformation

- *Derivation*: Are the original protection and use limitations maintained when data is transformed or further processed in the cloud?
- *Aggregation*: Is data in the cloud aggregated so that it is no longer related to an identifiable individual (and hence is no longer considered PII)?
- *Integrity*: Is the integrity of PII maintained when it is in the cloud?

Storage

- *Access control*: Are there appropriate controls over access to PII when stored in the cloud so that only individuals with a need to know will be able to access it?
- *Structured versus unstructured*: How is the data stored to enable the organization to access and manage the data in the future?
- *Integrity/availability/confidentiality*: How are data integrity, availability, and confidentiality maintained in the cloud?
- *Encryption*: Several laws and regulations require that certain types of PII should be stored only when encrypted. Is this requirement supported by the CSP?

Archival

- *Legal and compliance*: PII may have specific requirements that dictate how long it should be stored and archived. Are these requirements supported by the CSP?
- *Off-site considerations*: Does the CSP provide the ability for long-term off-site storage that supports archival requirements?
- *Media concerns*: Is the information stored on media that will be accessible in the future? Is the information stored on portable media that may be more susceptible to loss? Who controls the media and what is the organization's ability to recover such media from the CSP if needed?
- *Retention*: For how long will the data be retained by the CSP? Is the retention period consistent with the organization's retention period?

Destruction

- *Secure*: Does the CSP destroy PII obtained by customers in a secure manner to avoid potential breach of the information?
- *Complete*: Is the information completely destroyed? Does the destruction completely erase the data, or can it be recovered?

The impact differs based on the specific cloud model used by the organization, the phase (Figure 7-1, shown earlier) of personal information in the cloud, and the nature of the organization. The following analysis provides some of these considerations; however, every organization should consider performing a Privacy Impact Assessment (PIA) before embarking on a cloud computing initiative that involves personal information.

What Are the Key Privacy Concerns in the Cloud?

Privacy advocates have raised many concerns about cloud computing. These concerns typically mix security and privacy. Here are some additional considerations to be aware of:

Access

Data subjects have a right to know what personal information is held and, in some cases, can make a request to stop processing it. This is especially important with regard to marketing activities; in some jurisdictions, marketing activities are subject to additional regulations and are almost always addressed in the end user privacy policy for applicable organizations. In the cloud, the main concern is the organization's ability to provide the individual with access to all personal information, and to comply with stated requests. If a data subject exercises this right to ask the organization to delete his data, will it be possible to ensure that all of his information has been deleted in the cloud?

Compliance

What are the privacy compliance requirements in the cloud? What are the applicable laws, regulations, standards, and contractual commitments that govern this information, and who is responsible for maintaining the compliance? How are existing privacy compliance requirements impacted by the move to the cloud? Clouds can cross multiple jurisdictions; for example, data may be stored in multiple countries, or in multiple states within the United States. What is the relevant jurisdiction that governs an entity's data in the cloud and how is it determined?

Storage

Where is the data in the cloud stored? Was it transferred to another data center in another country? Is it commingled with information from other organizations that use the same CSP? Privacy laws in various countries place limitations on the ability of organizations to transfer some types of personal information to other countries. When the data is stored in the cloud, such a transfer may occur without the knowledge of the organization, resulting in a potential violation of the local law.

Retention

How long is personal information (that is transferred to the cloud) retained? Which retention policy governs the data? Does the organization own the data, or the CSP? Who enforces the retention policy in the cloud, and how are exceptions to this policy (such as litigation holds) managed?

Destruction

How does the cloud provider destroy PII at the end of the retention period? How do organizations ensure that their PII is destroyed by the CSP at the right point and is not available to other cloud users? How do they know that the CSP didn't retain additional copies? Cloud storage providers usually replicate the data across multiple systems and sites—increased availability is one of the benefits they provide. This benefit turns into a challenge when the organization tries to destroy the data—can you truly destroy information once it is in the cloud? Did the CSP really destroy the data, or just make it inaccessible to the organization? Is the CSP keeping the information longer than necessary so that it can mine the data for its own use?

Audit and monitoring

How can organizations monitor their CSP and provide assurance to relevant stakeholders that privacy requirements are met when their PII is in the cloud?

Privacy breaches

How do you know that a breach has occurred, how do you ensure that the CSP notifies you when a breach occurs, and who is responsible for managing the breach notification process (and costs associated with the process)? If contracts include liability for breaches resulting from negligence of the CSP, how is the contract enforced and how is it determined who is at fault?

Many of these concerns are not specific to personal information, but to all types of information and a broader set of compliance requirements. We address these questions in Chapter 10.

Who Is Responsible for Protecting Privacy?

There are conflicting opinions regarding who is responsible for security and privacy. Some publications assign it to providers;[†] but although it may be possible to transfer liability via contractual agreements, it is never possible to transfer accountability. Ultimately, in the eyes of the public and the law, the onus for data security and privacy falls on the organization that collected the information in the first place—the user organization. This is true even if the user organization has no technical capability to ensure that the contractual requirements with the CSP are met.

History and experience have proven that data breaches have a cascading effect. When an organization loses control of users' personal information, the users are responsible (directly or indirectly) for subsequent damages resulting from the loss. Identity theft is only one of the possible effects; others may include invasion of privacy or unwelcome solicitation. When an affected individual is dealing with the fallout, he will likely blame the one who made the decision to use the service, as opposed to the provider of the service. Full reliance on a third party to protect personal data is irresponsible and will inevitably lead to negative consequences.

† See *http://www.privacyrights.org/ar/cloud-computing.htm.*

Responsible data stewardship requires an in-depth understanding of the technology underlying cloud computing and the legal requirements and implications. As such, a cross-functional team is critical to adequately maintain security and privacy.

The accountability model (discussed earlier in this chapter) is similar to discussions around privacy in outsourcing or subcontracting relationships, and the conclusion is similar:

- Organizations can transfer liability, but not accountability.
- Risk assessment and mitigation throughout the data life cycle is critical.
- Knowledge about legal obligations and contractual agreements or commitments is imperative.

There are, however, many new risks and unknowns; thus, the overall complexity of privacy protection in the cloud represents a bigger challenge.

Changes to Privacy Risk Management and Compliance in Relation to Cloud Computing

The following topics describe analysis of the potential impact of cloud computing on the key OECD and other common privacy principles.

Collection Limitation Principle

This principle specifies that collection of personal data should be limited to the minimum amount of data required for the purpose for which it is collected. Any such data should be obtained by lawful and fair means and, where appropriate, with the knowledge or consent of the data subject.

In the privacy arena, lack of specifics on data collection with providers creates misunderstandings down the road. For instance, one global outsourcer said, "Clients come in expecting the right things in security, but the wrong things in privacy. They are expecting best practices, but they don't know what they are." There are comprehensive security frameworks and standards (such as the ISO 27000 series, NIST guidelines, etc.), and organizations know how to implement them. There is no universally adopted privacy standard—instead, there are conflicting laws, regulations, and views on what privacy is and what it requires from organizations to protect it. Many organizations want to do what they perceive to be "the right thing"; however, their perception may be different from the law. As a result, there may be different expectations regarding what privacy means between the organization and the CSP, and no agreed best practices.

It is essential that service-level agreements (SLAs) are initially defined before any information is provided or shared, because it is very hard to negotiate them later. If you start the request for proposal (RFP) process with an SLA target, you will be able to disqualify providers who cannot meet your stated needs. Well-defined security and privacy SLAs should be part of the statement of work (SOW). Ensure that your SLAs have teeth with specific penalty clauses. Do not cede command of service-level negotiation to the provider.

Moreover, organizations face the risk that, as different data elements about individuals are collected and later merged, the combined information is more than needed and the original purpose as well as the organization may be in potential violation of local laws.

Use Limitation Principle

This principle specifies that personal data should not be disclosed, made available, or otherwise used for purposes other than those with the consent of the data subject, or by the authority of law.

Cloud computing places a diverse collection of user and business information in a single location. As data flows through the cloud, strong data governance is needed to ensure that the original purpose of collection and limitation on use is attached to the data. This is critical when organizations create a centralized database, because future applications can easily combine the data via expanded views that are utilized for new purposes never approved by data subjects.

The ability to combine data from multiple sources increases the risk of unexpected uses by governments. Governments in different countries could ask CSPs to report on particular types of behaviors or to monitor activities of particular types or categories of users. The possibility that a CSP could be obliged to inform a government or a third party about user activities might be troubling to the provider as well as to its users.

Security Principle

Security is one of the key requirements to enable privacy. This principle specifies that personal data should be protected by reasonable security safeguards against such risks as loss or unauthorized access, destruction, use, modification, or disclosure of data.

For more information about security, see Chapter 6.

Retention and Destruction Principle

This principle specifies that personal data should not be retained for longer than needed to perform the task for which it was collected, or as required by laws or regulations. Data should be destroyed in a secure way at the end of the retention period.

How long data should be retained and when it should be destroyed is still a challenge for most companies. Data growth has led to definitions of policies and procedures for data retention and destruction. Most policies have been driven or imposed by legislation and regulations, such as the Health Insurance Portability and Accountability Act of 1996 (HIPAA), the Sarbanes-Oxley Act (SOX), and other federal and state compliance requirements.

The actual deletion process is sometimes loosely defined. But when data copies, data backups, or archives are deleted, are they really gone? Deleting a file only marks the space (or blocks) it occupies as usable. Until the blocks are actually overwritten, the data is still there and can be retrieved. In fact, the disk space occupied by deleted files must be overwritten with other data several times before the entirety of the files is deemed irretrievable (a minimum of seven times per the U.S. federal government's guidelines).

In many cases, disk or tape media is reused to store more data; therefore, data deletion typically does not constitute much of an issue. However, when leased IT assets, such as servers or disk arrays, must be returned, when obsolete systems are replaced, or when storage media has reached end-of-life, special care must be taken to ensure that any data once stored is irretrievable.

Encryption can play a key role in the destruction process. Encrypted data can be destroyed even when organizations lose track of their data by destroying the encryption key—data can no longer be decrypted and hence is rendered inaccessible. This is especially beneficial when the data is kept by CSPs—encrypted data can be destroyed without the involvement of the CSPs.

The problem begins when there is a lack of clearly defined policies around data destruction in cloud computing. Virtual storage devices can be reallocated to new users without deleting the data, and then allocated to new users. Personal information stored in this device may now be available to the new user, potentially violating individual rights, laws, and regulations. Servers or disks can be decommissioned without much thought as to whether data is still accessible. There are several approved methods of data destruction, including media destruction, disk degaussing, multiple data overwrites with random byte patterns, and destruction of keying ·material for encrypted data.

Transfer Principle

This principle specifies that data should not be transferred to countries that don't provide the same level of privacy protection as the organization that collected the information.

In a cloud computing environment, infrastructure is shared between organizations; therefore, there are threats associated with the fact that the data is stored and processed remotely, and there is increased sharing of platforms between users, which increases the need to protect privacy of data stored in the cloud. Another feature of cloud computing is that it is a dynamic environment; for example, service interactions can be created in a more dynamic way than in traditional e-commerce. Services can potentially be aggregated and changed dynamically by customers, and service providers can change the provisioning of services. In such scenarios, personal and sensitive data can move around within a single CSP infrastructure and across CSP organizational boundaries. The goal of integrated services provided by multiple CSPs is to enhance the possibility of data transfer to third parties. This transfer should be disclosed to the data subject prior to collection. In many cases there is a need for unambiguous consent by the individual to the data transfer. Typically the organization is required to agree to the provider's standard terms of service without any scope for negotiation. The terms are likely to be biased in the provider's favor, and the organization may not know all the entities that are involved in the process, and hence is rendered unable to provide an accurate notice to the data subjects.

The transfer challenge is further complicated because data can be anywhere in the world—usually, a company computing in the cloud does not know in what country its data resides at any given time. Instead of its data being stored on the company's servers, data is stored on the service provider's servers, which could be in Europe, China, or anywhere else. This tenet of cloud computing conflicts with various legal requirements, such as the European laws that require that a company know where the personal data in its possession is at all times, and there may be a need to report to data protection authorities on the data transfer. In some cases there may be a need to preapprove the transfer by data subjects.

The U.S. Safe Harbor Program—perhaps the most common means of compliance with EU requirements imposed when transferring the personal data of EU citizens to the United States—may not satisfy a multinational's EU legal obligations, because in cloud computing data could be stored on servers outside of both Europe and the United States, making the Safe Harbor Program ineffective. Furthermore, the Safe Harbor option may not be available for certain organizations not regulated by the Federal Trade Commission, such as those in the financial services industry. This may be the case even if the CSP is registered under the Safe Harbor Program.

One cloud computing application service provider (ASP) offers its customers the option to store their data only on European servers (for a higher fee, naturally). However, it is an impractical solution because it limits the very flexibility and efficiency that cloud computing is designed to provide. Given the enormous potential and benefits of computing in the cloud, it seems that, once again, the law needs to catch up with technology.

Accountability Principle

This principle states that an organization is responsible for personal information under its control and should designate an individual or individuals who are accountable for the organization's compliance with the remaining principles.

Accountability within cloud computing can be achieved by attaching policies to data and mechanisms to ensure that these policies are adhered to by the parties that use, store, or share that data, irrespective of the jurisdiction in which the information is processed.

The way to move onward is for organizations to value accountability and build mechanisms for accountable, responsible decision making while handling data. Specifically, accountable organizations ensure that obligations to protect data are observed by all processors of the data, irrespective of where that processing occurs.

Legal and Regulatory Implications

Across the globe, the legal and regulatory requirements for data privacy range from strictly enforced to non-existent, which can prove to be a daunting challenge for multinational companies or those serving customers from multiple jurisdictions. Some programs such as the OECD Guidelines‡ and the European Union Data Protection Directive§ are principle-based, where personal data processing is not permitted, except as directed in the statutes, whereas in countries such as the United States, certain types of processing are restricted, but activities are generally considered lawful unless specifically prohibited by applicable state and federal regulations. The jurisdiction of these laws is determined differently in different countries and states. Some of the laws are based on the location of the organization, some on the physical location of the data center, and some on the location of the data subjects. The only universal consistency is that the law has not caught up with the technology.

To further compound the challenge of processing personal data in a global environment, some requirements are conflicting. For example, compliance with the U.S. Federal Rules of Civil Procedure (FRCP) can breach the EU Directive. Differing attitudes on privacy have been the force behind countless cross-jurisdictional legal battles, international trade barriers, and long-standing political disputes.

In the next section, we will describe the implications of cloud computing on compliance with various privacy regulations. The scope is limited to aspects that are different in a public cloud environment, because many resources are available to help understand the full extent of the requirements.

U.S. Laws and Regulations

The U.S. regulatory environment is a complex combination of sector-specific federal privacy laws, state-specific laws, and other laws and regulations that can have a significant privacy impact on cloud computing environments.

Federal Rules of Civil Procedure

Rule 26‖ of the FRCP requires that parties involved in a civil lawsuit have a duty to disclose to the other party all information that will be used to support its claims or defenses. This includes electronically stored information (ESI), which creates a challenge in a cloud environment.

---

‡ OECD Guidelines on the Protection of Privacy and Transborder Flows of Personal Data (*http://www.oecd .org/document/18/0,3343,en_2649_34255_1815186_1_1_1_1,00.html*).

§ EU Directive 95/46/EC on the protection of individuals with regard to the processing of personal data and the free movement of such data (*http://www.cdt.org/privacy/eudirective/EU_Directive_.html*).

‖ See *http://www.law.cornell.edu/rules/frcp/Rule26.htm*.

When a lawsuit is filed, or even when it is reasonably anticipated, each party is required to invoke a *litigation hold* (a suspension of a company's document retention or destruction policies for documents that may be relevant to the lawsuit). There are provisions to exclude information destroyed in the normal course of business from the scope of discovery, but in many cases the courts have imposed monetary sanctions on companies that negligently destroy data—even when destruction is unintentional.#

Clearly, a records management strategy addressing archiving and secure data destruction is essential to reducing the burden of compliance. However, many small and medium-size enterprises (as many cloud computing users are) do not have a comprehensive strategy in place for lack of resources.

According to Rule 34(a)(2)(E)(i) of the FRCP, electronically stored documents must be produced in the form in which they are kept in the normal course of business.

Cloud computing environments often do not have the capability to support hold requirements in a way that both segregates the information subject to the hold and does not share information that is related to other individuals, causing a potential violation of the individuals' privacy and violation of privacy laws and regulations.

USA Patriot Act

Perhaps the most controversial privacy-related legislation, the USA Patriot Act has several implications for cloud computing.

At a high level, the challenge with the Patriot Act can be viewed as location, location, location. Exactly where is your data physically, and therefore whose government policies will your data be subject to? What law enforcement (including intelligence) practices, or perhaps conversely, privacy regulations, is the location of your data and your CSP required to abide by?

Specifically, the concern of many U.S. companies, and particularly foreign governments and organizations, is the legal ability of the U.S. government to access electronic information. The primary focus of media attention has been National Security Letters (NSLs). Although NSLs existed prior to the Patriot Act, their use greatly expanded as authority to issue NSLs was broadened to leaders of FBI field offices (e.g., Special Agents in Charge [SAICs]).

However, of greater concern to many foreign governments and organizations is the expanded use of (Patriot Act) Section 215 court orders. These court orders can be obtained from a magistrate judge and may require "... the production of any tangible things (including books, records, papers, documents, and other items) for an investigation to protect against international terrorism or clandestine intelligence activities, provided that such investigation of a United States person is not conducted solely upon the basis of activities protected by the first amendment to the Constitution."

Mosaid Technologies, Inc. v. Samsung Electronics (U.S. District Court of New Jersey, 2004).

For additional comparison of the various U.S. legal orders that can provide access to personal information stored in the cloud, see Table 7-1.

TABLE 7-1. Comparison of U.S. legal orders

Legal order	Who can authorize?	Scope of authority
Search warrant	Court writ (order)	Requires probable cause, although there are exceptions; under the (U.S.) Fourth Amendment, searches must be reasonable and specific, which means a search warrant must be specific as to the object to be searched for and the place to be searched. Other items, rooms, outbuildings, persons, vehicles, and so forth may require additional search warrants.
Subpoena *duces tecum*	Court (writ) order	Orders parties named to appear and produce tangible evidence (documents or otherwise) for use at a hearing or trial; *can be challenged in court.*
Administrative subpoena	Federal agencies—more than 300 instances where federal agencies have been granted administrative subpoena power in one form or another; *the FBI is not one of them*	Authorized use of subpoena power in conjunction with an agency's investigations or its administrative hearings or both. Failure to comply with an administrative subpoena may pave the way for denial of a license or permit or some similar adverse administrative decision in the matter to which the issuance of the subpoena was originally related. In most instances, however, administrative agencies ultimately rely on the courts to enforce their subpoenas.
NSL	Used by the FBI and other government agencies (e.g., CIA, DoD)	Form of administrative subpoena; does not require probable cause or judicial oversight. The scope is limited to telephone and email records (metadata only, not content), financial records, and credit information.
USA Patriot Act of 2001, §215 court order	Magistrate judge court order	"The Director of the [FBI] or a designee of the Director (whose rank shall be no lower than Assistant Special Agent in Charge) may make an application for an order requiring the production of any tangible things (including books, records, papers, documents, and other items) for an investigation to protect against international terrorism or clandestine intelligence activities, provided that such investigation of a United States person is not conducted solely upon the basis of activities protected by the first amendment to the Constitution."[a]

[a] Section 215 (a) (1) of the USA Patriot Act of 2001 (P.L. 107–56).

These changes to U.S. law have caused concern among foreign governments and organizations, and have hindered transborder (international) data flows. The Canadian provinces of British Columbia and Nova Scotia have already forbidden any government data from being stored or processed by providers located in the United States. Incidental information strongly suggests that several other foreign governments and companies have also decided not to store or process data by CSPs located in the United States, or legal entities based in the United States.

Many current CSPs do not provide their customers with control over data location, so the organizations are at risk that PII in their systems will be hosted in the United States and will be subject to the USA Patriot Act. In addition, even if an organization can control the location of its data, CSP management is typically centralized, and the information is accessible from the organization's U.S. location and may be at risk.

Electronic Communications Privacy Act

Fundamental to addressing all cloud computing risks (including those related to privacy) is the contractual agreement with the provider. It is absolutely critical for users to have a thorough understanding of the terms and conditions—from both a legal and a technical perspective. Agreements should clearly describe the services provided, limitations, liabilities, and rights of each party.

SLAs, contractual clauses, and a high-level understanding of applicable legislation can give user organizations, as well as data subjects, a false sense of security with regard to their rights to privacy. Users may assume that they are protected under the Electronic Communications Privacy Act (ECPA);[*] however, a legitimate court order exempts electronic communications and remote computing service providers from adhering to the law.

The following examples prove this point:

In *Psychopathic Records, Inc., v. Anderson* (2008 U.S. District Court of Michigan, Nov. 7, 2008), the court allowed the plaintiff to serve subpoenas on Yahoo! and Hotmail to obtain and preserve the defendant's email relating to alleged copyright infringement.

In *Warner Bros. Records, Inc., v. Does* (2007 U.S. District Court of Colorado, June 6, 2007), the court granted the plaintiff's request for permission to serve a subpoena on an Internet service provider (ISP) for logfiles to determine the defendants' (previously known only by their IP addresses) name, address, telephone number, email address, and Media Access Control (MAC) address. The ISP was given 10 days to contest the subpoena. Written more than two decades ago, the letter of the law does not fully address the spirit of the law due to drastic changes in technology. In this example, the legality of the request was not black and white, so the court left it up to the ISP to decide whether to contest. Users should evaluate vendors and enter into agreements with this possibility in mind.

It may seem that user organizations are at the mercy of cloud providers; however, the ECPA affords the right to file a civil suit[†] if a provider knowingly or intentionally violates the law. Restitution may include actual damages, any profits made by the violator, punitive judgments,

[*] United States Code Title 18, Part I.

[†] United States Code Title 18, Part I, Ch. 121, 2707.

and reasonable attorney fees. It is important to note that voluntary disclosure by the provider is in violation only if the provider is not authorized to access the contents[‡] and the customer has not given consent.[§] Clearly, it is important to pay attention to the fine print and watch out for clauses permitting the provider to change the terms of the agreement without notice.

The law differentiates between providers of electronic communication services and remote computing services, and between contents of communication and information about customers or subscribers. It is essential to seek legal advice when determining how the ECPA applies to an organization.

FISMA

The first thing to note when discussing the U.S. Federal Information Security Management Act of 2002 (FISMA) is that the act requires only U.S. federal agencies to develop, document, and implement an agency-wide information security program. It does not require this of state agencies or quasi-governmental agencies, such as the U.S. Postal Service; however, a contractor or other organization acting on behalf of a federal agency is also subject to FISMA, which is where the privacy implications of employing cloud computing begin to reveal themselves. Because FISMA outright requires compliance from federal agency vendors, with FISMA there is stronger vendor accountability than with HIPAA, and there is already guidance (OMB M-08-21) for use of contractor or outsourced services, which can be applied to cloud computing.

However, the guidance requires that security controls be provided commensurate with the risk impact level to the information system. Agencies must ensure that all FISMA policy requirements are met by providers (including identical security procedures and processes), and service providers must work with agencies to meet all requirements (including annual agency audits/evaluations). This, along with the requirement that the government obtains full productive use of anything it procures, or prohibition of vendor lock-in, effectively requires that agencies implement private clouds rather than use of public clouds. However, affected agencies should consider how their private clouds can interact with public clouds for activities, such as workload surge, segmentation of processing, and continuity of operations, and how that could then open an agency up to onward transfer questions, internal privacy law implications, and so forth. Agencies then should be aware, not only of the agreements with their third-party providers and whether these open them up to privacy issues, but also of any agreements with downstream providers that could have a potential impact on the agency in the event of a breach, legal action, or inconsistency in data retention issues, or whether the downstream provider is not compliant with FISMA. In addition, because FISMA does not address data ownership, agencies should ensure that they address the possible use of their data by a provider and how that may open up the agency to privacy litigation.

‡ United States Code Title 18, Part I, Ch. 121, 2702.

§ United States Code Title 18, Part I, Ch. 121, 2702 (c)(2).

GLBA

There are two key pieces to the Gramm-Leach-Bliley Act (GLBA) to consider when discussing the privacy implications of computing in the cloud: the Financial Privacy Rule and the Safeguards Rule.

The Financial Privacy Rule requires financial institutions to provide their customers with a privacy notice upon inception of the relationship and annually. The privacy notice must explain information collection, sharing, use, and protection. As previously described, the privacy implications of these activities within the cloud have many thorny issues and unanswered questions. GLBA also requires that the notice give a financial institution's customer the right to opt out of the information being shared with unaffiliated parties. It has yet to be determined legally whether CSPs are unaffiliated parties, because the law is frequently behind technology. But the implications of a financial institution using an open cloud model are that there is the distinct possibility that (in the future) CSPs would be deemed unaffiliated parties. The issue remains of how a CSP customer could opt out of the sharing while still using the service if the cloud is the platform employed. In addition, financial institutions are required to update their privacy policies when they change, and offer an opt-out at that time as well. How can a financial institution truly state the nature of the use and protection of such data, when it does not have full control over the data, may not have complete ownership of the data depending on the SLA, and may not be able to anticipate the dynamic use of the data in cloud applications?

The Safeguards Rule stipulates that a financial institution must perform risk management of the non-public information, implement an information security program, including periodic monitoring and testing of the program, and update safeguards as needed with the changes in how information is collected, stored, and used. In the cloud, how an enterprise manages the risk associated with non-public information becomes more complicated and more involved. The information security program of the financial institution must also consider the data security in the cloud—both in transit and at rest—and should work with its provider to ensure that the program is sufficient, is accurate, and is operating effectively. Finally, the institution should consider how to adequately update safeguards to allow for changes to collect, store, and use data in the dynamic cloud environment, or even determine whether updates are necessary.

HIPAA

One of the key privacy implications of the United States when using the cloud is similar to that already faced by health care providers using non-cloud third-party vendors for data storage. HIPAA regulates the use and disclosure of protected health information (PHI) by health care providers and health plans, but does not currently regulate their third-party providers. Organizations subject to HIPAA are required to enter into a business associate agreement with the third-party providers to transfer PHI, and this legally binds the providers to effectively be subject to HIPAA regulations. However, this agreement typically covers the transfer of data from the health plan organization to the CSP. Because it does not govern the use of data by the CSP, the CSP could store the data outside U.S. jurisdiction, and use the data in ways that are in conflict with HIPAA but are not in the terms of service. The ability for the enterprise to determine this, or determine where its data specifically is stored, is difficult if not impossible.

In addition, the HIPAA Privacy Rule stipulates the right of an individual to access his PHI and have any inaccuracies corrected. With the persistence of data, it can be difficult to be certain that data has been completely and accurately updated. The HIPAA Privacy Rule also requires health care providers to notify individuals of their information practices; however, with data being in the cloud, those notices may be incomplete or inaccurate (without the organization's knowledge), but would still be considered in violation of the act. Finally, governments and others may request data on an individual directly from the CSP, as a central collection point of data for individuals. The probability of such a request increases, as new services such as Google Health and Microsoft Health Vault may become large repositories of health information. When the CSP and the user organization are separate entities and are under the authorities for a gag order granted under the Patriot Act, it increases the likelihood that the CSP will not inform the user organization, and thereby the individual, even though HIPAA grants the individual this right, and the practical reality makes this harder to achieve than in an on-site data storage model. Ultimately, when considering the use of a CSP for PHI, review the CSP's terms of service carefully, as well as the business associate agreement.

HITECH Act

In early 2009, HIPAA was amended by the Health Information Technology for Economic and Clinical Health (HITECH) Act, a section of the American Recovery and Reinvestment Act of 2009 relating to health information technology. The goal of the law is, among others, to drive a transition to electronic health records (EHRs) so that by 2014 all U.S. residents will have an EHR. The law provides a privacy and security framework and safeguards to establish public trust so that individuals accept EHRs. From a privacy perspective, the law significantly expands the HIPAA Privacy Rule and security standards, changes the rules for business associates, and adds provisions for breach notification (see also Chapter 8). The immediate impact of the law is a significant expansion in the number of entities covered under HIPAA, as well as established increased accountability and liability to business associates.

This HITECH law has a significant impact on CSPs; under this law many of them are now business associates, and as such they are subject to privacy and safeguarding requirements. They are also now subject to the expanded rule on PHI breaches. These new requirements have a significant impact on the privacy and security safeguards that a CSP should implement. A key area is protection so that patient information does not fall under the definition of *unsecured PHI* (PHI that is unsecured by a technology standard that renders the PHI unusable, unreadable, or indecipherable to unauthorized individuals) and is developed or endorsed by a standard developing organization that is accredited by the American National Standards Institute (ANSI).

Organizations should closely review these requirements, and how they impact them, as well as the impact on their ability to use CSPs (and what new contractual requirements they should have). Organizations should also consider the impact from a customer service perspective; for example, the HITECH law requires covered entities that use or maintain EHRs to provide individuals with access to their PHI in electronic format, if requested.

It should be noted that several CSPs launched cloud-based EHR applications that provide individuals with the ability to manage their health information online. These providers claim that they don't fall under the HIPAA provisions, as they are not covered entities or business associates. The HITECH law expanded the definition of business associates—some claim that the law turns third-party data repositories, personal health records, and health information networks into business partners of care providers and health plans that provide them with the information, and hence requiring them to follow the business associate rules. The CSPs in the field claim that this isn't the case; however, we don't have a final legal resolution on this matter.

International Laws and Regulations

The international regulatory environment is driven by two approaches: one represented by EU Directive 95/46/EC on the protection of individuals with regard to the processing of personal data and on the free movement of such data (EU Directive), that was the model used by countries in Europe as well as Canada, and another reflected by the APEC Privacy Framework. The two approaches have a different privacy impact on cloud computing environments.

EU Directive

The most significant difference between the EU and U.S. legislation is the notion of personal privacy. In Europe, privacy is considered a basic human right and cannot be divorced from one's personal freedom. The EU Directive compels member states to implement and enforce data privacy legislation (national law) that (at a minimum) satisfies the requirements set forth in the EU Directive (community or supranational law). Processing of personal data is prohibited, unless it is in compliance with both sets of applicable regulation. The roles can be loosely compared to federal and state governments within the United States.

The EU Directive distinguishes between data controllers and data processors. If a CSP does not have the authority to make decisions regarding the processing of data (e.g., acting only on instructions from the data controller or owner), it is not subject to the same stringent rules. It is the controller (user organization) that is responsible for implementing an effective mechanism and, therefore, ensuring that its use of third-party service providers (such as CSPs) does not violate the law.

A key provision of the EU Directive is restriction on the transfer of personal data outside the European Union‖ (or countries designated by the European Commission as having adequate data protection standards in place). The regulators' objective is to prevent organizations from circumventing privacy rules by transferring data to places where it is not legally protected— not to limit trade or create unnecessary formalities. Organizations considering cloud computing as a solution should not automatically discount the idea based on this challenge.

The EU Directive contains several provisions to allow transfer of data,# including (among others):

- The data subject has given his consent unambiguously to the proposed transfer.
- The transfer is necessary for the performance of a contract between the data subject and the controller or the implementation of precontractual measures taken in response to the data subject's request.
- The transfer is necessary for the conclusion or performance of a contract concluded in the interest of the data subject between the controller and a third party.
- The transfer is necessary or legally required on important public interest grounds, or for the establishment, exercise, or defense of legal claims.
- The transfer is necessary to protect the vital interests of the data subject.

Member states also have the right to authorize transfers when the controller is deemed to have adequate safeguards as a result of contractual clauses. (Binding corporate rules and standard contractual clauses are mechanisms to streamline this process.) Although these requirements are complex, compliance with EU regulations in cloud computing can be met, provided the use of third-party service providers is well managed. The EU Directive's guidance on this matter is that the controller must, where processing is carried out on his behalf, select a processor providing sufficient guarantees in respect of the technical security measures and organizational measures governing the processing to be carried out, and must ensure compliance with those measures.*

Complying with this set of guidelines does not necessarily imply compliance with the EU Privacy law. Similar to the federal or state jurisdictions in the United States, EU member states must implement these laws locally, as a minimum effort. Each state has drafted its own legislation, and some are even more stringent than the supranational law. It is advisable to consult legal counsel when determining which stipulations must be adhered to.

The stringent requirements of the EU Directive may present legal limitations on the adoption of cloud computing, requiring organizations to increase the level of scrutiny on CSPs.

‖ EU Directive Chapter IV, Article 25.

EU Directive Chapter IV, Article 26.

* EU Directive Chapter VII, Article 17, Paragraph 2.

APEC Privacy Framework

The Asia Pacific Economic Corporation (APEC) Privacy Framework,[†] similar to the OECD Privacy Guidelines, is established as best practices for organizations operating within these economic areas. Unlike the EU Directive, these guidelines are not mandatory, and as such they may be adopted by participating economies as part of their laws. There is currently a significant effort by key APEC economies to drive broad adoption of the framework. Based on this effort, it is our view that any organization processing personal data will benefit from adherence to the framework. The APEC Privacy Framework is implemented via a pilot (pathfinder) led by multiple economies within the region. The pilot involves both governments and private sector organizations, and should provide a consistent approach for data transfer within the region. Successful implementation of the framework can provide a stronger basis for CSPs to operate seamlessly across borders.

These guidelines will provide a more flexible environment that supports transition to a cloud environment, where data flows between economies.

Summary

Cloud computing offers significant challenges for organizations that need to meet various global privacy regulations. As we discussed in this chapter, organizations need to adopt a systematic approach to addressing privacy in the cloud. Given the complexity of existing global legislation, it is advisable to seek in-country legal advice and develop a framework against which to design internal controls to manage processes, as shown earlier in Figure 7-1.

A problem that has existed for many years is how to deal with transborder data flows. Since these flows involve multiple international governmental jurisdictions, complexities develop due to conflicting rules. Cloud computing has these same issues, but can exacerbate the problem of knowledge of geographic location of specifically where cloud computing activities are occurring. An organization might be able to select which country the CSP uses to have its data stored and processed. However, determining which specific server or storage device will be used is extremely difficult to ascertain due to the dynamic nature of cloud computing.

---

† APEC Privacy Framework (*http://www.apec.org/apec/news___media/fact_sheets/apec_privacy_framework .html*).

We further explored the impact of cloud computing on OECD privacy principles and concluded that:

- Strong data governance (managing the entire life cycle of the data from creation to destruction) is needed by CSPs to be able to respond to disclosure of data by governments.
- Care must be taken to delete data and virtual storage devices, especially as it relates to device reuse.
- Transfer of data to third parties will require consent from the data owner.
- The European Union and U.S. Safe Harbor Program require knowledge of where data is stored at all times; this will encourage CSPs to store data on servers located outside Europe and the United States whenever legally possible.

CHAPTER EIGHT

Audit and Compliance

AUDIT AND COMPLIANCE REFERS TO THE INTERNAL AND EXTERNAL PROCESSES that an
organization implements to:

- Identify the requirements with which it must abide—whether those requirements are
  driven by business objectives, laws and regulations, customer contracts, internal corporate
  policies and standards, or other factors
- Put into practice policies, procedures, processes, and systems to satisfy such requirements
- Monitor or check whether such policies, procedures, and processes are consistently
  followed

Audit and compliance functions have always played an important role in traditional
outsourcing relationships. However, these functions take on increased importance in the cloud
given the dynamic nature of software-as-a-service (SaaS), infrastructure-as-a-service (IaaS),
and platform-as-a-service (PaaS) environments. Cloud service providers (CSPs) are challenged
to establish, monitor, and demonstrate ongoing compliance with a set of controls that meets
their customers' business and regulatory requirements. Maintaining separate compliance
efforts for different regulations or standards is not sustainable. A practical approach to audit
and compliance in the cloud includes a coordinated combination of internal policy compliance,
regulatory compliance, and external auditing.

Internal Policy Compliance

CSPs, like other enterprises, need to establish processes, policies, and procedures for managing their IT systems that are appropriate for the nature of the service offering, can be operationalized in the culture of the organization, and satisfy relevant external requirements.

In designing their service offerings and supporting processes, CSPs need to:

- Address the requirements of their current and planned customer base
- Establish a strong control foundation that will substantially meet customer requirements, thereby minimizing the need for infrastructure customization that could reduce efficiencies and diminish the value proposition of the CSP's services
- Set a standard that is high enough to address those requirements
- Define standardized processes to drive efficiencies

Figure 8-1 shows a life cycle approach for determining, implementing, operating, and monitoring controls over a CSP.

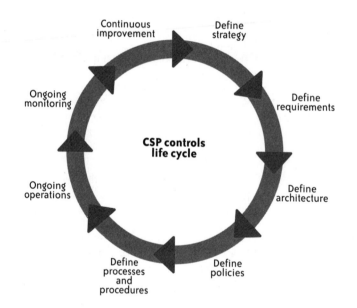

FIGURE 8-1. CSP life cycle approach

Here is an explanation of each stage of the life cycle:

Define strategy

As a CSP undertakes to build out or take a fresh look at its service offerings, the CSP should clearly define its business strategy and related risk management philosophy. What market segments or industries does the CSP intend to serve?

This strategic decision will drive the decision of how high the CSP needs to "set the bar" for its controls. This is an important decision, as setting it too low will make it difficult to meet the needs of new customers and setting it too high will make it difficult for customers to implement and difficult for the CSP to maintain in a cost-effective manner. A clear strategy will enable the CSP to meet the baseline requirements of its customers in the short term and provide the flexibility to incorporate necessary changes while resisting unnecessary or potentially unprofitable customization.

Define requirements

Having defined its strategy and target client base, the CSP must define the requirements for providing services to that client base. What specific regulatory or industry requirements are applicable? Are there different levels of requirements for different sets of clients?

The CSP will need to determine the minimum set of requirements to serve its client base and the incremental industry-specific requirements. For example, the CSP will need to determine whether it supports all of those requirements as part of a base product offering or whether it offers incremental product offerings with additional capabilities at a premium, now or in a future release.

Define architecture

Driven by its strategy and requirements, the CSP must now determine how to architect and structure its services to address customer requirements and support planned growth. As part of the design, for example, the CSP will need to determine which controls are implemented as part of the service by default and which controls (e.g., configuration settings, selected platforms, or workflows) are defined and managed by the customer.

Define policies

The CSP needs to translate its requirements into policies. In defining such policies, the CSP should draw upon applicable industry standards as discussed in the sections that follow. The CSP will also need to take a critical look at its staffing model and ensure alignment with policy requirements.

Define processes and procedures

The CSP then needs to translate its policy requirements into defined, repeatable processes and procedures—again using applicable industry standards and leading practices guidance. Controls should be automated to the greatest extent possible for scalability and to facilitate monitoring.

Ongoing operations

Having defined its processes and procedures, the CSP needs to implement and execute its defined processes, again ensuring that its staffing model supports the business requirements.

Ongoing monitoring

The CSP should monitor the effectiveness of its key control activities on an ongoing basis with instances of non-compliance reported and acted upon. Compliance with the relevant internal and external requirements should be realized as a result of a robust monitoring program.

Continuous improvement

As issues and improvement opportunities are identified, the CSP should ensure that there is a feedback loop to guarantee that processes and controls are continuously improved as the organization matures and customer requirements evolve.

Governance, Risk, and Compliance (GRC)

CSPs are typically challenged to meet the requirements of a diverse client base. To build a sustainable model, it is essential that the CSP establish a strong foundation of controls that can be applied to all of its clients. In that regard, the CSP can use the concept of GRC that has been adopted by a number of leading traditional outsourced service providers and CSPs.[*] GRC recognizes that compliance is not a point-in-time activity, but rather is an ongoing process that requires a formal compliance program. Figure 8-2 depicts such a programmatic approach to compliance.[†]

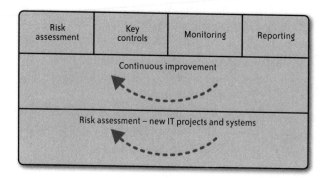

FIGURE 8-2. A programmatic approach to compliance

Key components of this approach include:

Risk assessment

This approach begins with an assessment of the risks that face the CSP and identification of the specific compliance regimes/requirements that are applicable to the CSP's services. The CSP should address risks associated with key areas such as appropriate user authentication mechanisms for accessing the cloud, encryption of sensitive data and

---

[*] KPMG LLP, GRC Discussion Document, March 2009.

[†] KPMG LLP. "Industry Issues and Standards—Effectively Addressing Compliance Requirements." ISACA San Francisco Chapter, Consumer Information Protection Event, April 1, 2009.

associated key management controls, logical separation of customers' data, and CSP administrative access.

Key controls

Key controls are then identified and documented to address the identified risks and compliance requirements. These key controls are captured in a unified control set that is designed to meet the requirements of the CSP's customers and other external requirements. The CSP drives compliance activities based on its key controls rather than disparate sets of externally generated compliance requirements.

Monitoring

Monitoring and testing processes are defined and executed on an ongoing basis for key controls. Gaps requiring remediation are identified with remediation progress tracked.

The results of ongoing monitoring activities may also be used to support any required external audits. Refer to "Auditing the Cloud for Compliance" on page 194 for a discussion of external audit approaches.

Reporting

Metrics and key performance indicators (KPIs) are defined and reported on an ongoing basis. Reports of control effectiveness and trending are made available to CSP management and external customers, as appropriate.

Continuous improvement

Management improves its controls over time—acting swiftly to address any significant gaps identified during the course of monitoring and taking advantage of opportunities to improve processes and controls.

Risk assessment—new IT projects and systems

The CSP performs a risk assessment as new IT projects, systems, and services are developed to identify new risks and requirements, to assess the impact on the CSP's current controls, and to determine whether additional or modified controls and monitoring processes are needed.

The CSP also performs an assessment when considering entry into a new industry or market or taking on a major new client with unique control requirements.

Benefits of GRC for CSPs

CSPs must adhere to a variety of IT process control requirements including external requirements and internal requirements. As we examine these requirements, we find numerous points of intersection. By combining compliance efforts to address all of these requirements and taking a more uniform and strategic approach, increased efficiencies and compliance can be attained. Instead of performing control review and testing cycles separately, control language and testing can be structured to address the needs of multiple sets of requirements. Therefore, control review and testing need to be completed only once to meet the demands of multiple sets of requirements. This strategic approach results in a decreased level of effort to meet control requirements and increased compliance due to the control language being defined in a more efficient manner to support many compliance needs.

CSPs often struggle to meet the many demands of compliance requirements. These efforts are often in silos, unstructured, and reactive in nature. Repeatedly non-compliant controls are discovered during the course of an audit or as a result of a security incident. By implementing a structured compliance program and organization, significant benefits can be derived.

Achieving periodic silos of compliance mostly as a result of third-party reviews will be replaced by an ongoing focus on compliance to increase overall IT process compliance in a more efficient manner.

The use of KPIs and compliance-based risk assessments will provide valuable insight into areas of IT control weaknesses. Improved visibility into IT control weaknesses can greatly enhance decision making for new investments, placing precious resources where there is the greatest need.

Continuous controls monitoring will be performed to shift from a detective approach discovering compliance failures to a more preventive approach of regularly reviewing control effectiveness and thereby avoiding compliance failures before they can occur.

With proactive compliance management performed by control and compliance subject matter professionals, control changes required through the introduction of new regulations, threats, and IT systems can be more smoothly managed and integrated into the control environment.

Compliance benefits can be further extended by more effectively using automation to improve control compliance.

In summary, a GRC approach helps a CSP to:

- Reduce risks through a structured risk management approach
- Improve monitoring of IT compliance
- Improve security
- Rationalize compliance requirements and control assessment processes
- Reduce the burden of compliance monitoring and testing

GRC Program Implementation

To implement a GRC program several major scope elements must be developed, approved, and put in place. The major components of work have been broken down into the following work streams: governance, risk management, compliance, and continuous improvement.

Figure 8-3 depicts a typical process for implementing a unified IT compliance program.

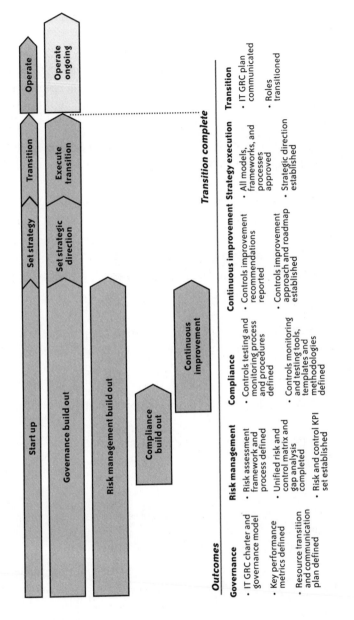

FIGURE 8-3. Implementing a GRC program

Start-up involves building out all the major work components necessary to define and operate the program. This is generally led and performed by the GRC team working with guidance and input from IT management. This will include the following:

Governance build-out

- The operating scope/charter, procedures, and governance mechanisms for the GRC team will be developed.

- An organizational change management and transition plan will be developed to assist the organization in communicating how the GRC team will integrate with the CSP as a whole.

Risk management build-out

- A risk assessment framework will be developed leveraging existing methodologies. This framework will be tailored to the CSP's processes and will be accompanied by a risk assessment process definition.

- The CSP's compliance requirements will be rationalized to support the development of the unified control matrix.

- The unified control matrix will be developed and mapped against current control processes with gaps identified.

- KPIs will be defined to monitor progress and provide a basis for ongoing measurement and project management office dashboard reporting.

Compliance build-out

The testing/monitoring processes and procedures, tools, templates, and methodologies will be developed to support effective compliance utilizing a standardized and efficient approach.

Continuous improvement

Controls improvement recommendations will be developed, risk-rated, and prioritized.

Set strategy

The set-strategy phase will encompass the GRC team presenting the program as a whole to the GRC oversight group and acquiring consensus and approval for the program strategy and approach.

Transition

The transition phase will comprise a short period of communicating the new GRC roles and introducing resources and activities to the broader organization.

Operate

The operate phase is when the ongoing services are made operational and the program executes its charter, strategy, and approach as defined and approved in previous phases.

Illustrative Control Objectives for Cloud Computing

This section describes illustrative control objectives for cloud computing that CSPs should consider as they develop or refine their compliance programs. A variety of industry standards and frameworks for IT controls can be used when designing IT control sets, as we will discuss in "Regulatory/External Compliance" on page 182. In that regard, the ISO 27001 standard (Information technology—Security techniques—Information security management systems—Requirements) has gained broad international acceptance as a solid framework for information-security-focused controls. ISO 27001 contains a solid foundation of IT/security control objectives (summarized in the following sections) and supporting control activities for a CSP to build on.‡ In addition, the ISO 27002 standard (Information technology—Security techniques—Code of practice for information security management) contains more detailed supporting guidance for each topic covered in ISO 27001.§ Refer to these standards for a listing of control activities and additional good practices guidance for the topics listed in the following sections.

A.5 Security policy

Information security policy
> Provides management direction and support for information security in accordance with business requirements and relevant laws and regulations

A.6 Organization of information security

Internal organization
> Manages information security within the organization

External parties
> Maintains the security of the organization's information and information processing facilities that are accessed, processed, communicated to, or managed by external parties

A.7 Asset management

Responsibility for assets
> To achieve and maintain appropriate protection of organizational assets

Information classification
> To ensure that information receives an appropriate level of protection

‡ ISO/IEC 27001:2005, Information technology—Security techniques—Information security management systems—Requirements.

§ ISO/IEC 27002:2005, Information technology—Security techniques—Code of practice for information security management.

A.8 Human resources security

Prior to employment
>To ensure that employees, contractors, and third-party users understand their responsibilities and are suitable for the roles they are considered for, and to reduce the risk of theft, fraud, or misuse of facilities

During employment
>To ensure that all employees, contractors, and third-party users are aware of information security threats and concerns and of their responsibilities and liabilities, and are equipped to support an organizational security policy in the course of their normal work, and to reduce the risk of human error

Termination or change of employment
>To ensure that employees, contractors, and third-party users exit an organization or change employment in an orderly manner

A.9 Physical and environmental security

Secure areas
>To prevent unauthorized physical access, damage, and interference to the organization's premises and information

Equipment security
>To prevent loss, damage, theft, or compromise of assets and interruption to the organization's activities

A.10 Communications and operations management

Operational procedures and responsibilities
>To ensure the correct and secure operation of information processing facilities

Third-party service delivery management
>To implement and maintain the appropriate level of information security and service delivery in line with third-party service delivery agreements

System planning and acceptance
>To minimize the risk of system failures

Protection against malicious and mobile code
>To protect the integrity of software and information

Backup
>To maintain the integrity and availability of information and information processing facilities

Network security management
> To ensure the protection of information in networks and the protection of the supporting infrastructure

Media handling
> To prevent unauthorized disclosure, modification, removal, or destruction of assets and interruption to business activities

Exchange of information
> To maintain the security of information and software exchanged within an organization and with any external entity

Electronic commerce services
> To ensure the security of electronic commerce services and their secure use

Monitoring
> To detect unauthorized information processing activities

A.11 Access control

Business requirement for access control
> To control access to information

User access management
> To ensure authorized user access and to prevent unauthorized access to information systems

User responsibilities
> To prevent unauthorized user access, and compromise or theft of information and information processing facilities

Network access control
> To prevent unauthorized access to networked services

Operating system access control
> To prevent unauthorized access to operating systems

Application and information access control
> To prevent unauthorized access to information held in application systems

Mobile computing and teleworking
> To ensure information security when using mobile computing and teleworking facilities

A.12 Information systems acquisition, development, and maintenance

Security requirements of information systems
> To ensure that security is an integral part of information systems

Correct processing in applications
> To prevent errors, loss, unauthorized modification, or misuse of information in applications

Cryptographic controls
> To protect the confidentiality, authenticity, or integrity of information by cryptographic means

Security of system files
> To ensure the security of system files

Security in development and support processes
> To maintain the security of application system software and information

Technical vulnerability management
> To reduce risks resulting from exploitation of published technical vulnerabilities

A.13 Information security incident management

Reporting information security events and weaknesses
> To ensure that information security events and weaknesses associated with information systems are communicated in a manner that allows timely corrective action to be taken

Management of information security incidents and improvements
> To ensure that a consistent and effective approach is applied to the management of information security incidents

A.14 Business continuity management

Information security aspects of business continuity management
> To counteract interruptions to business activities and to protect critical business processes from the effects of major failures of information systems or disasters and to ensure their timely resumption

A.15 Compliance

Compliance with legal requirements
> To avoid breaches of any law, statutory, regulatory, or contractual obligations and of any security requirements

Compliance with security policies and standards, and technical compliance
> To ensure compliance of systems with organizational security policies and standards

Information systems audit considerations
> To maximize the effectiveness of and to minimize interference to/from the information systems audit process

Incremental CSP-Specific Control Objectives

Building on the general-purpose IT/security control objectives defined in ISO 27001, the following are additional illustrative control objectives of particular relevance to CSPs. Additional control objectives may be applicable depending on the nature of the services offered by the CSP.

Asset management, access control

Data protection/segregation/encryption

To provide logical segregation of CSP customers' data

To enable customer classification of sensitive data

To enable protection of data commensurate with risk and defined information classifications

Information systems acquisition, development, and maintenance

Encryption standards

To enable encryption of sensitive data using consistent mechanisms

To enable access to current and archived data regardless of which keys were used for encryption

Communications and operations management

Logging

To securely provide audit logs of relevant actions (e.g., user activity, configuration changes) for internal or external review

To periodically review higher-risk audit events with appropriate action taken where required

Access control

Authentication to the cloud

To provide authentication mechanisms commensurate with the associated risk

To strictly limit CSP administrative access to customer data, including IT and customer support personnel

Compliance

Monitoring/compliance function

> To provide ongoing monitoring of compliance with policies, procedures, and standards

> To provide proactive risk identification and mitigation

Additional Key Management Control Objectives

Where encryption is used, effective key management controls are critically important to help ensure the confidentiality and availability of sensitive data. Here are the relevant key management control objectives.[||]

Key management

Key generation practices

> Cryptographic keys are generated in accordance with industry standards, including:

- Random or pseudorandom number generation

- Prime number generation

- Key generation algorithms

- Hardware and software components

- References to the key generation procedural documentation

Key storage, backup, and recovery practices

> Asymmetric private keys and symmetric keys remain secret and their integrity and authenticity are retained, including:

- Key separation mechanisms

- Hardware and software components

- References to key storage, backup, and recovery procedures

- Business continuity management documentation

Key distribution practices

> Secrecy of asymmetric private keys, symmetric keys, and keying material, and the integrity and authenticity of all keys and keying material, are maintained during key distribution, including:

- Initial key distribution processes

- Subsequent key replacement processes

- Key synchronization mechanisms

- References to the key distribution procedural documentation

---

‖ KPMG LLP, Key Management Policy and Practice Framework, January 2002.

Key use practices

Cryptographic keys are used only for their intended purpose, including:

- Business applications
- Key separation mechanisms
- Related crypto-periods
- References to the business and system description documentation

Key destruction and archival practices

All active instances of cryptographic keys are properly erased (destroyed) at the end of their designated crypto-periods and archived keys are handled appropriately, including:

- Controls to maintain confidentiality, integrity, and authenticity
- Mechanisms to prevent an archived key from being reinstalled
- Inclusion of references to the business and system documentation

Cryptographic hardware life cycle practices

Access to cryptographic hardware is limited to properly authorized individuals, and the hardware is functioning properly. The description should include:

- Controls for the device life cycle (e.g., shipping, inventory controls, installation, initialization, repair, and de-installation)
- References to device documentation (e.g., product specifications, users' manual) and certification (e.g., FIPS 140)

Certificate life cycle management

Subscribers are properly identified and authenticated, and certificate request information is accurate and complete.

Certificates are generated and issued securely and accurately.

Upon issuance, complete and accurate certificates are available to subscribers and relying parties.

Certificates are revoked based on authorized and validated certificate revocation requests.

Certificates and certificate chains are properly verified.

Initialization, distribution, usage, and termination of portable tokens (e.g., smart cards) are properly managed.

Control Considerations for CSP Users

The following are illustrative control objectives of particular relevance to users of CSPs. Additional control objectives may be applicable depending on the nature of the services offered by the CSP.

Access control

Managing access to the cloud
> To restrict user access to cloud resources based on job function/responsibilities

> To properly administer users throughout the life cycle from hire, to role change, to termination

Configuration management
> To clearly define responsibilities for configuration management between the CSP and CSP user

> To restrict access to change virtual system configurations and provide logging of any such changes

Information systems acquisition, development, and maintenance

Change management
> To clearly define responsibilities for infrastructure change management between the CSP and CSP user

> To ensure that administrative privileges are properly restricted

> To ensure that changes are properly documented, authorized, approved, tested, and implemented

Application maintenance
> To clearly define responsibilities for application change management between the CSP and CSP user

> To ensure that administrative privileges are properly restricted

> To ensure that changes are properly documented, authorized, approved, tested, and implemented

Organization of information security

Vendor management
> To assess, monitor, and manage risks associated with the use of CSPs

Regulatory/External Compliance

CSPs face an increasingly complex array of external compliance requirements from their customers, whether those include industry standards, regulatory regimes, or customer-specific frameworks. Frequently, those requirements are based on or refer to industry standards. As a result, using industry standards can be an effective compliance approach for CSPs if they can navigate through the ever-increasing number of standards that exist or are under development (see Figure 8-4).

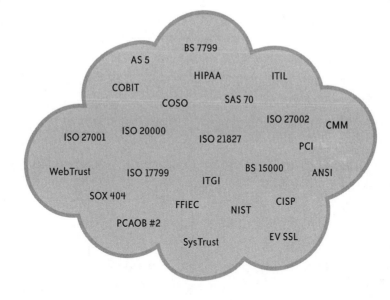

FIGURE 8-4. So many standards

From an information technology and security controls perspective, it can be helpful to look at these standards in terms of their focus and objective. The matrix in Table 8-1 was developed to summarize how a number of leading industry standards/regulatory requirements fit together.# Understanding these standards in their proper context helps an organization to determine their applicability and how they might be used.

TABLE 8-1. High-level standards road map

	Control environment/ company level controls	Information security	IT service delivery/ operations	Systems development	Financial reporting systems	Specific technologies or incremental requirements
Best practices Guidance	COBIT					
	COSO	ISO27002	ITIL ISO 20000-2	CMM/ISO 21827	ITGI-SOX	ISO various ANSI various NIST various

Lundin, Mark. "Industry Issues and Standards—Effectively Addressing Compliance Requirements." ISACA San Francisco Chapter, Consumer Information Protection Event; April 1, 2009.

	Control environment/ company level controls	Information security	IT service delivery/ operations	Systems development	Financial reporting systems	Specific technologies or incremental requirements
Certification/ audit criteria/ requirements		ISO 27001	ISO 20000-1			
Regulatory/ industry requirements		FFIEC HIPAA HITRUST NIST PCI ISO 2700X			SOX PCAOB	EV SSL
Audit framework	SAS 70 SysTrust WebTrust BITS FISAP				PCAOB	WebTrust CA WebTrust EV GAPP

As Table 8-1 shows, many IT standards have a specific area of focus, such as:

- Overall control environment/company-level controls
- Information security
- IT service delivery/operations
- Systems development
- Financial reporting systems
- Specific technologies

In addition, the nature of individual standards can generally be characterized as:

- Best Practices Guidance
- Certification/Audit Criteria/Requirements
- Regulatory/Industry Requirements
- Audit Framework

When developing a controls framework or assessing how to address the requirements of a particular standard/set of requirements, it is desirable to base the framework on the standard that is most relevant. For CSPs, where security is a paramount concern, ISO 27001 is used as a baseline. The CSP may refer to ISO 27002 for additional best practices guidance. It may then be necessary to add to the control framework incremental requirements from relevant regulatory or industry requirements or topics covered in the illustrative control objectives. As the CSP enters new markets or industries and inherits new requirements, it is essential that the CSP critically analyze such requirements to determine whether they truly give rise to needed additional controls or whether they are already covered by the CSP's control set. Relevant audit frameworks should be considered when designing the CSP's control set and periodic external audits should cover the most relevant aspects of the CSP's controls.

The following sections discuss a selection of common industry/regulatory requirements (Sarbanes-Oxley, PCI DSS, HIPAA) and their applicability in a cloud computing environment.

Sarbanes-Oxley Act

In response to significant financial reporting fraud in 2001–2002, the Sarbanes-Oxley Act of 2002 (SOX) was passed and signed into law. As a result of SOX:

- Public company CEOs and CFOs are required to certify the effectiveness of their internal controls over financial reporting (ICOFR) on a quarterly and annual basis.
- Management is required to perform an annual assessment of its ICOFR.
- External auditors are required to express an opinion on the effectiveness of management's ICOFR as of the company's fiscal year end.[*]

SOX also led to the creation of the Public Company Accounting Oversight Board (PCAOB) which was charged with establishing audit standards. PCAOB Auditing Standard No. 2 called attention to the importance of information technology general controls (ITGCs). The following paragraph gave rise to public companies' renewed focus on the effectiveness of their ITGCs:

> Some controls ... might have a pervasive effect on the achievement of many overall objectives of the control criteria. For example, information technology general controls over program development, program changes, computer operations, and access to programs and data help ensure that specific controls over the processing of transactions are operating effectively.[†]

Ultimately, the IT Governance Institute developed a set of IT Control Objectives for Sarbanes-Oxley that became the de facto industry standard for ITGC needed to achieve the requirements of SOX. This included control objectives and recommended supporting control procedures in the following areas:

Program Development and Program Change
    Acquire or develop application system software.

---

[*] Sarbanes-Oxley Act of 2002, sections 302, 404.

[†] PCAOB Auditing Standard No. 2—An Audit of Internal Control Over Financial Reporting Performed in Conjunction with an Audit of Financial Statements, March 9, 2004.

Acquire technology infrastructure.

Develop and maintain policies and procedures.

Install and test application software and technology infrastructure.

Manage changes.

Computer Operations and Access to Programs and Data

Define and manage service levels.

Manage third-party services.

Ensure system security.

Manage the configuration.

Manage problems and incidents.

Manage data.

Manage operations.

From an IT perspective, key application controls supporting financial reporting processes would also be within the scope of a company's internal and external SOX compliance efforts.

PCAOB Audit Standard No. 5 in 2007 emphasized a risk-based approach, thereby enabling most companies to narrow the scope of their SOX compliance activities. Although SOX applies to U.S. public companies with a certain market capitalization, the concept has also been adopted in Japan (J-SOX), in the insurance industry (NAIC Model Audit Rule), and elsewhere.

Cloud computing impact of SOX

SOX focuses on the effectiveness of a company's financial reporting process—including finance and accounting processes, other key business processes (e.g., the order-to-cash process), and controls over IT systems that have a material impact on financial reporting (e.g., the company's enterprise resource planning or ERP system and transaction processing systems that feed into the general ledger). The scope includes internally managed systems and outsourced systems that can materially impact financial reporting. The SOX compliance scope for each public company is ultimately defined by the company's management with input from its external auditor. Whether or not a CSP becomes relevant to a specific corporate customer's SOX audit activities will depend on the nature of service provided by the CSP to that corporate customer.

Services provided by a CSP could be relevant to a corporate customer from a SOX perspective. For example, an organization might utilize a SaaS application that plays a significant role in financial reporting serving as the system of record for various transactional activities. If those transactional activities are financially significant to the customer, the SaaS application would likely be part of the customer's SOX scope. As a result, the customer and its external auditor would be required to test relevant CSP controls—by performing test procedures at the CSP site, reviewing the CSP's current audit report, or a combination of both. Such controls would typically include the aforementioned topics and may include application controls as described shortly. (We discuss relevant CSP audit reports in "Auditing the Cloud for Compliance" on page 194.)

In another scenario, an organization might utilize PaaS to underlie an important financial application. An organization might use IaaS to support traditional applications or cloud-based applications that are used for processing or reporting on financial transaction activities. In each of these cases, SOX control requirements would be applicable.

From an IT general controls perspective, it is important to have robust processes for user management/segregation of duties, systems development, program and infrastructure change management, and computer operations (e.g., monitoring, backup, and problem management). Effective IT general controls are imperative to enable application controls.

Application controls will vary depending on the nature of the application. Typical controls focus on segregation of duties for key functions, completeness and accuracy of reports, system configurations for transaction processing, logging of activities, and so on.

In addition, it is important for the CSP to clearly define which control activities are the CSP's responsibility and which are the responsibility of the customer. Consequently, the CSP and its customers need to define boundaries where there is shared responsibility. This enables the CSP to focus its compliance efforts on areas it controls, while helping customers to do the same.

Where the CSP supports services that are likely to be in scope for SOX, the CSP should build those key controls into its control framework and provide guidance for customers as to how the CSP helps the customer otherwise meet its compliance requirements.

PCI DSS

Companies that process credit card transactions are required to comply with the Payment Card Industry (PCI) Data Security Standard (DSS) as evidenced through third-party assessments and/or self-assessments depending on the volume of card processing activity. These requirements apply whether cardholder data is processed and stored by the company or by a third party.

PCI DSS contains the following set of 12 high-level requirements that are supported by a series of more detailed requirements:[‡]

- Install and maintain a firewall configuration to protect cardholder data.
- Do not use vendor-supplied defaults for system passwords and other security parameters.
- Protect stored cardholder data.
- Encrypt transmission of cardholder data across open, public networks.
- Use and regularly update antivirus software.

‡ Payment Card Industry (PCI) Data Security Standard Requirements and Security Assessment Procedures, Version 1.2, October 2008.

- Develop and maintain secure systems and applications.

- Restrict access to cardholder data based on the business's need to know.

- Assign a unique ID to each person with computer access.

- Restrict physical access to cardholder data.

- Track and monitor all access to network resources and cardholder data.

- Regularly test security systems and processes.

- Maintain a policy that addresses information security.

Cloud computing impact of PCI DSS

Organizations are also required to ensure that their contracts with third-party service providers include PCI DSS compliance where such service providers store or process cardholder data. In a cloud environment, the organization and the supporting CSP should clearly define their responsibilities for protection of cardholder data, whether those responsibilities are shared or can be attributed to one party.

A fundamental component of PCI DSS is the need to segment systems and networks that store or process cardholder data from other systems and networks. Limiting the number of systems that process or store cardholder data, and isolating them on separate network segments, has the double benefit of reducing exposure to breaches and narrowing the scope of systems that must be assessed for compliance with the PCI DSS requirements as they are applicable only to systems used to store or process cardholder data. If the CSP provides services including processing of credit card transactions, it is important that the CSP clearly define its information flows and segment credit card processing and storage activities from other activities, thereby narrowing the scope of the infrastructure that would be subject to PCI compliance requirements. In addition, utilizing end-to-end encryption of sensitive data, such as cardholder data, is a desirable approach to mitigate risk.

From the perspective of a CSP, it is important to be aware of the PCI requirements. Although it is important for organizations to take a programmatic approach to PCI compliance, it is equally important for a CSP to do the same where the CSP supports processing of credit card transactions. The ultimate objective of PCI is to protect cardholder data, prevent breaches, and quickly contain a breach if it occurs. These objectives, as applied to all sensitive data, ring true for the cloud computing environment as well.

HIPAA

Entities that process protected health information (PHI) are required to comply with the security and privacy requirements established in support of HIPAA. The HIPAA security and privacy rules focus on health plans, health care clearinghouses, health care providers, and system vendors.

The following is a summary of the topics addressed by the HIPAA Security Standards.[§]

Administrative safeguards

Security management process
    Risk analysis

    Risk management

    Sanction policy

    Information system activity review

Assigned security responsibility

Workforce security
    Authorization and/or supervision

    Workforce clearance procedure

    Termination procedures

Information access management
    Isolation of health care clearinghouse function

    Access authorization

    Access establishment and modification

Security awareness and training
    Security reminders

    Protection from malicious software

    Log-in monitoring

    Password management

Security incident procedures
    Response and reporting

Contingency plan
    Data backup plan

    Disaster recovery plan

    Emergency mode operation plan

    Testing and revision procedure

    Applications and data criticality analysis

[§] Department of Health and Human Services, Office of the Secretary, 45 CFR Parts 160, 162, and 164, Health Insurance Reform: Security Standards; Final Rule, February 20, 2003.

Evaluation

> Business associate contracts and other arrangements

> Written contract or other arrangement

Physical safeguards

Facility access controls

> Contingency operations

> Facility security plan

> Access control and validation procedures

> Maintenance records

Workstation use, workstation security, device and media controls

> Disposal

> Media reuse

> Accountability

> Data backup and storage

Technical safeguards

Access control

> Unique user identification

> Emergency access procedure

> Automatic logoff

> Encryption and decryption

Audit controls, integrity

> Mechanism to authenticate electronic PHI

Person or entity authentication, transmission security

> Integrity controls

> Encryption

The following is a high-level summary of the topics addressed in the HIPAA Privacy Standards.‖

Summary of HIPAA privacy standards

- Uses and disclosures of PHI: General rules
- Uses and disclosures: Organizational requirements

‖ Department of Health and Human Services, Office of the Secretary, 45 CFR Parts 160 and 164, Standards for Privacy of Individually Identifiable Health Information; Final Rule, December 28, 2000 and August 14, 2002.

- Consent for uses or disclosures to carry out treatment, payment, and health care operations
- Uses and disclosures for which an authorization is required
- Uses and disclosures requiring an opportunity for the individual to agree or to object
- Uses and disclosures for which consent, an authorization, or an opportunity to agree or object is not required
- Other procedural requirements relating to uses and disclosures of PHI
- Notice of privacy practices for PHI
- Rights to request privacy protection for PHI
- Access of individuals to PHI
- Amendment of PHI
- Accounting of disclosures of PHI
- Administrative requirements
- Transition requirements

Cloud computing impact of HIPAA

The HIPAA security and privacy rules emphasize health organizations' (covered entities) obligations to ensure that individually identifiable health information (PHI) is adequately protected when entrusted to business associates (e.g., third-party service providers).

The level of security afforded particular electronic PHI should not decrease just because the covered entity has made the business decision to entrust a business associate with using or disclosing that information in connection with the performance of certain functions instead of performing those functions itself.#

As we discussed in Chapter 7, business associate agreements (contracts) are generally used by organizations to extend the HIPAA requirements to their third-party service providers that process or store health information. Accordingly, where the CSP processes or stores individually identifiable health information on behalf of entities which are subject to HIPAA, the HIPAA security and privacy requirements apply. In addition, further regulations regarding the protection of health information and breach notification requirements are under development in support of the 2009 Health Information Technology for Economic and Clinical Health (HITECH) Act.

As the move toward electronic medical records accelerates, CSPs serving the health care industry should be mindful of these emerging requirements. A GRC program can provide a

---

Department of Health and Human Services, Office of the Secretary, 45 CFR Parts 160, 162, and 164, Health Insurance Reform: Security Standards; Final Rule, February 20, 2003.

strong foundation to adequately safeguard sensitive medical information and a means to effectively address new requirements.

Other Requirements

CSPs may be subject to a variety of other requirements depending on industry and jurisdiction. Adopting the GRC approach and critically reviewing such requirements, as well as incorporating the truly incremental elements into the overall framework, will inevitably be the most effective way to address such requirements. Separate, siloed efforts focused on compliance with individual standards/regulations often result in duplication of efforts.

The Control Objectives for Information and Related Technology (COBIT)

COBIT is an IT governance framework and supporting tool set that allows managers to bridge the gap between control requirements, technical issues, and business risks. COBIT enables clear policy development and good practice for IT control throughout organizations. COBIT emphasizes regulatory compliance, helps organizations to increase the value attained from IT, enables alignment, and simplifies implementation of the COBIT framework.

Cloud computing impact of COBIT

The COBIT framework has been used in the past as a basis for formulating the baseline of control definitions. The most recent example is the IT Control Objectives for Sarbanes-Oxley which was designed to provide guidance on which control objectives from COBIT are relevant to Section 404 of SOX. In fact, COBIT has been mapped to the following standards: ITIL v3, NIST SP800-53 Rev. 1, TOGAF8.1, CMMI, ITIL, PRINCE2, ISO/IEC 17799, and SEI's CMM. This level of mapping illustrates the comprehensive nature of the COBIT framework and so can be used to explore the relevant components required in a cloud computing environment.

Figure 8-5 illustrates an overview of the COBIT framework. Almost all of the components illustrated here can apply to a cloud computing environment. However, the key question will be determining who owns and performs the control activities. In some cases, such as "Manage third party services (DS2)," it is obvious that the customer of the CSP owns and performs this control activity. However, the control activities relating to "Monitor and evaluate IT performance (ME1)" are most likely jointly owned and performed jointly between the CSP and the customer. A clear governance model needs to be determined to understand how the COBIT framework could be applied to the cloud computing environment.

Cloud Security Alliance

The Cloud Security Alliance (CSA) is a grassroots effort to create and apply best practices to help secure and provide assurance within cloud computing. The group is striving to provide security practitioners with a comprehensive roadmap for being proactive in developing positive and secure relationships with cloud providers. Much of this guidance is also quite relevant to the cloud provider to improve the quality and security of their service offerings.

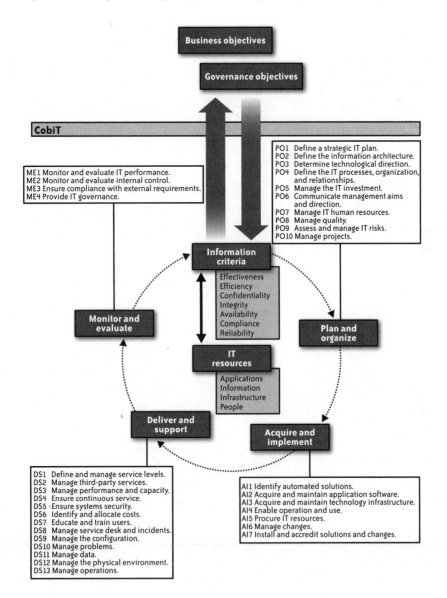

FIGURE 8-5. Overall COBIT framework

The primary objective of CSA are:

- Promote a common level of understanding between the consumers and providers of cloud computing regarding the necessary security requirements and attestation of assurance.
- Promote independent research into best practices for cloud computing security.
- Launch awareness campaigns and educational programs on the appropriate uses of cloud computing and cloud security solutions.
- Create consensus lists of issues and guidance for cloud security assurance.

CSA has published a white paper (available at *http://www.cloudsecurityalliance.org*) that focuses on areas of concern that are either unique to cloud computing or are greatly exacerbated by the model.

The white paper attempts to discuss cloud computing practice, relevant security issues, and guidance, organized under 15 domains:

- Cloud Computing Architectural Framework
- Governance and Enterprise Risk Management
- Legal
- Electronic Discovery
- Compliance and Audit
- Information Lifecycle Management
- Portability and Interoperability
- Traditional Security, Business Continuity, and Disaster Recovery
- Data Center Operations
- Incident Response, Notification, and Remediation
- Application Security
- Encryption and Key Management
- Identity and Access Management
- Storage
- Virtualization

Auditing the Cloud for Compliance

When it comes to auditing cloud computing against the compliance requirements discussed earlier, there are two perspectives that must be dealt with. First is what your organization's internal audit department's expectations are for meeting requirements, as well as, of course, the expectations that your external auditors have with regard to meeting requirements. The "Right to Audit" (RTA) clause is often used in outsourcing contracts to ensure that clients can conduct audits for various assurance reasons. In the case of a CSP, the RTA can be applied. Customers need to define the scope of the RTA. For example, customers should validate service level performances, the security of data-at-rest, and the physical security of the data center. However, due to multitenancy and shared logical environment, it becomes difficult to conduct an audit without the CSP breaching the confidentiality of other tenants sharing the infrastructure. In such cases, the CSP should adopt a compliance program based on standards such as ISO27001 and provide assurance via SysTrust or ISO certification to its customers.

Internal Audit Perspective

As we discussed earlier, a programmatic approach to compliance is particularly important in a cloud computing environment as the impact of a control failure could be quite severe. The CSP cannot afford to wait until the annual external audit to determine whether controls have operated effectively during the past year, because of the increased potential for control failures impacting multiple customers. Key controls must be identified early on and proactively monitored so that any potential issues can be investigated and addressed in a timely manner. For example, a failure to detect errors in the automated system configuration and activity logging processes on a near-real-time basis could lead to system downtime, breached security, or data loss. Although controls should be designed to prevent the occurrence of such issues, near-real-time detection and rapid correction of any such issues will go a long way toward demonstrating the CSP's commitment to security and continuous improvement.

Combined with an emphasis on automated preventive controls, proactive monitoring of key controls will help the CSP to make risk-based IT investment decisions, meet its customer commitments, and at least keep pace with emerging developments. Whether control monitoring activities are performed by the internal audit department, the information security function, the IT organization, or a combination thereof, it is important that a disciplined approach be implemented as described in "GRC Program Implementation" on page 172.

External Audit Perspective

An external audit of the CSP will likely be required for customers to gain comfort in the effectiveness of the CSP's controls. Historically, a variety of audit frameworks have been used to assess the controls of outsourced service providers, including CSPs. Some of the most common audit frameworks are summarized here and described in the section that follows. Although some CSPs have been completing such external audits for five or more years, an increasing number of CSPs are now initiating external audits for the first time in response to increasing market pressure.

Audit framework

SAS 70

Audit of controls based on control objectives and control activities (defined by the service provider).

Auditor opinion on the design, operational status, and operating effectiveness of controls.

Intended to cover services that are relevant for purposes of customers' financial statement audits.

SysTrust

Audit of controls based on defined principles and criteria for security, availability, confidentiality, and processing integrity.

Intended to apply to the reliability of any system.

WebTrust

Audit of controls based on defined principles and criteria for security, availability, confidentiality, processing integrity, and privacy.

Intended to apply to online/e-commerce systems.

ISO 27001

Audit of an organization's Information Security Management System (ISMS), as defined in a documented ISMS.

SAS 70

Statement on Auditing Standards No. 70 (SAS 70) was developed by the American Institute of Certified Public Accountants (AICPA) to provide a mechanism for service organizations to complete one audit of their controls resulting in a report that could be provided to their customers and their customers' auditors. This audit framework was designed to facilitate completion of the service organizations' customers' financial statement audits while reducing the need for multiple audits of the service organization's controls. Intended primarily for transaction processing operations, over time SAS 70 has increasingly been used for audits of other types of service providers that have a less direct impact on their customers' financial reporting activities.

There are two types of SAS 70 examinations (audits): Type I and Type II. The SAS 70 Type I audit report focuses on the design of controls and whether such controls were in operation at a specific point in time. The SAS 70 Type II audit report focuses on the effectiveness of controls over a period of time and whether such controls were properly designed and in operation as of the period end. (Refer to Appendix A for example SAS 70 Type II report content.)

SAS 70 is often misconstrued to be a "certification," but it is not. The service organization defines its control objectives and describes its supporting control activities in the SAS 70 report. The auditor then test-audits such controls. Because the service provider is not being audited against an external set of criteria, a user must read the SAS 70 report to understand the scope.

The service provider may choose to align its controls with a standard such as ISO 27001 and reflect this in the SAS 70 report, but this is not required. Refer to the "Illustrative Control Objectives for Cloud Computing" on page 174 for discussion of relevant control areas.

Given the importance of outsourced control activities, the concept of the SAS 70 audit has broad international acceptance. Historically, some countries have developed their own local standards modeled on SAS 70 while others use the SAS 70 standard in combination with local auditing standards. In response to increasing use of service organizations globally, the International Auditing and Assurance Standards Board (IAASB) released a proposed International Standard on Assurance Engagements—ISAE 3402, *Assurance Reports on Controls at a Third Party Service Organization*, in December 2007. The proposed standard describes an audit framework very similar to SAS 70. For example, the proposed standard refers to Type A and B reports rather than Type I and II reports.[*]

At the time of this writing, the IAASB and national bodies are working to finalize the international standard and to develop localized guidance for its use. In the United States, the AICPA is developing a new standard based on ISAE 3402 to replace SAS 70 in the next few years. It is expected that the nature and content of the SAS 70 audit report will not substantially change.

SysTrust

SysTrust is an audit framework that was developed by the AICPA and Canadian Institute of Chartered Accountants (CICA) to provide a mechanism for service providers to complete an audit based on a predefined set of criteria for security, availability, processing integrity, and confidentiality. Whereas SAS 70 was intended to focus on financial transaction processing, SysTrust was designed to apply to the reliability of any system—focusing on the principles of security, availability, confidentiality, and processing integrity. As a result, it is particularly well suited to CSPs serving enterprise customers. SysTrust reports focus on the operating effectiveness of controls over a period of time. (Refer to Appendix B for example SysTrust report content.)

The Trust Services Security, Availability, Confidentiality, and Processing Integrity Criteria, as summarized in the following list, form the foundation of the SysTrust audit.[†] Refer to the Trust Services Principles and Criteria for additional details.[‡]

---

[*] International Auditing and Assurance Standards Board, Proposed International Standard on Assurance Engagements—ISAE 3402, Assurance Reports on Controls at a Third Party Service Organization, December 2007.

[†] Trust Services Principles, Criteria, and Illustrations for Security, Availability, Processing Integrity, Confidentiality, and Privacy (Including WebTrust® and SysTrust®).

[‡] American Institute of Certified Public Accountants, Inc., and Canadian Institute of Chartered Accountants, Trust Services Principles, Criteria and Illustrations for Security, Availability, Processing Integrity, Confidentiality, and Privacy (Including WebTrust® and SysTrust®), 2006.

Policies

Review and approval

Specific security, availability, confidentiality, and processing integrity topics addressed

Responsibility and accountability

Recovery and continuity of service

Monitoring of system capacity

Communications

System description (defines audit scope)

Communication of security, availability, confidentiality, and processing integrity obligations to users

Responsibility and accountability communicated to responsible individuals

Security breach process

Communication of changes that impact system security, availability, confidentiality, and processing integrity

Procedures

Logical access procedures and restrictions, allow users to access only their data

Physical access procedures and restrictions

Protection of systems and data against unauthorized logical access

Virus protection

Protection of authentication information

Security breach/incident handling procedures

Procedures for addressing non-compliance

Design and implementation of systems in accordance with policies

Personnel qualifications

Configuration management

Change management, including emergency changes

Protection of systems against availability risks

Integrity and completeness of backups

Disaster recovery/business continuity

Completeness, accuracy, timeliness, and authorization of inputs, system processing, and outputs

Monitoring

Periodic review of systems/controls based on policies

Identification of potential impairments to ability to meet policies

Monitoring of environmental and technological changes

In contrast with SAS 70, SysTrust includes defined criteria that must be met by the service provider. The service provider can optionally include a detailed description of controls as part of the SysTrust report. Depending on the nature of services provided and their applicability, the CSP can elect to include one or more of the Trust Services principles within the audit scope.

At the time of this writing, a relatively minor revision to the Trust Services Principles and Criteria has been published as an exposure draft for comment.[§]

WebTrust

WebTrust is another AICPA/CICA audit framework, very similar to SysTrust, but is intended to focus on e-commerce services—often where there is a direct interaction with individual end users. WebTrust utilizes the same criteria as SysTrust (the Trust Services Security, Availability, Confidentiality and Processing Integrity principles and criteria). It can also include privacy criteria (based on the Generally Accepted Privacy Principles) where the service provider is interacting with and collecting personal information from individual end users in accordance with a Privacy Policy.[||] WebTrust results in an audit report indicating whether the specific criteria were met.

Here is a summary of the topics covered by generally accepted privacy principles:

- Management
- Notice
- Choice and consent
- Collection
- Use and retention
- Access
- Disclosure to third parties
- Security for privacy
- Quality
- Monitoring and enforcement

ISO 27001 certification

ISO 27001 certification is another available audit approach. With this approach, the auditor assesses whether the organization has a formal ISMS in place—including documentation of the ISMS, completion of a risk assessment, development of a risk treatment plan, and implementation of processes for responding to identified issues. Typically, the certification is

---

§ See *http://www.webtrust.org*.

|| American Institute of Certified Public Accountants, Inc., and Canadian Institute of Chartered Accountants, Generally Accepted Privacy Principles—A Global Privacy Framework, May 2006.

valid for three years and involves an initial audit with smaller update audits performed approximately annually during the remainder of the three-year period. The ISO 27001 certification is more focused on the overall security program rather than the effectiveness of specific control activities.

Comparison of Approaches

Table 8-2 compares and contrasts key elements of these audit approaches.[#] The most applicable approach will depend on the nature of services provided by the CSP. For certain CSPs, a unified audit approach—completing one set of audit activities but issuing multiple reports—may be required to satisfy a diverse customer base.

SAS 70 was designed as a tool to support the financial audits of customers that use service organizations. It is most applicable where the CSP plays a significant role in transaction processing or financial reporting for customers.

ISO 27001 was designed to provide a mechanism for organizations to demonstrate that they have an information security management system in place—much like ISO 9001 is used to demonstrate that organizations have quality management systems in place. ISO 27001 certification is generally most applicable where global customers and prospects seek comfort with the CSP's overall security program.

Trust Services (SysTrust and WebTrust) are most applicable where the CSP needs to demonstrate to customers and prospects that its specific security, availability, confidentiality, processing integrity, and privacy controls are operating effectively over a period of time.

TABLE 8-2. Comparison of common external audit approaches

Topics to consider	SAS 70 (Type II)	Trust Services (SysTrust and WebTrust)	ISO 27001 certification
Intended audience for the report	Restricted to service organizations, customers of the service organization, and their auditors. The report is not intended for non-customers	Applicable to any stakeholder of the system. The report is designed such that it can be posted online or distributed manually	Applicable to any stakeholder of the system, though organizations typically publicize their certification status but limit distribution of supporting details
Intended purpose	Provides user auditors with information about controls at the service organization that may affect assertions in the	Provides assurance that an organization's system's controls meet one or more of the Trust	Provides assurance that an organization has an ISMS in place

[#] AICPA, Building Trust and Reliability—SAS 70, SysTrust, and WebTrust.

Topics to consider	SAS 70 (Type II)	Trust Services (SysTrust and WebTrust)	ISO 27001 certification
	user organizations' financial statements	Services principles and related criteria	
Subject matter coverage	Focuses on systems and controls at the service organization that affect user organizations' financial statements	Focuses on internal controls related to any financial or non-financial system by specific subject matter	Provides an ISMS to monitor and maintain internal controls related to any financial or non-financial system based on the ISO 27001 domains
Nature of the report	Provides assurance about whether the description of the service organizations' controls is fairly stated, whether the controls are suitably designed, and whether the controls are operating effectively	Provides assurance that a company's controls over a defined system meet the Trust Services criteria for the specific principle(s) being examined. May also provide assurance on compliance with those controls	Provides assurance that an organization has an ISMS in place
Comparability of reports	No customized control objectives and criteria are used for each engagement	Standardized principles and criteria are used for all engagements	Standardized criteria are used for all engagements, though the service provider determines which requirements are applicable in its ISMS
Frequency of the audit	Audits are typically performed every 6 or 12 months	An audit must be performed at least annually to maintain the WebTrust or SysTrust seal	The certification is typically valid for three years—with surveillance visits generally conducted annually
Coverage of Business Continuity Management (BCM)	Cannot be included. Identifying and testing the operating effectiveness of such controls (such as BCM) that could affect processing in future periods is not permitted	Included as part of the availability criteria. Identifying and testing forward-looking criteria (such as BCM) as part of the framework of SysTrust and WebTrust engagements is permitted	Included as part of the ISO 27001 criteria

When finalized, ISAE 3402 and related localized guidance may permit the use of this approach for services/systems that are not applicable to financial reporting. However, specific criteria will need to be developed to support such cases.

Summary

To support internal business and risk management objectives and to support customer requirements, it is essential that CSPs take a programmatic approach to monitoring and compliance. Maintaining separate compliance efforts for different regulations or standards is not sustainable. Relying on after-the-fact audits to identify problems will not enable the CSP to properly manage risk. Supporting individual customer audits will be particularly challenging—from a CSP resource perspective, from a client confidentiality perspective given the high degree of shared infrastructure, and from a data collection perspective given the virtual nature of many cloud environments. To drive efficiency, risk management, and compliance, CSPs need to implement a strong internal control monitoring function coupled with a robust external audit process. To gain comfort over their in-cloud activities, CSP users need to define their control requirements, understand their CSP's internal control monitoring processes, analyze relevant external audit reports, and properly execute their responsibilities as CSP users.

The cloud computing environment presents new challenges from an audit and compliance perspective, but much can be used from traditional outsourcing models and from existing industry standards and frameworks. A programmatic approach to monitoring and compliance will help prepare CSPs and their users to address emerging requirements and the evolution of cloud business models.

CHAPTER NINE

Examples of Cloud Service Providers

THROUGHOUT THIS BOOK, WE HAVE REFERENCED CLOUD SERVICE PROVIDERS (CSPs) and have explored the three service delivery offerings (SPI). This chapter will provide you with an overview of eight providers (in alphabetical order), their service offerings, and use cases.

Amazon Web Services (IaaS)

Amazon Web Services (AWS) provides infrastructure-as-a-service (IaaS) offerings in the cloud for organizations requiring computing power, storage, and other services. According to Amazon, AWS allows you to "take advantage of Amazon.com's global computing infrastructure," which is the heart of Amazon.com's retail business and transactional enterprise.

AWS offers a number of infrastructure-related services, including the following:

Elastic Compute Cloud (EC2)
> EC2 is a web service that provides resizable compute capacity in the cloud. EC2 allows scalable deployment of applications by providing a web services interface through which customers can create virtual machines (VMs)—that is, server instances—on which the customer can load any software of her choice. A customer can create, launch, and terminate server instances as needed, paying by the hour for active servers.

Simple Storage Service (S3)
> S3 provides a web services interface that can be used to store and retrieve unlimited amounts of data, at any time, from anywhere on the Web.

Simple Queue Service (SQS)

SQS is a distributed queue messaging service that supports the programmatic sending of messages via web services applications as a way to communicate over the Internet. The intent of SQS is to provide a scalable hosted message queue that resolves issues arising from the common producer-consumer problem or connectivity between producers and consumers.

CloudFront

CloudFront is a content delivery network that delivers your content using a global network of edge locations. Requests for objects are automatically routed to the nearest edge location, so content is delivered with the best possible performance. CloudFront works with S3 which durably stores the original, definitive versions of files.

SimpleDB

SimpleDB is a web service providing the core database functions of data indexing and querying. This service works in close conjunction with S3 and EC2, collectively providing the ability to store, process, and query data sets in the cloud, making web-scale computing easier and more cost-effective for developers.

There are a number of potential use cases to consider when discussing AWS, as outlined in Table 9-1.

TABLE 9-1. AWS use cases

Use case	Use case description	Service(s)
Web/application hosting	Web/application vendors can leverage the AWS infrastructure for computing power and storage as an alternative to internally hosting their applications. This can result in cost savings and efficiencies associated with managing infrastructure and time to market.	EC2, S3, SimpleDB, SQS
Backup and storage	Organizations can leverage AWS as an option for managing internal backup and storage as an alternative to an on-site storage infrastructure. Though storage hardware costs are generally decreasing, the size of productivity and media files is growing, which is resulting in exponential increases in storage needs.	S3
Content delivery	Organizations involved in content delivery, such as streaming media, can leverage the AWS worldwide network of edge servers to minimize degradation of delivery and service.	CloudFront, S3
High-performance computing	Organizations that have high-performance computing requirements can leverage AWS computing power on demand to process large amounts of data without having to create an internal infrastructure. This can result in cost savings and efficiencies associated with usage and time to market.	EC2, S3

Use case	Use case description	Service(s)
Media hosting	Organizations that are involved in the distribution and storage of media files can leverage AWS to offset the unpredictable requirements related to storage and processing.	EC2, S3, SQS, CloudFront
MapReduce	This is a web service that enables businesses, researchers, data analysts, and developers to process a vast amount of data utilizing a Hadoop framework.	EC2, S3
Cloud "bursting"	This is the ability to deal with rapid spikes in processing demands.	EC2

With regard to pricing, AWS is based on consumption as defined by the type of service provided, and the rates are posted online. Additionally, AWS services are based on platform flexibility, allowing the customer to choose the appropriate operating system, programming model, and so forth to meet her needs.

Google (SaaS, PaaS)

Google App Engine is Google's platform-as-a-service (PaaS) offering for building and hosting web applications on the Google infrastructure. Currently, the supported programming languages are Python and Java. App Engine is free up to a certain level of used resources, after which fees are charged for additional storage, bandwidth, or CPU cycles required by the application.

Google Apps is Google's software-as-a-service (SaaS) offering for business email and collaboration. It features several applications with similar functionality to traditional office suites, including Gmail, Google Calendar, Talk, Docs, and Sites. Additionally, Google Apps has a number of security and compliance products to provide email security and compliance for existing email infrastructures. The Standard Edition is free and offers the same amount of storage as regular Gmail accounts; the Premier version is based on a per-user license model and associated storage level.

There are a number of potential use cases to consider when discussing Google services, as noted in Table 9-2.

TABLE 9-2. Google use cases

Use case	Use case description	Service(s)
Messaging	Organizations can leverage Google Apps for internal email and calendar services without the investment and maintenance of a messaging architecture.	Gmail, Google Calendar
Securing existing email systems	Organizations can leverage Google Apps for securing existing email systems by filtering out messaging threats including spam and viruses without the investment and maintenance of hardware and software.	Google Email Security

Use case	Use case description	Service(s)
Email retention and legal discovery for existing email systems	Organizations can leverage Google Apps for managing email retention with a searchable archive so that they can locate email quickly in the event of legal discovery without the investment and maintenance of hardware and software.	Google Email Archiving and Discovery
Collaboration	Organizations can leverage Google Apps for office productivity and collaboration without the need to install software on local machines and/or servers.	Google Docs, Google Sites
Application development	Organizations can leverage the Google App Engine platform to develop custom applications based on Java and Python, and the associated services, without investing in internal infrastructure.	App Engine

Microsoft Azure Services Platform (PaaS)

Azure Services Platform is Microsoft's PaaS offering that is part of the company's strategy of lessening its emphasis on the desktop and shifting more resources to web-based products. It provides an operating system called Windows Azure that serves as a runtime for the applications and provides a set of services that allows development, management, and hosting of managed applications at Microsoft data centers.

The platform includes the following services:

.NET Services

A set of developer-oriented services that provide basic pieces required by many cloud-based applications (access control, service bus, workflow, etc.).

SQL Services

A set of services that extend the capabilities of Microsoft SQL Server into the cloud as a web-based, distributed relational database. It provides web services that enable relational queries, search, and data synchronization with mobile users, remote offices, and business partners.

Live Services

A set of services that provide developers the ability to connect their applications to Windows Live users. In addition, Live Services let users log in using Live ID, access and share contacts, feed content into Windows Live, and so on.

In regard to pricing, the Azure Services Platform is based on a consumption model including compute time, storage, API calls, and so forth.

There are a number of potential use cases to consider when discussing the Azure Services Platform, as noted in Table 9-3.

TABLE 9-3. Azure Services Platform use cases

Use case	Use case description	Services
Application vendor to offer SaaS version	Organizations can leverage the Azure Services Platform to enhance the functionality of existing applications without investing in internal infrastructure. For example, instead of continuing to leverage the in-house deployment model, the vendor can leverage the Azure Services Platform to develop a SaaS version of the product.	Windows Azure, .NET Services, SQL Services
Application development	Organizations can leverage the Azure Services Platform to develop custom applications based on Windows Azure and associated services without investing in internal infrastructure.	Windows Azure, .NET Services, SQL Services

Proofpoint (SaaS, IaaS)

Proofpoint provides SaaS and IaaS services in the cloud related to securing the enterprise email infrastructure, with solutions for email security, archiving, encryption, and data loss prevention. Proofpoint's solutions are priced on a per-user, per-year basis, depending on the specific product features deployed.

Proofpoint offers a number of SaaS and IaaS services, including the following:

Enterprise
> The Enterprise email security and data loss prevention solution provides security for both inbound and outbound email, without the need for on-premises hardware or software. This customizable solution can be deployed with a variety of options including a "Protection" bundle (with antispam, antivirus, email firewall, and email policy enforcement features), a "Privacy" bundle (with data protection features including detection of private identity, health care and financial information detection, preconfigured data protection policies, and incident management), and an "Encryption" bundle that adds policy-based email encryption features.

Shield
> The Shield SaaS connection management and frontline spam protection service defends against malicious and spam email connections, reducing inbound spam volumes and preventing denial of service (DoS) and directory harvest attacks.

Archive
> Archive is an on-demand email archiving solution that addresses email storage management, legal discovery, and regulatory compliance. Patented encryption technology is used to ensure that messages are secure while being transmitted to Proofpoint's data centers and also while stored in the archive. At the same time, archived messages remain fully searchable by authorized users. The solution makes it possible for enterprises to create and enforce legal holds during e-discovery (i.e., to find all relevant email related to a legal

case and to ensure the retention of that data during a lawsuit), and it gives end users easy, self-service access to their historical email.

There are a number of potential use cases to consider when discussing Proofpoint services, as noted in Table 9-4.

TABLE 9-4. Proofpoint use cases

Use case	Use case description	Service
Inbound email security	Organizations can leverage Proofpoint email security solutions to block spam, viruses and other malware, phishing attacks, and inappropriate content in incoming email messages, and enforce basic corporate email policies for outgoing email.	Enterprise
Data loss prevention	Organizations can protect confidential information from inappropriate distribution via email. Outgoing email and attachments are scanned for confidential information and blocked from transmission if they are found to contain such content. Blocked messages can be quarantined for review by security or compliance personnel.	Enterprise
Compliance with data protection regulations	Organizations can ensure that private information such as customer financial data and personal health care information is protected against inappropriate exposure. Outgoing email and attachments are scanned for the presence of protected financial, health care, or identity data and then automatically encrypted or blocked as appropriate.	Enterprise
Email archiving	Organizations can enforce corporate policies for email retention, ease email storage burdens on local servers, and enable rapid searching of historical email for e-discovery (including the ability to enforce legal holds) and give end users essentially an "unlimited" inbox.	Archive

RightScale (IaaS)

RightScale provides IaaS-related services in the cloud to assist organizations in managing cloud deployments offered by other CSPs, including vendors such as AWS, FlexiScale, and GoGrid. The RightScale Cloud Management Platform allows organizations to manage and maintain their cloud deployments through one web-based management platform, while at the same time taking advantage of offerings by more than one CSP. RightScale's pricing is based on a number of editions from Developer through Enterprise level, and associated features and server times.

> NOTE
> Server usage and other charges from cloud infrastructure providers, such as AWS, are billed separately by the cloud provider and are not included in monthly RightScale usage fees.

The RightScale Cloud Management Platform includes the following:

Cloud Management Environment

The Cloud Management Environment provides control, administration, and life cycle support for cloud deployments via a dashboard for real-time management of deployments across one or more clouds, including public and private clouds. The dashboard provides transparent access to and control over all aspects of cloud deployment, including the ServerTemplates, underlying scripts, input parameters, real-time monitoring, and automatic or manual response.

Cloud Ready ServerTemplates

ServerTemplates and the Best Practice Deployment Library help to simplify deployment management. ServerTemplates, developed by RightScale, incorporate standard cloud configurations for common application deployment components such as scalable web and application servers, database master/slave pairs, and grids for batch processing. Partner ServerTemplates, developed by RightScale partners, help incorporate RightScale's partners' applications, tools, and components into deployments. Customer ServerTemplates can be cloned, customized for specific needs, and then saved in a custom library. Over time, an organization will build a repository of ServerTemplates representing valuable corporate knowledge for the organization.

Adaptable Automation Engine

The Adaptable Automation Engine executes and manages deployments that adapt to situations as required by system demand, system failure, or other specified events. As demand changes, servers can be added or decommissioned. As components fail, existing servers can adopt their roles or the system can deploy new servers. As queues fill or empty, grids can expand or contract automatically. Active monitoring, alerts, and escalations ensure real-time adaptation based on the rules and automatic responses defined by the organization.

Multi-cloud Engine

The Multi-cloud Engine interacts with cloud infrastructure application programming interfaces (APIs) and manages the unique aspects of each cloud. As a result, organizations are not locked into any one cloud; instead, they are free to choose among several cloud providers, deploy across multiple clouds, or move an application from one cloud to another.

There are a number of potential use cases to consider when discussing RightScale services, as noted in Table 9-5.

TABLE 9-5. RightScale use cases

Use case	Use case description	Service
Complexity in managing the cloud infrastructure	Organizations can leverage RightScale as an option for managing the complexities involved in deploying and managing a CSP's infrastructure services. This can result in efficiencies associated with managing services and time to market, as the organization can focus on core strengths rather than learning how to deploy within the CSP's environment.	Cloud Management Platform
Single management platform	Organizations can leverage RightScale as an option for managing and maintaining cloud deployments through one management platform. This can result in efficiencies and costs savings related to personnel costs as the organization can more effectively and efficiently address head count related to managing cloud deployments.	Cloud Management Platform
Portability	Organizations can leverage RightScale to manage cloud infrastructure APIs and the unique aspects of each cloud so that they can freely choose among a variety of CSP offerings based on their unique needs, manage and migrate deployments across these clouds (public or private), and avoid vendor lock-in.	Cloud Management Platform

Salesforce.com (SaaS, PaaS)

Salesforce.com is a provider of SaaS-based CRM products, as well as having a PaaS offering, Force.com. Salesforce.com's CRM solution is divided into several applications including Sales, Marketing, Service, and Partners. Pricing is on a per-user basis, and the rates and different support packages are posted online.

Salesforce.com has more recently begun to provide PaaS-based services through the Force.com platform. Force.com allows external developers to create add-on applications that integrate into the main Salesforce.com applications, and are hosted on Salesforce.com's infrastructure. Applications are built using Apex, a proprietary programming language for the Force.com platform. Pricing is on a per-developer basis, and different support packages allow for varied levels of storage, API calls, and so forth. AppExchange is a directory of applications built for Salesforce.com by third-party developers which users can purchase and add to their Salesforce environments. As of May 2009, approximately 800 applications are available from more than 450 independent software vendors (ISVs) via AppExchange.

There are a number of potential use cases to consider when discussing Salesforce.com services, as noted in Table 9-6.

TABLE 9-6. Salesforce.com use cases

Use case	Use case description	Service(s)
On-demand CRM	Organizations can leverage Salesforce.com CRM applications to centralize, manage, and efficiently share prospective client information without investing in internal infrastructure.	CRM
Extend functionality of Salesforce.com CRM	Organizations can leverage Force.com to develop add-on applications that extend the functionality of the Salesforce.com CRM or leverage the existing directory of applications within AppExchange without investing in internal infrastructure.	Force.com, AppExchange
Application development	Organizations can leverage the Force.com platform to develop custom applications based on the Force.com platform without investing in internal infrastructure.	Force.com

Sun Open Cloud Platform

As the company that coined the phrase "The Network is the Computer," Sun Microsystems envisions a world of many clouds, both public and private, that are open and compatible. Sun takes an inclusive view that there are many different types of clouds, and many different applications that can be built using them. To that end, according to Sun, it plans to offer an extensive portfolio of products (hardware and software) and services under the umbrella of an "Open Cloud Platform" to foster open communities and partner ecosystems. According to Sun, the Open Cloud Platform is an open architecture (APIs, open format) and infrastructure encompassing technologies such as Java, MySQL, OpenSolaris, and Open Storage software. Sun believes that its Open Cloud Platform offering will foster an ecosystem of partners, developers, and others, because cloud computing can be successful only if you can leverage maximum reuse of others' technologies and components.

According to Sun, the Open Cloud Platform will offer the necessary cloud service ingredients (hardware, software, and management capabilities) to help customers and partners wishing to become CSPs for any of the cloud delivery models—SaaS, PaaS, or IaaS (SPI). Sun is working with service providers and enterprises to build their own clouds to service their respective customers and users.

One of the things driving cloud computing is the wide availability of open source software and components; developers can rapidly assemble applications out of open source components and run them in the cloud. According to Sun, it has developed foundational technologies (software and hardware) to enable the three emerging cloud business models: public clouds, private clouds, and hybrid clouds.

Sun's foundation technologies include OpenSolaris, MySQL, the open source GlassFish application server, Crossbow (a network virtualization technology and an OpenSolaris component), the Sun xVM hypervisor (based on the open source Xen), the Solaris Zetta File System (ZFS), the Sun xVM VirtualBox, and NetBeans (an IDE for developers). Sun's hardware portfolio encompasses an array of servers based on X86, SPARC, and energy-efficient chip-multithreaded (CMT) UltraSPARC processors and Open Storage with a range of densities and I/O capacities.

Sun's implementation of a public cloud, initially targeting the developer community, is an IaaS, with a public compute and storage infrastructure service (future delivery). Developers will access the Sun public cloud services from a web browser to provision resources on their platform of choice—Linux, Windows, or OpenSolaris operating systems. For its initial offering, Sun plans to support a RESTful API for creating and managing cloud resources, including compute, storage, and networking components. Sun will also provide client libraries for Java, Ruby, and Python development. Sun's X86 virtual box supports the Open Virtualization Format (OVF), which makes VMs portable across clouds that support the OVF open standard.

Sun's cloud offerings also include Project Kenai (beta):

> Project Kenai host[s] projects and code to be deployed on [the] Sun Cloud, [and] facilitates collaboration with like-minded developers to access or initiate projects directly from the NetBeans. Project Kenai also has [a] repository of APIs for the Sun Cloud service. These APIs are posted for review (at *http://www.kenai.com*) and comment using the Creative Commons license.

There are a number of potential use cases to consider when discussing the Sun cloud platform, as noted in Table 9-7.

TABLE 9-7. Sun use cases

Use case	Use case description	Service(s)
High-performance computing and elasticity	Organizations that have high-performance computing requirements can leverage the Sun Open Cloud Platform to process large amounts of data.	Sun Open Cloud Platform, private cloud services
Development and testing	Organizations, start-ups, social network developers, and enterprises trying to experiment with disruptive ideas or wanting to experiment with hosting applications in the public cloud can leverage the Sun public cloud services and open source components to develop applications in Java, Ruby, Python, and MySQL.	Sun compute and storage cloud, Project Kenai, NetBeans, VirtualBox
Surge computing	Organizations can offload an overburdened IT infrastructure (temporarily or permanently) to accommodate peak loads, batch processing jobs, or anticipated spikes in demand for services.	Sun Open Cloud Platform, compute and storage cloud, Project Kenai, NetBeans, VirtualBox

Workday (SaaS)

Workday is a provider of SaaS-based human resources and financial management products. Workday pricing is on a per-user basis and functionality. Workday's solutions are divided into several modules, including the following:

Human Capital Management

> Workday's HR and Human Capital Management software is designed to help companies organize, staff, pay, and develop the global workforce.

Payroll

> Workday Payroll allows companies to group employees, manage payroll calculation rules, and pay employees according to organizational, policy, and reporting needs.

Worker Spend Management

> Workday Worker Spend Management combines Workday Expense, Procurement, and Business Resource Management capabilities into one solution that extends Workday Human Capital Management and helps companies understand and manage total workforce cost—spend on, by, and for workers.

Financial Management

> Workday Financial Management offers a financial services solution to address internal and external requirements by combining support for business and HR accounting transactions, a framework for internal control and audit, and robust financial reporting and business-performance management.

Benefits Network

> Workday Benefits Network provides HR organizations with a catalog of prebuilt integrations that connect to benefits providers, giving HR management organizations the ability to evaluate, select, and offer the most appropriate plans for their workforce.

Table 9-8 notes a use case to consider when discussing Workday services.

TABLE 9-8. Workday use case

Use case	Use case description	Services
On-demand HR	Organizations can manage various aspects of HR and financial management processes without investing in internal infrastructure.	HR and Financial Management modules

Summary

As we have discussed, the cloud computing market is becoming increasingly crowded each day. Amazon, Google, Microsoft, Salesforce.com, and Sun are considered some of the key players in the cloud computing market, but they represent only a handful of the providers in this space. Table 9-9 summarizes their respective service offerings and focus areas.

TABLE 9-9. Summary of offerings by example providers

CSP	Offering	Focus area
Amazon	Core offerings include the AWS infrastructure related to servers, storage and bandwidth, databases, and messaging for interfaces. Differentiators vis-à-vis competitors: • Supports varied operating systems/programming languages • Content Delivery Network	SMB focus
Google	For creating and running web applications. Supports only Python and Java (does not support Microsoft and others). Also provides SaaS-related productivity applications.	SMB focus
Microsoft	Operating system with a set of developer services. Allows the building of new cloud applications and the enhancement of existing applications for the cloud. Platform for Microsoft application development.	Enterprise/SMB focus
Proofpoint	Core offerings include on-demand services related to email security and archiving.	Enterprise/SMB focus
RightScale	Core offering is a Cloud Management Platform for managing the cloud infrastructure from multiple vendors. Differentiators vis-à-vis competitors: • Transparent access and control over multiple cloud offerings to best meet organizational needs • Portability	SMB focus
Salesforce.com	Allows the building and integration of business and CRM applications within the Salesforce.com infrastructure. Supports only the Apex proprietary programming language.	Enterprise focus
Sun	Core offerings include infrastructure related to servers, storage, and databases. Differentiators vis-à-vis competitors: • Supports varied operating systems/programming languages • Open cloud concept to support other CSPs (public, private, and hybrid clouds) • Virtual data center capabilities	Enterprise/SMB focus
Workday	Core offerings include on-demand services related to HR.	Enterprise/SMB focus

The question we haven't asked yet is: what is the current focus group for CSPs? Are their customers at the enterprise level or at the small and medium-size business (SMB) level? It would appear that the cloud is already a viable and sensible solution for many SMBs. However, as we have discussed in this book, there are still a number of questions around security, availability, and so on. Will these issues need to be overcome before cloud computing takes off for enterprise-level organizations? We will address these issues and others in the concluding chapter. However, before addressing these issues, we will look at another aspect of cloud computing security in Chapter 10—that is, security-as-a-service. Service-as-a-service is security offered as a service and delivered in the cloud, as opposed to the security of CSP offerings discussed in the rest of the book. Additionally, in Chapter 11 we will look at the impact of cloud computing on the role of traditional corporate IT. How is corporate IT being affected by cloud computing, and what is the relationship between the two?

CHAPTER TEN

Security-As-a-[Cloud] Service

So far, we have addressed the security provided by cloud service providers (CSPs) as well as the security provided by customers using cloud services. In this chapter, the focus is on security provided *as* cloud services; that is, security delivered through the cloud, also known as security-as-a-service.

Just like software-as-a-service (SaaS), the business model with security-as-a-service is subscription-based. In addition, security-as-a-service is also sometimes referred to as "SaaS," which is how we will address it specifically in this chapter.

With SaaS, there are two emerging provider types. The first type comprises established information security vendors who are changing their delivery methods to include services delivered through the cloud. The second type comprises start-up information security companies that are also emerging in this field as pure, play CSPs—that is, these companies provide security only as a cloud service, and do not provide traditional client/server security products for networks, hosts, and/or applications.

Among established information security companies that are changing their business models to also include SaaS, the most prominent are traditional anti-malware vendors. However, other established information security companies are also involved in the delivery of SaaS, especially with regard to email filtering.

Origins

Three points of impetus help to explain how security-as-a-[cloud] service began. The earliest impetus is a decade old now: spam, or unsolicited email. As early as 1999, companies (such as Postini*) were offering email services as follows:

> Postini was founded with the idea that email should be better. While email is the most popular Internet resource, service providers and software developers aren't making email better, and worst of all, aggressive marketers are targeting any email user as a potential customer. Postini services are designed to extend the capability of your service providers' email offering. Junk mail services are only the first step. Over the coming months, you will see more Postini services that make email even better.†

A number of other companies now provide email filtering services, both standalone security companies, as well as many Internet service providers (ISPs) which are often reselling the services of standalone security companies with their own brand.

A second impetus for SaaS is managed security services (MSSs). Managed security service providers (MSSPs) have been providing outsourced services to customers for several years, whereby the MSSPs manage an organization's network security devices, such as firewalls and intrusion detection systems (IDSs). The impetus for using MSS was, and is, the same as cloud computing: lower costs compared to in-house solutions through shared resources. The difference between MSSPs and CSPs, however, is that the shared resources for MSSPs are personnel, and not infrastructure. Additionally, because many organizations are not staffed to handle round-the-clock support for such services and do not have the expertise to fully staff such positions, the shared services (i.e., personnel) model of MSSPs can be financially attractive. The MSSP model became an impetus for CSPs because it broke the strong but informal barrier to outsourcing parts of an organization's information security program. And in this case, that outsourcing also meant off-premises management of information security devices. (Although outsourcing information security is often an option, initially it tended to be outsourcing on-premises—that is, within the customer's own facilities—as opposed to off-premises. Of course, now outsourcing can be on-premises, off-premises, onshore, offshore, and other variations in delivery.)

Although this network security work is outsourced in this model, the responsibility for a customer's security remains with the customer. It is the customer who is responsible for managing and monitoring the MSSP, and the customer dictates what security policies are to be enforced. The MSSP monitors and manages devices (e.g., firewalls, IDSs) and data flows

---

* Postini was acquired by Google in September 2007. See *http://googleblog.blogspot.com/2007/09/weve-officially -acquired-postini.html*.

† According to the Internet Archive's Wayback Machine for Postini.com, May 10, 2000. MessageLabs, another email filtering company, founded in 1999 and acquired by Symantec in May 2008, even used to refer to itself as an application service provider—an earlier evolution of cloud computing.

(e.g., Web, content, or email filtering). But these devices (including the devices that manage and monitor data flows) belong to the customer. As a result, cost savings and efficiency improvements go only so far. Although this is a subscription-type service (an operational expense, or OpEx), there is still the associated capital expense (CapEx) of the customer's on-premises hardware. With cloud computing, CapEx is further reduced because most of the devices and the monitoring and management are the responsibilities of the SaaS provider.

A third point of impetus for SaaS is the declining organizational efficiency of trying to provide security on the endpoints directly. Not only is there is a huge proliferation of endpoints, but they have so many configuration variables that organizational IT departments simply cannot manage them effectively. Additionally, because many of these endpoints are mobile, trying to troubleshoot configuration problems and keep security software up-to-date is a huge task. Add to those problems the fact that many mobile devices lack sufficient resources (e.g., processing power, memory, and storage capacity) to adequately handle today's endpoint protection suites and the endpoint protection situation is not looking positive.

Because of these issues, and the explosive growth in malware, protecting endpoints on the endpoints is an increasing problem. For example, "In 2008, Symantec detected 1,656,227 malicious code threats.... This represents over 60 percent of the approximately 2.6 million malicious code threats that Symantec has detected over time."‡ This has led to a change in thinking about how to protect those endpoints. Instead of protecting endpoints on the endpoints, why not protect them through the cloud? That is, why not clean the traffic to and from the endpoints as it transits the cloud? Instead of dealing with all the complications of trying to monitor and manage the endpoints themselves, move the monitoring and management of traffic to and from the endpoint (not the monitoring and management of devices themselves) to the cloud.

This concept of moving anti-malware protection to the cloud, instead of being endpoint-resident, gained considerable traction with the presentation of a paper at the July 2008 USENIX Conference in San Jose, California. That paper, titled "CloudAV: N-Version Antivirus in the Network Cloud" and available at *http://www.eecs.umich.edu/fjgroup/pubs/cloudav-usenix08.pdf*, showed that cloud-based antivirus (i.e., anti-malware) provides 35% better detection against recent threats than endpoint-based single engines, and an overall detection rate of 98%. That overall detection rate is significantly better than the results of a single engine running on an endpoint. (Endpoints are generally limited to running only a single anti-malware engine at a time because of constraints on endpoint resources, as well as incompatibilities of running multiple engines.)

‡ Symantec's Global Internet Security Threat Report: "Trends for 2008," Volume XIV, published April 2009, p. 10.

Today's Offerings

Today's offerings in the SaaS segment involve several services to improve information security: email filtering (including backup, archival, and e-discovery§); web content filtering; vulnerability management; and identity-as-a-service (spelled in this chapter as *IDaaS*).

Email Filtering

SaaS for email primarily involves cleansing spam, phishing emails, and malware included in email from an organization's incoming email stream, and then delivering that clean email securely to the organization so that it is effectively not repolluted. The touted benefits of this approach are not only more comprehensive security for clients due to the use of multiple engines, but also better performance of those client devices (because the anti-malware runs in the cloud and not on the endpoint directly), as well as far better anti-malware management. The anti-malware management is superior to endpoint solutions because that anti-malware is OS- and processor-agnostic, so it can be managed centrally through the cloud rather than working with multiple management systems, probably from multiple anti-malware vendors. This cleansing-in-the-cloud service has corollary benefits: reduced bandwidth used by email, reduced loads on organizational email servers, and improved effectiveness of a (recipient) organization's own anti-malware efforts.

Although most attention on SaaS involving email tends to focus on inbound email, it is also often used with outgoing email. Many organizations want to ensure that they are not inadvertently sending malware-infected emails, and cleansing outbound email through SaaS is a good method for preventing such problems and embarrassments. Additionally, outside SaaS email can be used to enforce organizational policies around the encryption of email (e.g., between specified [email] domains, such as those belonging to business partners or customers). This email encryption is generally performed at the (email) server-to-server level so that individual user actions and key management are not required. This is accomplished by using either Secure Sockets Layer (SSL) or Transport Layer Security (TLS) on network communications at the transport layer.

A further benefit of SaaS anti-malware is the collective intelligence that is gained from the visibility of all malware threats to all endpoints across an enterprise, irrespective of type (e.g., server, desktop, laptop, or mobile device), location, OS, or processor architecture. Having this greater view in a timely manner is a significant help to organizational information security teams.

---

§ *E-discovery* refers to discovery in civil litigation of information in an electronic format. Because so much of an organization's information is transmitted via email, email becomes an obvious best place to start an e-discovery program, though e-discovery is not (or should not be) limited to email.

SaaS for email also includes email backup and archiving. This service usually involves storing and indexing an organization's email messages and attachments in a centralized repository. That centralized repository allows an organization to index and search by a number of parameters, including date range, recipient, sender, subject, and content. These capabilities are particularly useful for e-discovery purposes, which can be extremely expensive without such capabilities.

Web Content Filtering

As endpoints belonging to an organization—whether they are within an organization's facilities, at home, or on the road—try to retrieve web traffic, that traffic is diverted to a SaaS provider that scans for malware threats and ensures that only clean traffic is delivered to end users. Organizations can also enforce their web content policies by allowing, blocking, or throttling traffic (use of bandwidth for that traffic reduced). Because of the number of websites accessible today, earlier URL filtering solutions deployed on organizations' premises are increasingly inefficient. SaaS providers supplement that URL filtering with the examination of Hypertext Transfer Protocol (HTTP) header information, page content, and embedded links to better understand site content. Additionally, these services use a collective reputation scoring system to bolster the accuracy of this filtering.

SaaS for web content also involves scanning outbound web traffic for sensitive information (e.g., ID numbers, credit card information, intellectual property) that users could send externally without appropriate authorization (data leakage protection). Web traffic is also scanned for content analysis, file type, and pattern matching to prevent data exfiltration.

Figure 10-1 illustrates SaaS web content filtering.

Vulnerability Management

As the Internet-facing presence of organizations has grown in size and complexity, as well as in importance to their operations, ensuring the secure configuration and operation of the systems involved has become more difficult and more important. There are SaaS providers that discover, prioritize, and assess systems for vulnerabilities, and then report and remediate those vulnerabilities and verify the systems' secure operation. Such information is also used to monitor for and report on compliance with some regulatory requirements (e.g., the Payment Card Industry's Data Security Standard).

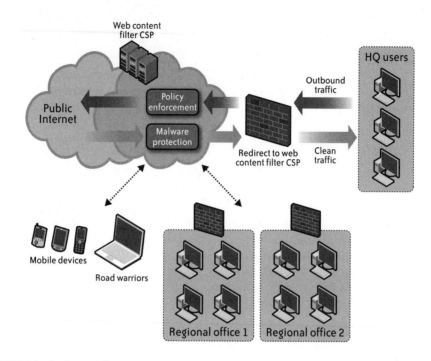

FIGURE 10-1. SaaS web content filtering

Identity Management-As-a-Service

Identity management-as-a-service (IDaaS) only recently emerged as an example of SaaS, in comparison to email filtering, web content filtering, and vulnerability management, which are more established as SaaS offerings. As Chapter 5 describes, there are some significant deficiencies in today's identity and access management (IAM) capabilities with regard to uses in cloud computing (e.g., scalability). IDaaS attempts to provide some IAM services in the cloud. Today's relatively early IDaaS offering tends to focus on authentication, because this is the most critical problem for customers; see Figure 10-2. However, the most significant problem for CSPs concerns IDaaS providers, and developing some form of collaborative meta system. (Just as meta directories did not scale within organizations, virtual directories will not scale to a cloud level.) IDaaS providers will also need to provide other IAM services for cloud customers, including authorization (groups and roles at a minimum), provisioning, and auditing.

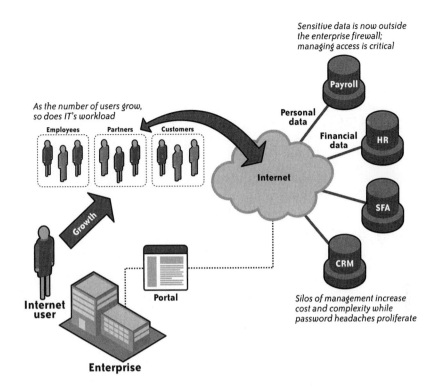

Sensitive data is now outside
the enterprise firewall;
managing access is critical

As the number of users grow,
so does IT's workload

Silos of management increase
cost and complexity while
password headaches proliferate

FIGURE 10-2. IDaaS model

Summary

Several of today's SaaS offerings are not only viable but in fact quite mature. Email and web content filtering have been provided for several years, and the methods of providing such services have been well developed. Some other SaaS offerings are newer and still maturing (e.g., IDaaS). Today, these offerings are provided to multiple organizations with the providers using their own specialized clouds. None of today's regular or established CSPs (for examples of providers see Chapter 9) yet offer SaaS as an integrated offering.

CHAPTER ELEVEN

The Impact of Cloud Computing on the Role of Corporate IT

CLOUD COMPUTING HAS THE POTENTIAL TO BE THE NEXT DISRUPTIVE TECHNOLOGY with consequence of significant change. Depending on the perspective and situation of the organization or the individual, this represents both opportunity and crisis. Such change may be resisted, even if it is a good idea and it works.

The role of the corporate IT department will be impacted significantly by a company's adoption of cloud computing. The degree of change will relate to the current approach to IT governance and management, and to the level and speed of adoption.

What are the driving forces and resisting forces that will drive adoption, and which is stronger? In this simplistic analysis, the driving forces need to outweigh the resistance to make individuals and organizations adopt the cloud as the enabling technology platform of the next decade or so. Understanding the driving forces to maximize benefit and the way resistance is managed will impact the speed of adoption and the ultimate role that corporate IT professionals perform. In this chapter we discuss:

- Driving forces for adopting the cloud
- Resisting forces to maintain the status quo
- How cloud computing will affect the role of IT

Why Cloud Computing Will Be Popular with Business Units

There are a number of reasons why business units will see cloud computing as an alternative way of using information technology. These reasons may well change the role of IT in the near future, and some of IT's traditional service delivery models and organizational structures will need to be changed to accommodate the power of computing that can be easily deployed through cloud computing. Some of the reasons include the following:

- Cloud computing is a low-cost solution.
- Cloud computing offers responsiveness and flexibility.
- The IT expense matches the transaction volumes.
- Business users are in direct control of technology decisions.
- The line between home computing applications and enterprise applications will blur.

We explore each of these in turn.

Low-Cost Solution

First and foremost, cloud technologies have to be cost-effective in terms of total cost, and they must improve the ratio between maintenance cost and discretionary spending on value-added projects. Most of the annual budgets in the vast majority of IT departments today are consumed by maintenance and depreciation—providing no new value add. This balance between maintenance and depreciation versus new value add is critical; there is no benefit in reducing infrastructure costs and paying more for application development through increased cost of integration. This leads to the importance of taking a holistic view of the true costs of IT: including integration cost, reporting cost, disaster recovery planning, IT staff costs, and the cost of swapping out a poorly performing cloud service provider (CSP). Compelling cost benefit equations will drive the adoption; disastrous contractual relationships will slow the adoption for individuals and companies that are impacted. The potential that cloud computing has for economies of scale and innovation will provide a strong cost-effectiveness driver. The low cost of technology offered by CSPs will encourage business units to go directly to CSPs rather than using traditional IT departments (because doing the latter would cost more and most likely it would take longer to adopt such changes). This may have a profound impact on the role of IT. IT may no longer be seen as an implementation provider, but rather as a risk advisor and guidance provider. This would require different IT skill sets and a new IT structure to support business units. Instead of silos of groups or liaison roles, IT needs to be more closely embedded within business units and be seen as part of the business unit instead of aligned to IT. Core IT would provide training and mentorship for these IT resources and educate them on the compliance requirements as they adopt the new technologies.

Responsiveness/Flexibility

Provided that IT meets availability and reliability goals within acceptable costs, perhaps a more critical driver than cost is responsiveness and flexibility. A new company is acquired, a new product is launched, a layoff happens, and the sales force is reorganized. All of these events can occur within short notice, command resources, and can consume an entire IT budget. Technology support for process improvement becomes a lower priority than keeping the lights on and responding to a "must-do" project.

In the acquisition scenario, it may well be that your payroll provider is more experienced at combining two companies' payrolls than an in-house IT department would be. It may be that the email provider is also well versed in taking on such a consolidation project and can scale the infrastructure with ease. The CSP's experience may lead to a cost-effective solution, and be more responsive than that of traditional IT departments. The argument for CSP responsiveness can be seen by what is in many ways a virtual IT organization. This "delegation" to a CSP gives IT management the bandwidth to deal with the hard stuff, such as people, combining processes, product lines, and getting value out of the acquisition.

This argument also applies to the IT business-as-usual operation. If most of IT's funds are spent on routine or commodity functions, performance of critical business processes will degenerate. If users do not have the ability to adapt or take advantage of evolving technology, satisfaction with IT will also decline. Responsiveness may also be enhanced by a broad customer base for an application contributing new solutions to run on the platform and extend software-as-a-service (SaaS) functionality. This allows a business group to adapt to new regulations, respond to new requirements, and find a better way of doing things. Do all companies then end up with the same systems and processes? Maybe some of that happens, but the way they combine and apply components leads to tremendous variety in operational approach. The bigger risk is getting left behind by not taking advantage of the responsiveness, flexibility, and adaptability that a combination of CSPs can offer.

IT Expense Matches Transaction Volume

A company may have a critical and urgent requirement to mobilize a new sales force, in a new region. The requirements include having a high degree of visibility into the sales pipeline to manage sales execution and the quality of the demand signal. Other investments will be made based on this data. On top of the responsiveness argument is the impact on cash flow, one of the most important business metrics. A company can buy as many Salesforce.com applications as it needs to support a hopefully growing but possibly dwindling sales force.

In another example, a company performs Sarbanes-Oxley (SOX) Section 404 IT control testing once a year. Renting an IT Governance, Risk, and Compliance (GRC) application for that period may reduce costs, and the company may take advantage of increasing levels of automation and adaptation to new regulations through an evolving SaaS provider.

Matching investment to revenue using a SaaS model is an attractive proposition. Some enterprise resource planning (ERP) vendors are using this model to price on-premises software, validating the strength of this approach but also offering an alternative scenario to achieve this benefit. That's a good thing from a cloud adoption perspective, as it increases competition in responding to this business driver.

Business Users Are in Direct Control of Technology Decisions

In the future, business users will be able to purchase services from a service catalog, and they will be in control of the services they use. In this scenario, there may be little to zero touch from the IT department in transacting services, and costs may be directly billed to the business user for transactions and services consumed. In that scenario, business users would have an incentive to discontinue obsolete functions, so accountability and alignment of IT costs will be improved. Will business users really make those kinds of decisions? Should they be allowed to? What are the implications of this? Answers will vary across the various industries and the relative maturity of the CSP customer.

The Line Between Home Computing Applications and Enterprise Applications Will Blur

In many scenarios, knowledge worker tools delivered by the Internet are used more efficiently to run the home than to run the workplace. We tend to collaborate more effectively with our friends at home than we do with our colleagues at work. It's a hassle to key in my telephone numbers when I change phones, so I store them in the cloud. My smart phone gives me stock quotes, and allows me to make trades from wherever I am. In my private life, I assess the value of the application and invest time in assimilating it into my way of operating. If it does not work or I don't like it, I don't use it or I find an alternative. In this way, adopting tools in your personal life on a self-selecting basis from CSPs can educate and raise expectations.

The personal productivity of the knowledge worker in business life and in private life feeds off each other and adds another push to adoption. The boundary between personal and work life merges.

Potential Threats of Using CSPs

A number of threats from CSPs may promote the existing role of the IT function and dissuade businesses from using CSPs.

Vested Interest of Cloud Providers

CSPs have made considerable investments in data centers and infrastructure. The cost of capturing the customer has been expended and needs to be recouped. The price for initial service may have been low. The business model relies on a continual and expanding revenue stream from each customer. The big CSPs become bigger as cloud services grow. They "partner" with their clients, but no one customer holds very much sway. In some cases, the CSP, often out of necessity, uses proprietary technology. This can be a significant risk that may exist if a CSP goes bankrupt, or starts to raise prices to compensate for loss of revenue, or is unresponsive to business needs. In some cases, the customer may be locked in, and exiting from a CSP may prove costly.

Loss of Control Over the Use of Technologies

Loss of control may be a reality if competitive forces are not maintained during the entire life of a cloud service, and it is costly to switch CSPs. Assume that cost-effectiveness and responsiveness can be maintained. Should a company outsource its critical IT function to a third party or many third parties? It may not be clear whether one or many are optimal. However, as customers rely more on the CSP, they may have less control over their use of technology. The IT function will most likely resist this change, as it has a direct impact on its function.

Perceived High Risk of Using Cloud Computing

Through cloud computing's association with the Internet, and the fact that it is a new service, there is a perception that cloud computing has significant risks and challenges. A central question that drives uncertainty toward the adoption of cloud computing concerns where the data is being processed or stored at any given time. Any replacement of in-house services with CSP-based services may add measurably to this risk.

Portability and Lock-in to Proprietary Systems for CSPs

The deployment of cloud services offers the possibility of spending less money on routine IT operations, and more in adding value to the business. A prerequisite for this is realized cost improvement in data center operations. This requires migration costs from a data center to a CSP to be sufficiently low. It also relies on lower upfront costs to establish a new customer on the platform. This will enable contract time frames to be shorter and be cost-effective for both parties. Lock-in concerns will need to be removed by better standards to migrate data and allow multiple service providers to cooperate in meeting customer needs. If this flexibility does not exist as hardware and storage becomes cheaper, this will not be passed on to the consumer; new customers will get better rates, fueling dissatisfaction. Supplier dominance in the market would inhibit widespread growth. This concern is explored in the Open Cloud Manifesto.[*]

---

[*] See *http://www.opencloudmanifesto.org/*.

Lack of Integration and Componentization

Prior to ERP, the scope of package solutions comprised individual applications, such as finance, payroll, or manufacturing. The packages sat alongside custom applications and most of the data exchange was through custom programs. The level of automation was low and the level of integration was low. ERPs sought to improve integration, and they became a central component of the majority of IT strategies. One driving force for ERP vendors was to extend their software footprint, and effectively lock in a customer to that vendor.

Coexistence of ERP implementation strategies came later. This was partly driven by customer demand for new functionality and the reaction time of ERP vendors, and by mixed ERP environments that developed through user companies' acquisitions including a different ERP platform. ERP vendors are now responding with more open, non-proprietary architectures. That also makes it possible for ERP vendors who acquire niche software providers to integrate that code as is, without rewriting their application and leaving existing customers high and dry. So, tools and standards that enable integration, componentization of applications, and service-oriented architecture have led to marked shifts in ERP positioning. These position changes by ERP vendors are examples of the way customer demand and expediency drive changes. There are parallels with the adoption of cloud computing.

ERP Vendors Offer SaaS

The major ERP vendors now have SaaS offerings. Such expanded offerings in the past have been conceived as both an offensive and a defensive measure. Emphasis on the middle market in the past five years was driven partly to keep Microsoft from establishing an enterprise ERP presence as well as to gain additional revenue. Customers can assume that both dynamics are operating in the SaaS scenario, and as base ERPs become more componentized and sophisticated this will help with interoperability issues.

A Case Study Illustrating Potential Changes in the IT Profession Caused by Cloud Computing

To illustrate a company's adoption of cloud computing and its impact on IT, we have painted a picture of a fictional cloud-enabled company called Nimbus Systems, a small to medium-size business (SMB). Here are some factors pertaining to the company:

- Core ERP is hosted in a private cloud in a data center in Colorado. Functions are limited to finance, reporting, master data maintenance, budgeting, and planning.

- There is no single order management solution. Customer interaction is highly customized and demand comes through in a variety of modes, but uses a standard format.

- Direct procurement uses strategic sourcing agreements, online auctions, and links with the supply chain. This is a hosted B2B application with a combination of public and private clouds. Vendor records and product catalogs are stored in this application.
- Manufacturing is outsourced to 23 companies worldwide.
- Distribution is outsourced to two global carriers.
- A hosted supply chain solution orchestrates the "virtual supply chain," and is managed by the planning department in the Bahamas.
- Three alternative sales force automation systems are available on a SaaS model. Customer data is stored in the ERP.
- Indirect purchasing and travel management are cloud applications.
- Netbook computers are the default workstations, with all "desktop" applications and storage in the cloud.
- Collaboration tools are available on a pay-per-use basis as a service paid directly by the business consumer.
- R&D has retained its own research machines, but product development is in a cloud application that brings all parties the design, source, and price, and plans product launch information.
- Each product shipped is tailored to a specific customer need. A custom variant configuration application has been developed and the rules are maintained in-house.
- All documents, emails, and voice mails are archived and managed by a specialist CSP.
- HR, payroll, and benefits management are outsourced.
- The help desk is maintained in-house, but all second- and third-level support is routed to the appropriate third-party provider.

What is interesting about this scenario is that the individual components already exist in production at different companies. The Nimbus Systems IT department does not operate or house the infrastructure; building of applications is limited to the specialized customer-facing application, and support and maintenance functions are provided by the CSP. The Nimbus Systems IT organization now spends fewer resources on building and maintaining commoditized functions and more on the differentiated functions. The skills have become more oriented around architecture, procurement, accreditation, a common vocabulary, and inspection and monitoring. In many cases, these are new skills in the IT department that need to be acquired. For IT services to support the business goals of Nimbus Systems there is a more sophisticated need for IT governance and management.

In the Nimbus Systems model, someone from the company needs to take responsibility for critical functions such as:

- Developing the IT strategy, and in particular, any shared investments to support business goals

- Defining the architecture and standards
- Adding new suppliers and services
- Negotiating with individual suppliers
- Maintaining the service catalog
- Integrating services to form an end-to-end process
- Monitoring data integrity, security, and privacy
- Conducting disaster recovery planning
- Monitoring IT costs and alignment to delivered value
- Conducting IT supplier management and contingency planning if a supplier fails or is unresponsive

A critical component will be an approach to the governance of IT to create an environment for services to be delivered effectively. ISO/IEC 38500:2008,[†] corporate governance of information technology standard, provides a framework for effective governance of IT to assist those at the highest level in an organization to understand and fulfill their legal, regulatory, and ethical obligations in respect of the organization's use of IT.

This standard provides guiding principles for directors of organizations on the effective, efficient, and acceptable use of IT within their organizations. It is organized into three prime sections: Scope, Framework, and Guidance.[‡]

The framework comprises definitions, principles, and a model. It sets out six principles for good corporate governance of IT:

- Responsibility
- Strategy
- Acquisition
- Performance
- Conformance
- Human behavior

It also provides guidance to those advising, informing, or assisting directors.

An established governance mechanism will be essential to prevent cloud computing from becoming the next generation of "shadow IT" (i.e., IT functions performed outside of IT, and not under the control of the established IT department).

IT governance creates an environment for effective IT management processes to be established and operated. Implementing service management frameworks, such as the Information

---

† *http://en.wikipedia.org/wiki/ISO_38500#cite_note-0*

‡ *http://en.wikipedia.org/wiki/ISO_38500#cite_note-1*

Technology Infrastructure Library (ITIL), provides a mechanism to manage the portfolio of services and ensure that there is comprehensive coverage of IT processes such as disaster recovery planning, change control, and capacity management. It will be useful to refer to some of the ITIL definitions and concepts to make the explicit connection with the ITIL service management framework and the requirements that cloud computing will place on IT management.

ITIL v3 defines a set of IT management processes and functions as part of a service life cycle (see Table 11-1). IT organizations are covering these functions in some way, perhaps not formalized and not with a service management orientation.

TABLE 11-1. ITIL management processes and functions

Service strategy	Service transition
Financial management Service portfolio management Demand management	Knowledge management Service asset and configuration management Change management Release and deployment management Validation and testing
Service design	**Service operations**
Service catalog management Service-level management Capacity management Availability management IT service continuity management Information security management Supplier management	Incident management Problem management Event management Request fulfillment Access management
	Continual service improvement (CSI)
	Service-level management Service measurement and reporting CSI improvement process

We have listed these processes to make the following key points:

Responsibility for specific aspects of IT may be delegated to managers within the organization. However, accountability for the effective and acceptable use and delivery of IT by an organization remains with the directors and cannot be delegated, according to ISO/IEC 38500:2008.

Responsibility for managing IT will be delegated throughout the corporation and, in some cases, to third parties. This is true now and will continue to be true as the driving forces of cloud adoption place more control in the customer's hands. The company itself is accountable for IT service effectiveness, not the CSP.

ITIL is process-oriented and the processes are designed to support a services-oriented approach from internal and external providers. This means ownership for processes such as information security and availability is managed across services, and responsibility can be made clear for those complicating aspects of the cloud architecture.

A critical concept concerns the service portfolio containing all services (live, in-process, and retired), the service catalog (live services), and service-level agreements (SLAs) that define the agreement of the service to be delivered to meet a specific customer need. Within the structure of a service catalog is both a business service component and a technical service catalog. This supports the concept of business managers who are responsible for an organization's business objectives and performance and for engaging IT to support those goals and appropriate IT services. These concepts support the increased level of ownership for defining, procuring, and paying for the services, and IT providing the necessary support to ensure that the service operates effectively in the overall context of the company's IT environment.

Discussions about responsibility for specific IT processes and how specific risks are dealt with help to construct the overall IT organization. Who are the process owners? Where do they report? How are they measured? Who makes what decision?

Frameworks for IT governance and service management are already prepared and handle many of the complicated IT management aspects proposed by adoption of cloud computing. Implementation of complete service life cycle management practices as presented in ITIL v3 is rare given the recent date of introduction in 2008. However, many individual processes and functions have been adopted and IT organizations are transforming to a process orientation. The ability of an IT organization to deal with cloud computing will depend to a large extent on the adoption of a service management type of approach to IT.

Giving up IT responsibility for certain decisions to business counterparts, and working with business units to determine specific requirements and concerns about security and privacy, provides a mechanism for IT to respond to IT's changing role in the corporation. The risk is that the cost of managing the CSP is not a value add and becomes a bureaucracy unto itself, standing in the way of responsiveness to business needs. The roles of the IS governance group are to direct and monitor the use of IT, acquire new technology, and assess the competence of the staff managing the business and technical aspects of IT. As with any transformational change, a clear vision of the nature of the change and the ability to sponsor the change will be required from company leadership.

In summary, the new IT function will spend fewer resources on building and maintaining commoditized functions and more on differentiated functions. Skills become more oriented around governance, IT service management, architecture, procurement, accreditation, a common vocabulary, and inspection and monitoring. In many cases, these are new skills in an IT department that need to be acquired or may come from outside the IT department. Given this, IT function skills will migrate to CSPs as new skills are acquired in organizational IT departments.

Without this type of IT change, there is a risk of going back to the stovepipes, duplicating inconsistent data as happened before deployment of ERP systems. The balance between control to achieve effective integration and speed of response will be the art and skill of the new IT group function.

Governance Factors to Consider When Using Cloud Computing

The CSP and its customer have a number of processes to manage. As explained in earlier chapters, such processes include:

- Managing identity
- Provisioning access
- Defining data storage requirements
- Managing key management
- Monitoring and managing service levels
- Monitoring and maintaining availability
- Providing assurance on internal controls
- Providing secure connectivity
- Providing for data governance
- Managing for problem management and incident response
- Developing, maintaining, and, when necessary, executing a business continuity program

It is important for the CSP and the customer to understand the various levels of responsibilities as they relate to the aforementioned processes. Some of these processes may be achieved by the CSP itself, or by the customer itself. In some cases, they may be jointly performed. As a basic rule, during early adoption of the CSP it would be prudent for customers to take on as many of the processes as they can. As the customer gets more familiar with the services of the CSP the customer may slowly transition some of the processes to the CSP where the CSP shows competency and a proven track record to take on these processes. Clear metrics, boundaries of responsibilities between the customer and the CSP, as well as adequate policies need to be in place for the processes to be well managed.

A critical question to address is which part of an organization should manage these processes and which function and executive officer should own the relationship of the CSP? Should this be an operational concern where the chief operating officer becomes the owner? Should this be a technology concern where the chief information officer becomes the owner? Should this be a business-led concern where the most relevant business executive (e.g., finance, sales, legal, human resources, logistics, etc.) becomes the owner?

To answer these questions, look at the nature of the service being provided by the CSP, the culture of the customer, the competency and skills of the customer and the CSP, and the level of executive sponsorship at the customer organization. It is clear that the role of IT may change with the adoption of cloud computing from pure implementation and maintenance of technology to integration of cloud computing into the organization.

Look at a software company that has a traditional IT group. This IT group would manage IT resources to help sustain, grow, and manage business needs. This would typically involve providing back office support in managing the network, application development, and help desk support. Often the software development of the company's own products would be managed by engineering, and in most cases, the related infrastructure would also be managed by engineering. However, with the advent of cloud computing there is a potential for traditional IT groups to play a larger role. For example, the IT group could be seen as a facilitator with the adoption of CSPs to benefit both business initiatives as well as product development. IT groups can promote more common standards and ensure that appropriate measures are in place to mitigate and manage enterprise risks. This will free up resources in other areas to focus more on their core competencies and thereby increase the productivity of the company. Business units and engineering should not be concerned with confidentiality, integrity, and availability concepts as IT professionals are well rehearsed in these areas and are best positioned to define and manage these principles.

Summary

Just as outsourcing, collocation facilities, and application service providers (ASPs) have had an impact on corporate IT, cloud computing will do the same. In many respects, that cloud computing impact will be an extension or continuation of the trend that the other factors listed have had as well: more work formerly done in-house by corporate IT will shift to outside the organization. Corporate IT departments will become more like managers of the IT services provided than the actual providers of those services.

Particular attention should also be paid to the economics of cloud providers. It is inevitable that many start-ups will go out of business, but the growing competition that is being seen creates business models with razor-thin margins that create challenges to invest in appropriate support and quality. Ultimately, this becomes a major governance issue for internal IT, who now become consultants and business analysts. They need to take steps to ensure that their cloud provider is a healthy business and can provide a sustainable solution for the long term.

However, there are two differences worth noting. First, delineation of responsibilities between providers and customers is much more nebulous than that between customers and outsourcers, collocation facilities, or ASPs. Given the newness of the cloud computing business model and its nascent stage of development, this lack of clarity on responsibilities is to be expected. With time, more maturity in defining those responsibilities between CSPs and customers will occur. The other difference between cloud computing and other, earlier trends in shifting IT services is that cloud computing is likely to involve much more direct business unit interaction with CSPs than with other providers previously. In fact, there will be many instances where business units go directly to CSPs without even consulting corporate IT departments. Essentially, IT is being cut out of the business loop—deliberately. Many business units see a diminishing value of corporate IT departments to provide for the services that business units need—not only in direct IT skills, but even in management or oversight of IT operations. This diminished view of IT's value directly to business units is reinforced by cloud computing's "pay as you go" business model and the shift from capital expenditures (CapEx) to operational expenditures (OpEx).

CHAPTER TWELVE

Conclusion, and the Future of the Cloud

As we have noted throughout this book, cloud computing has the potential to be a disruptive force by affecting the deployment and use of technology. The cloud could be the next evolution in the history of computing, following in the footsteps of mainframes, minicomputers, PCs, servers, smart phones, and so on, and radically changing the way enterprises manage IT. Yes, plenty of questions are still left to be answered regarding security within the cloud and how customers and cloud service providers (CSPs) will manage issues and expectations, but it would be a severe understatement to say simply that cloud computing has generated interest in the marketplace.

The hype regarding cloud computing is unavoidable. It has caught the imagination of consumers, businesses, financial analysts, and of course, the CSPs themselves. Search for "cloud computing" on the Internet and you will uncover thousands of articles defining it, praising it, ridiculing it, and selling it.

So powerful is the term *cloud computing* that according to some, just the mere mention of it may help to drive additional attention and revenues for providers. Take, for example, the case of Salesforce.com. According to Marc Benioff, CEO of Salesforce.com, his software-as-a-service (SaaS) organization did not embrace the use of the term until he read an article that referred to Google and Amazon as cloud computing leaders in December 2007. Soon afterward, Salesforce.com started to leverage the term in its marketing efforts and collateral. In the full fiscal year since Salesforce.com started using the term *cloud computing*, its revenues grew 44%.

"I think it's the most powerful term in the industry," said Benioff.*

OK, what does all this mean? Does this mean enterprise adoption of the cloud is a "sure thing"? Maybe. Or maybe not. As we noted in the previous chapters, a number of key drivers for cloud computing may make the move compelling for enterprises, including low levels of initial investment and ongoing costs, economies of scale, open standards, and sustainability. Additionally, there are some potential barriers to adoption that we have discussed, including concerns regarding security, privacy, and compliance and governance.

At the end of the day, you are probably going to make your own assessment regarding the future of the cloud and whether the use cases and associated value propositions are appropriate for you and/or your organization. The objective of this chapter is to give you a snapshot of analyst and IT leadership thoughts regarding the potential of the cloud and our thoughts regarding the future of the cloud.

Analyst Predictions

Most financial analysts feel that cloud computing will be a huge growth area in terms of IT spending and revenue streams over the next few years, but the estimates vary.

According to a May 2008 forecast by Merrill Lynch, the volume of the cloud computing market opportunity will amount to $160 billion by 2011, including $95 billion in business and productivity applications and $65 billion in online advertising.†

According to a March 2009 forecast by Gartner, worldwide cloud services are on pace to surpass $56.3 billion in 2009, a 21.3% increase from 2008 revenues of $46.4 billion. The market is expected to reach $150.1 billion in 2013.‡

"Cloud computing is a broad and diverse phenomenon. Much of the growth represents a transfer of traditional IT services to the new cloud model, but there is also scope for creation of substantial new businesses and revenue streams," said Ben Pring, research vice president for Gartner. "Cloud computing enables a shift in IT provision from direct purchase and payment for services to provision of services which are free at point of use and where revenue is derived from advertising. Services supported by advertising are currently, and will remain, the largest component of the overall cloud services market through 2013."

According to an IDC October 2008 forecast, spending on IT cloud services is growing at five times the rate of traditional, on-premises IT. Also according to IDC, even more striking than this high growth rate is the contribution that the cloud offering's growth will soon make to the

---

* "The Internet Industry Is on a Cloud—Whatever That May Mean," by Geoffrey A. Fowler and Ben Worthen. *The Wall Street Journal,* March 2009.

† "The Cloud Wars: $100+ billion at stake," by Merrill Lynch, May 2008.

‡ See *http://www.gartner.com/it/page.jsp?id=920712.*

IT market's overall growth. As illustrated in Figure 12-1, cloud computing services will generate approximately one-third of the net new growth within the industry.

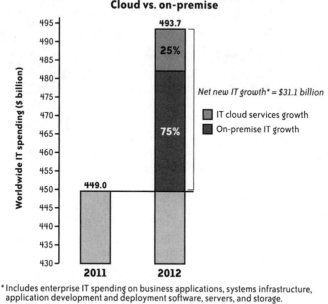

Net new IT growth* = $31.1 billion

Source: IDC, October 2008 (revised)

FIGURE 12-1. Sources of incremental IT spending growth

Additionally, according to IDC and illustrated in Figure 12-2, projected spending on cloud services will nearly triple by 2012, and will continue to be dominated by SaaS offerings over this period of time. But as you can see from the sheer scale of the increase in overall cloud services spending, platform-as-a-service (PaaS) and infrastructure-as-a-service (IaaS) services will also experience strong growth.§

So, the analysts seem to be sold on the growth potential of cloud computing. What about IT and business leaders?

§ See *http://blogs.idc.com/ie/?p=224*.

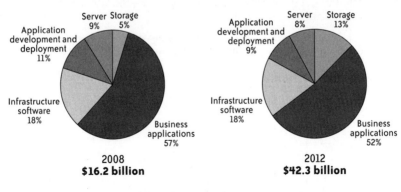

Worldwide IT cloud services spending* by product/service type

2008
$16.2 billion

2012
$42.3 billion

* Includes enterprise IT spending on business applications, systems infrastructure, application development and deployment software, servers, and storage.

Source: IDC, October 2008

FIGURE 12-2. Worldwide IT cloud services spending

Survey Says?

In October 2008, CIO Research released the results of its cloud computing survey[||] for which it polled 173 IT executives to get their thoughts on cloud computing and its applicability to their enterprises.

As you can see from Table 12-1, a majority of the respondents felt that cloud computing will cause a shift in the way enterprises use IT, and only 18% felt that it is not going to have a major impact in the short or near term.

TABLE 12-1. Survey results #1 on cloud computing[a]

The cloud: your view	
Cloud computing will cause a radical shift in information technology driving the next wave of innovation	58%
Cloud computing is an evolving concept that will take years to mature	54%
Current on-demand offerings are not appropriate for my business	36%
Cloud computing is a passing fad	18%

[a] Source: CIO Research

|| "Forecast: Cloud Computing Looms Big on the Horizon," by *CIO Focus*, October 2008.

However, as you will note from Table 12-2, fewer than one-third of the respondents stated that their organizations are currently utilizing or implementing cloud computing.

TABLE 12-2. Survey results #2 on cloud computing[a]

Is cloud computing on your organization's tech roadmap?	
Yes, currently using or implementing	30%
No, not on our technology roadmap	29%
Yes, on the radar or actively researching	17%
Yes, plan to use within one year	10%
Yes, plan to use within one to three years	5%
Not sure	5%
Yes, plan to use within three to five years	2%

[a] Source: CIO Research

Table 12-3 summarizes at a high level the use cases for leveraging the cloud and the respondents' feedback on how their respective organizations are currently using cloud computing. As you can see from the survey, the SaaS model is currently the most common example of the usage of cloud computing, as we might expect. Most financial estimates mirror the results of this survey by pointing out that the SaaS model currently accounts for more than 50% of IT spending associated with cloud services.

TABLE 12-3. Survey results #3 on cloud computing[a]

How is your organization currently using cloud offerings?	
Running applications using a software-as-a-service (SaaS) model	51%
Do not currently use any cloud computing offerings	37%
Storage	24%
Access to extra computing power on demand	19%
Other	8%

[a] Source: CIO Research

As you can see from Table 12-4, for those respondents who noted that they are currently using or are planning to use the cloud, the drivers were varied but the common theme was centered on elasticity and reduction of costs associated with capital expenditures.

TABLE 12-4. Survey results #4 on cloud computing[a]

Primary reasons you're using or plan to use cloud	
Scalability on demand/flexibility to the business	50%
Reduced hardware infrastructure costs	38%
Reduced IT staffing/administration costs	35%
Access to skills capabilities we have no interest in developing in-house	28%
Not using or planning to use cloud computing offerings	19%
Capacity—data center	16%
Capacity—storage	11%
Frequent software updates	10%
Other	5%

[a] Respondents selected up to three criteria. Source: CIO Research

In regard to barriers, Table 12-5 notes that security is far and away the single largest potential barrier to cloud adoption as seen by IT executives. But as we have noted, there are also major concerns regarding privacy, governance, and compliance. CSPs, both established and new entrants, will need to better address how their service offerings will deal with these concerns if they expect to convince enterprises of the value proposition associated with the various cloud use cases.

TABLE 12-5. Survey results #5 on cloud computing[a]

Greatest concerns surrounding cloud adoption at your company	
Security	45%
Integration with existing systems	26%
Loss of control over data	26%
Availability concerns	25%
Performance issues	24%
IT governance issues	19%
Regulatory/compliance concerns	19%
Dissatisfaction with vendor offerings/pricing	12%
Ability to bring systems back in-house	11%
Lack of customization opportunities	11%
Measuring ROI	11%
Not sure	7%

Greatest concerns surrounding cloud adoption at your company	
Other	6%

a Respondents selected up to three criteria. Source: CIO Research

If you compare the analysts' predictions and the survey of IT leaders, you will note that they are at odds in terms of their thoughts regarding the near-term future of the cloud. The analysts seem to be banking on the growth potential of the cloud and what it could mean in terms of spending and service increase, whereas the IT leaders seem to be hedging their bets that a number of questions and concerns, such as security, still need to be resolved before cloud computing truly takes off. Which camp will prove to be prophetic? Only time will tell....

Security in Cloud Computing

Since the premise of our book is that security is a concern when discussing cloud computing, let's revisit the security considerations we previously discussed and conclude with our thoughts on the current and future states of these considerations for the cloud:

- Infrastructure security
- Data security and storage
- Identity and access management
- Security management
- Privacy
- Audit and compliance
- Security-as-a-[cloud] service
- Impact of cloud computing on the role of corporate IT

Infrastructure Security

During our discussion of infrastructure security, we looked at network-, host-, and application-level security and the issues surrounding each level with specific regard to cloud computing. At the network level, although there are definitely security challenges with cloud computing, none of those challenges are caused specifically by cloud computing. All of the network-level security challenges associated with cloud computing are instead exacerbated by cloud computing, not specifically caused by it. Likewise, security issues at the host level, such as an increased need for host perimeter security (as opposed to organizational entity perimeter security) and secured virtualized environments, are exacerbated by cloud computing but not specifically caused by it. And the same holds true for the application level. Certainly, there is an increased need for secure software development life cycles due to the public-facing nature of (public) cloud applications and the need to ensure that APIs have been thoroughly tested for security, but those application-level security requirements are again exacerbated by cloud computing and not specifically caused by it.

Therefore, the issues of infrastructure security and cloud computing are about understanding which party provides which aspects of security (i.e., does the customer provide it or does the CSP provide it)—in other words, defining trust boundaries.

With regard to infrastructure security, an undeniable conclusion is that trust boundaries between customers and CSPs have moved. When we see poll after poll of information executives (e.g., CIOs) and information security professionals (e.g., CISOs) indicating that security is their number one concern with cloud computing, the primary cause for that concern is really over moved trust boundaries. To be more specific, the issue is not so much that the boundaries have moved, but more importantly that customers are unsure where those trust boundaries have moved to. Many CSPs have not clearly articulated those trust boundaries (e.g., what security is provided by the CSP versus what security still needs to be provided by the customer), nor are those new trust boundaries reinforced in operational obligations such as service-level agreements (SLAs).

Although the CSPs have the primary responsibility for articulating these new trust boundaries, some current confusion about this is also the fault of information security personnel. There are some information security professionals who, either fearing something new or not fully understanding cloud computing, are engaging in FUD (fear, uncertainty, and doubt) with their business customers.

Similar to confusion over moved trust boundaries is the fact that the established model of network tiers or zones no longer exists. That model has been replaced with domains, which are less precise and afford less protection than the old model. (Domain names are used in various networking contexts and application-specific naming and addressing purposes based on DNS.) If we can no longer trust the network (organizational) perimeter to provide sufficient protection and are now reliant on host perimeter security, what is the trust model between hosts?

An analogy of this problem already exists and was dealt with 20 years ago—STU- (Secure Telephone Unit) IIIs used by the U.S. Department of Defense and the intelligence community. In that model, each STU-III unit (a host) was responsible for its own "perimeter security" (i.e., the device's electronic components were tamper-resistant), and each device had a secure authentication mechanism (i.e., a dongle with an identity written to it, protected and verified by asymmetric encryption and Public Key Infrastructure or PKI). Additionally, each device would negotiate a common level of authorization (classification level) based on an attribute included with the identity in the dongle.

Today, we have no such model in cloud computing. The STU-III model simply is not viable for cloud computing, and there is no trusted computing platform for virtual machine (VM) environments. Therefore, host-to-host authentication and authorization is problematic in cloud computing since much of it uses virtualization. Today the use of federated identity management is focused on trust, identity, and authentication of people. The identity management solutions of today do assist in managing host-level access; however, there is no viable solution today that addresses the issue of host-to-host trust. The host-to-host trust issue is exacerbated in cloud computing because of the sheer number of resources available.

Conceptually similar to the trust boundary problem at the application level is ensuring that one customer's data is not inadvertently provided to another, unauthorized customer. Data has to be securely labeled to ensure that it remains separated among customers in a multitenancy environment. Today, data separation in cloud computing is logical, not physical, as was done previously, and there are valid concerns about the adequacy of that logical separation.

Data Security and Storage

During our discussion of data security and storage, we looked at several aspects of data security and the storage of data. If cloud computing customers are concerned about the security afforded by infrastructure security and are counting on data security to provide compensating controls, those customers will be disappointed. A major reason for the lack of effective data security is simply the limitations of current encryption capabilities. However, efforts to adequately detail data lineage (mapping) are simply not possible in today's cloud computing offerings. The amount of effort (and cost) to provide such mapping runs counter to the economic incentives of cloud computing. Another major problem with current cloud computing offerings is a lack of serious attention (effective action) to customers' concerns about data remanence (i.e., data residue left behind and possibly becoming available to unauthorized parties).

These concerns with data security do not negate the capabilities or advantages of utilizing storage-as-a-service in the cloud—for non-sensitive, non-regulated data. If customers do want to (simply) store organizational data in the cloud, they must take explicit actions, or at least verify that the provider will and can adequately provide such services, to protect their data stored in the cloud.

We know how to effectively encrypt data-in-transit, and we know how to effectively encrypt data-at-rest. But because encrypted data cannot be processed, indexed, or sorted, to do any of those important activities requires that the data be unencrypted—hence, a security concern, especially if that data is in the cloud and is beyond the data owner's direct control.

Even efforts to effectively manage data that is encrypted are extremely complex and troublesome due to the current inadequate capabilities of key management products. Key management in an intra-organizational context is difficult enough; trying to do effective key management in the cloud is frankly beyond current capabilities and will require significant advances in both encryption and key management capabilities to be viable. Claims of key management products being effective currently are naïve at best.

Identity and Access Management

From the discussion points in Chapters 3 and 5, we established the premise that traditional network controls are no longer relevant in the cloud and should be superseded by data security and identity-based controls.

Managing access control and governance within identity and access management (IAM) to meet today's business needs in the cloud remains one of the major hurdles for enterprise adoption of cloud services. IAM support for business needs ranges from secure collaboration with global partners to secure access for global employees consuming sensitive information from any location and any device at any time. Thanks to the proliferation of consumer technologies (e.g., Apple iPhone) into the enterprise (consumerization of IT) and the steady dissolution of the network perimeter, enterprises are faced with greater risks in protecting their intellectual property and sensitive information as well as sustaining compliance. Easily accessible, user-friendly Web 2.0 technologies delivered via browsers is one other catalyst that is accelerating the trend of "consumerization of identity and access management" services (e.g., consumer-based identity services such as OpenID). In short, IT is constantly challenged to support today's business needs with yesterday's technologies and static processes. And the information protection challenges are exacerbated by increasingly mobile, dynamic, replicated, and scattered data on a variety of media ranging from USB memory sticks to storage-as-a-service.

On the other hand, IT is grappling with user access management dissatisfaction issues among business users who are increasingly frustrated with today's "user-unfriendly" IAM techniques (e.g., carrying a token card that performs two-factor authentication, remembering a variety of user IDs and passwords for various services, and forcing users to choose a strong password that they write down and carry in a wallet). And it is no secret that users will do anything to side-step identity or any other security controls that slow their productivity and business agility. Hence, IAM solutions need to strike a balance and act as enablers of security controls to increase user adoption and compliance.

Although the basic technology building blocks (trusted identity stores, provisioning processes, authorization and authentication methods, federation) for IAM exist today, the migration and extension of those technologies into cloud services in their current form will not yield the purported IAM benefits of efficiency, efficacy, and business agility. The sheer volume of dynamic cloud compute resources (compute nodes, storage, network policies) combined with the magnitude of users and services accessing those resources are challenging the scalability, automation, and availability requirements of today's directory and identity infrastructure services. The primary reason is that today's IAM solutions deployed in the enterprise are complex, require extensive customization, are expensive, and are not easily extendable to cloud services. Furthermore, the trusted source of identity in the cloud is still an issue and needs to be addressed. On the other hand, support for IAM practices and standards by CSPs is sparse and is not adequate for most enterprises. Although large SaaS cloud services are showing signs of support for federation standards such as the Security Assertion Markup Language

(SAML), they are largely absent from PaaS and IaaS services. A word of caution: viral adoption of cloud services driven by business units that don't leverage your own federated identity management infrastructure and IAM processes risks repeating the mistakes (e.g., provisioning of multiple credentials per user) that caused you to implement enterprise identity management solutions in the first place.

Today's early adopters—small and medium-size businesses (SMBs)—who are driven by the economic advantages of cloud computing have silently embraced the basic low-assurance authentication methods, leaving the enterprises waiting on the sidelines. Enterprises are hoping that the CSPs will offer IAM capabilities that are standard within their enterprise, and have come to expect this in any new service.

As we discussed in Chapter 5, enterprise cloud adoption barriers include lack of support for federation (single sign-on or SSO), integration with corporate directories, risk-based authentication, scalable identity services, and the extension of the IAM practice to the CSP. Hence, IAM solution design for cloud services will require careful consideration of cloud use cases, investment in processes and architecture that address cloud user access provisioning (including privileged users), service-to-service authentication and user-to-service authentication, and management of the user and access life cycle.

A small set of CSPs (mostly large SaaS service providers, such as Salesforce.com) are beginning to pay attention to enterprise IAM requirements, including support for standards such as SAML that facilitate SSO using federation. However, given the early adoption cycle by large enterprises, from an enterprise perspective IAM capabilities are primitive at best. Customers should continue to demand IAM features, including support for SAML, user provisioning using the Service Provisioning Markup Language (SPML) standard, and an open application programming interface (API) to support various user and access automation requirements. This IAM capability chasm has given birth to a new breed of cloud-based identity services; for example, identity services and frameworks such as secure token services (STSs) from Microsoft's Azure support basic federation from Active Directory to Microsoft's cloud services and facilitate user SSO from on-premises Active Directory to Microsoft's cloud services. Although these cloud-based identity services are lowering the barriers to entry for SMBs, they are deemed inadequate to meet most enterprise requirements such as custom reporting and compliance management. Trust and user data management are other barriers, and most enterprises are not willing to store their trusted source for identity outside controlled enterprise boundaries. This issue is further exacerbated by use cases in which attribute data associated with identities is either copied or stored in the cloud service. Synchronizing multiple identity repositories remains a key challenge for enterprises. Working with cloud-based services and addressing synchronization issues by way of federation, virtual directories, and an open API will reduce these barriers.

To avoid costly retrofits and integration with aftermarket products, organizations looking to adopt cloud-based services should embed an IAM strategy into the cloud service strategy road map. Organizations that have been investing in directories, IAM capabilities, and practices should therefore stand to gain by leveraging an optimized internal IAM strategy and practice in the cloud. The most important success factor for an enterprise to effectively manage identities and access control in the cloud is the presence of a robust directory and federated identity management capability within the organization (an internal or cloud-based identity service)—for instance, architecture and systems, user and access life cycle management processes, and audit and compliance capabilities. When it comes to authenticating users and services to the cloud, organizations need to pay attention to simplicity and ease of use in addition to risk-based authentication methods (e.g., look up when sensitive data is accessed). Another premise to keep in mind is that "all clouds are not created equal," so enterprises need to have a strategy for employing risk-based IAM methods, including strong authentication, automated provisioning, deprovisioning, auditing, and monitoring to address risks that are specific to a CSP.

Although identification and authentication challenges can be overcome (when those capabilities are made available by the service provider) with a well-architected IAM infrastructure and IT processes, authorization services in the cloud are very basic and evolving. Cloud users should be aware that granular application authorization is immature at this point. Where it does exist, it is usually implemented using CSP proprietary profiles and primitive roles—often CSPs offer primitive roles such as "user" and "administrator." As a long-term strategy, customers should be advocating for greater support of eXtensible Access Control Markup Language (XACML)-compliant entitlement management on the part of cloud providers, even if XACML has not been implemented internally. XACML provides a standardized language and method of access control and policy enforcement across all applications that enforce a common authorization standard. At the very least, CISOs should be thinking about authorization standards and avoid any temptation to customize a solution based on the provider's capability.

Business and IT stakeholders should also be advocating standardization of enterprise roles within the enterprise—in other words, roles mapped to user business functions (e.g., accounts payable manager, people manager, and purchase order approver). In the future, well-defined enterprise roles should be mapped to the cloud service roles or profiles supported by the CSPs. We believe SPML and XACML will play a role in that regard. (Currently, we are not aware of any effort to standardize the naming conventions of enterprise roles.)

IT architects should be advocating externalization of authentication and authorization components from applications (loosely coupled) as this can aid in the rapid adoption of cloud-based services including cloud identity services, policy-based authentication, centralized logging, and auditing (e.g., OpenSSO from Sun Microsystems and Microsoft's Geneva claims-based authentication framework can help externalize authentication).

Security Management

With the adoption of cloud services, a large part of your network, system, applications, and data will move to a third-party provider's control. The cloud services delivery model brings new challenges to the IT operations and management staff in the area of availability, access control, vulnerability, security patching, and configuration management. As a first step, cloud customers will have to understand all the layers they own, touch, or interface with—network, host, application, database, storage, and web services, including identity services. To tackle these challenges, you will need to understand the interfaces and the scope of IT system management responsibilities, including your responsibilities for access, change, configuration, patch, and vulnerability management.

Although you may be transferring some of the operational responsibilities to the provider, you may still own some of the responsibilities whose scope will depend on a variety of factors, including the type of cloud service. Major factors to consider are the SLA, monitoring capability, and provider-specific security management capabilities to support the extension of your internal operations management processes and tools.

Today, customers largely rely on CSPs for the service instrumentation to measure and manage the security, availability, and performance of their services in the cloud. Most CSPs are sharing the overall service metrics via a dashboard (e.g., Amazon's service health dashboard at *http:// status.aws.amazon.com/*). Although a CSP may be publishing the most up-to-the-minute information of its overall system status across all customers, the onus is on you to keep abreast of the service status. To manage the availability of your application you will need to measure, monitor, and manage service levels from your perspective (i.e., for your virtual environment). Unfortunately, the lack of standards and weak capabilities from CSPs to help customers place probes into their virtualized environment have exacerbated cloud service management. Hence, as a tenant of a *aaS service, you will have to understand what instrumentation and dashboards are made available to you by the service provider to help manage service levels to your users.

From a security management perspective, a key issue is the lack of enterprise-grade access management features. Since access control features will vary with the service delivery model and provider, customers will have to understand what access control features are available (strong authentication, user provisioning) and what their responsibilities are in managing the life cycle of user access to the cloud service. Some service providers are making an effort to keep their customers informed of new threats and educating them on ways to protect the information hosted in their cloud (e.g., Salesforce.com publishing threat and security practice information via *http://trust.salesforce.com/*).

In a virtualized environment where infrastructure is shared across multiple tenants, your data is commingled with that of other customers at every phase of the life cycle—during transit, processing, and storage. Even if you are able to install monitoring probes at infrastructure layers available to you, the resource bottlenecks that are visible to your instrumentation may not be able to give the necessary information to perform root-cause analysis (e.g., latency of packets between your system nodes in the cloud). Outages that impact the entire population will be visible to all users. Another dimension in cloud computing is the issue of monitoring and measuring disruptions across your users—depending on the cloud service architecture, failures of the infrastructure components may impact only a subset of the population and it would be hard to detect the service disruption unless the affected users report it (e.g., Google mail disruption events that impact only a subset of users). Hence, it is important to understand the location of the service, service-level guarantees such as internode communication, and storage access (read and write) latency.

The scope of security management of cloud services will vary with the service delivery model, provider capabilities, and maturity. Customers will have to make trade-offs with respect to the flexibility and control offered by the SPI services. The more flexible the service (i.e., the lower the service abstraction), the more control you can exercise on the service, and with that come additional security management responsibilities. Given that most cloud service offerings lack transparency in the area of SLA, provider management capabilities, and security responsibilities, the management functions will continue to challenge enterprises that have established IT governance, tools, and processes. Those frameworks, processes, and tools that address systemic qualities including reliability, availability, and security may not be extensible to the CSP. If you have adopted standard IT frameworks including the Information Technology Infrastructure Library (ITIL) and ISO 27002 in your organization, they should be reviewed and continuously adjusted based on the cloud service capabilities, sensitivity of information, and SLA that govern various management functions.

Privacy

Cloud computing offers significant challenges for global organizations that are facing multiple global and sometimes conflicting privacy rules, regulations, and guidance. Organizations need to adopt a systematic approach to addressing privacy in the cloud. Given the complexity of existing global legislation, it is advisable to seek in-country legal advice and develop a framework against which to design internal controls to manage processes, as we showed in Figure 7-1 in Chapter 7.

Cloud computing is facing a challenge that has existed for many years: how to deal with cross-border data flows. Since this involves a number of foreign jurisdictions, complexities start to develop due to conflicting rules among foreign governments (or even among various states within the United States). The nature of, and one of the major benefits of, cloud computing just expands this challenge. It is worth noting that an organization can define to the CSP in which country it would like to have its data stored and processed. However, determining which specific server or storage device will be used is difficult to ascertain due to the dynamic nature of cloud computing.

We further explored the impact of cloud computing on Organization for Economic Cooperation and Development (OECD) and other privacy principles, and we concluded that:

- The CSP requires strong data governance (managing the entire life cycle of the data from creation to destruction) to enable client organizations to respond to requests for government disclosure of data.

- Care should be taken to delete storage devices, especially as it relates to virtual storage devices where storage is constantly being reused.

- Transferring data to third parties will require consent from the data owner.

- Multiple privacy laws and regulations, such as the European Union and U.S. Safe Harbor Program, require knowledge of where data is stored at all times. This will encourage CSPs to store data on servers located in specific jurisdictions that minimize legal risk (potentially outside Europe and the United States).

- Data protection and privacy policies should be applied to data and should follow through the data's life cycle to ensure that original commitments are met and to create accountability and knowledge of what happens to data.

Organizations are expected to be responsible for knowing and managing how data is being handled and stored at all times. This becomes difficult in a cloud computing environment since IT resources are often shared and used on demand. There are a few steps that a CSP can take to improve data privacy and security. This includes improving security solutions such as IAM (restricting access), key management (encrypting data), secure event and incident monitoring (monitoring for security breaches), and data loss prevention solutions (monitoring for data breaches). The organization's privacy commitments (legal, regulatory, and contractual) should be attached to the data elements across their life cycle. There are many debates regarding who should be responsible for privacy—perhaps the CSPs?

However, it is a commonly held belief that the accountability for privacy protection falls on the organization that collected the information in the first place. To fulfill this role, it is essential for these organizations to understand the privacy and security policies and security architecture of the service the CSP is delivering, to have the right contractual arrangements in place, and to monitor the CSP's compliance. The various reporting standards we explained in Chapter 8 can help satisfy the multiple requests that organizations will have from the CSP. However, these reports tend to be generic and may not explain the specific nature of the processes and controls associated with the specific data in mind. There is a need for a globally consistent privacy standard that the CSPs will adopt and independent third parties will monitor for compliance.

It is worth noting that payroll processing has been around for a long time and data is regularly sent to payroll bureaus for processing. Such data is sensitive and contains a lot of personally identifiable information (PII). Most organizations have relied on SAS 70 reports to gain comfort regarding the processes and controls supporting the payroll process. These payroll processors have multiple customers and process a number of payrolls at the same time. The current SAS 70s, however, don't provide user organizations with comfort regarding the privacy of the data.

The risks and issues around payroll processing are very similar to concepts being introduced by cloud computing. However, since payroll processing has been around for a longer time, organizations have gotten used to relying on it for security. Granted, organizations can recalculate the accuracy of the processing, but the payroll service provider is still responsible for securing the data.

Audit and Compliance

It is clear that the CSP will face a large number of requests from its customers to prove that the CSP is secure and reliable. There a number of audit and compliance considerations for both the CSP and the customer to consider in cloud computing. First, which compliance framework should a CSP adopt to satisfy its customers and manage its own risks? The customer base will largely determine the framework that the CSP would choose. Most IT service providers are adopting a combination of ITIL, ISO 27001, and specific industry standards such as the Health Insurance Portability and Accountability Act of 1996 (HIPAA) and the Payment Card Industry (PCI). It is expected that the CSP will adopt the same approach.

It is possible that the adoption of cloud computing may impact an organization's Sarbanes-Oxley (SOX) program. At the moment, most organizations are resisting putting any data relating to financial reporting systems into cloud computing. However, email is often used as the means for communicating the authorization or approval of a control activity, and this may end up in the cloud. Alternatively, smaller organizations with finite resources may use PaaS and thereby bring software development life cycle controls into scope.

Many forms of reporting are available to satisfy these requests, as we explored in Chapter 8. The most relevant standard for the CSP to adopt would be SysTrust, or eventually, SAS 70, once new changes are made to this standard.

For the CSP to be successful it will be necessary to establish an appropriate framework of processes and controls. This framework needs to be comprehensive and globally accepted to meet the challenges of the various industry verticals. Imagine if the CSP customer is a health care provider or a bank. The requirements will be different for each and it can be expensive for a CSP to meet the various industry requirements.

A growing concept in the industry is the development of an IT Governance, Risk, and Compliance (GRC) program. The intent of such a program is to develop an IT uniformed compliance framework. A number of tools are available today that can automate this process. Such tools have:

- A library of controls covering standards such as ISO 27001, PCI, Control Objectives for Information and Related Technology (COBIT), ITIL, the National Institute of Standards and Technology (NIST), and many others

- Built-in connectors to leverage existing security tools deployed in the IT environment
- A flexible, real-time reporting engine that can report on various standards and organizational units

Figure 12-3 illustrates an overview of the capabilities of an IT GRC program and its relationship to the broader enterprise GRC. A large proportion of its function relates to security, and such programs result in the adoption of compliance dashboards that can be configured to various levels of management and show real-time compliance and an indicator of where risk exists.

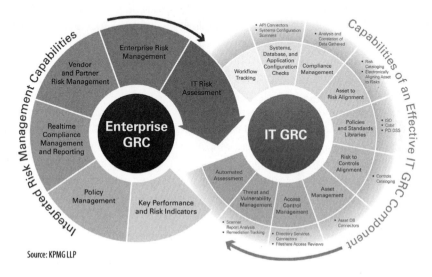

Source: KPMG LLP

FIGURE 12-3. An overview of IT GRC

Such tools can report on specific organizational units against a specific standard, or a combination of standards against a tailored framework. This would allow a CSP to reduce its cost of compliance and create a more sustainable solution. The adoption of IT GRC will allow the CSP to deliver more custom reports to reflect the standards relevant to the customer and in a timelier manner.

Security-As-a-[Cloud]-Service

Security-as-a-service is already well established in the nascent cloud computing space. In fact, it is likely to continue to grow both in terms of market share against traditionally delivered security capabilities and in terms of depth of offerings. For example, not only is the relatively new identity-as-a-service (IDaaS) a needed alternative for individual organizations, but IDaaS will become even more desirable for growing organizational types, such as increasingly multistatus organizations (i.e., employees, contractors, interns, other companies' employees, and vendors, all working in the same shared workspace), co-opetition (cooperative competition), and virtual organizations. Additionally, other important security services could be outsourced and provided in a cloud environment, such as logging, auditing, and security incident and event management (SIEM).

Security-as-a-service is likely to see significant future growth for two reasons. First, it is likely that a continuing shift in information security work from in-house to outsourced will continue. What started with email filtering and managed security services will continue and expand as organizations look to reduce capital expenditures (CapEx) further and increasingly concentrate on their core capabilities. Second, several other information security needs are present for organizations currently, but they will accelerate in need and complexity with the growing adoption of cloud computing. That growing complexity will further fuel the growth of SaaS. Specifically, we are referring to two preventive (proactive) controls and two detective (reactive) controls. The two proactive controls are also important to the growth of cloud computing: identity management that is intercloud and scalable to the cloud size, and (encryption) key management. Significant improvement in both is needed for cloud computing, and that will make potential solutions very valuable. The two reactive controls are needed for audit and compliance purposes as well: scalable and effective SIEM, and data leakage prevention (DLP). Trying to provide solutions to each of these controls will be difficult and requires significant complexity that must be hugely scalable and yet easy to use. However, all of these needs also pose significant and growing opportunities for vendors as cloud computing continues to grow in adoption.

Impact of Cloud Computing on the Role of Corporate IT

Almost certainly, many corporate IT departments will continue to be redefined by this latest model of outsourcing. As with earlier outsourcing (e.g., to large IT services firms such as CSC, EDS, and IBM Global Services, or application development to China or India), use of collocation facilities or application service providers (ASPs) and IT functions previously done in-house are moving outside corporate IT departments. With growing IT needs at the cost of growing complexity, many organizations are deciding that IT is not a core competency for their organizations and much of the IT work required to run today's organizations is being turned over to specialist companies. Cloud computing is a further example of this.

However, cloud computing is in some respects also a repudiation of traditional corporate IT departments. Business units are tired of hearing CIOs and IT departments telling them that the costs of their desired projects are excessively high and that there will be an excessive time delay until those projects can be implemented. Part of cloud computing's appeal is the speed with which business units can be up and running on their desired platform or application, along with the perceived lower costs of "pay as you go" and lack of upfront capital expenditures. As such, it really should be no surprise that the push for the use of cloud computing in most organizations is coming from business units and not from within IT. The long-standing tech mantra of better, faster, cheaper has come home to roost for corporate IT departments.

Program Guidance for CSP Customers

It is important for customers of CSPs to develop a strategy to manage the security issues mentioned earlier. We suggest that the strategy be based on developing capabilities in the manner illustrated in Figure 12-4.

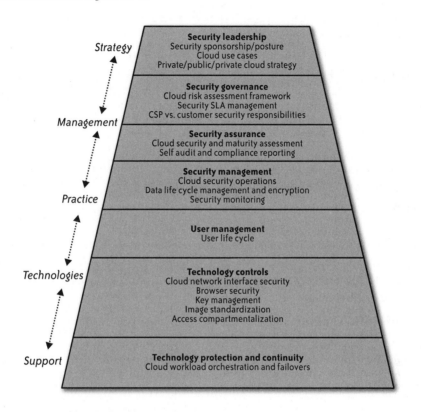

FIGURE 12-4. An enterprise security architecture for cloud computing

Let's briefly examine each component of this enterprise security architecture.

Security Leadership

Appropriate leadership needs to be involved with any strategy involving cloud computing. This applies to both CSPs and their customers. Customers are likely to have a decentralized approach as each business unit adopts its own plans for addressing the CSP. It is important to centralize this planning to ensure that consistent practices are adopted and that the maximum purchasing power is leveraged. Considerations of using the public, private, or hybrid clouds need to be standardized. Today, some customers of CSPs have IT departments whose staff members have little knowledge of how the CSPs are being used.

It is important for management to have a deep understanding of the issues around cloud computing and it is vital that they are educated on the latest solutions and challenges with cloud computing. The traditional security paradigm is different for cloud computing, so it is essential for leadership to fully understand the complexities and capabilities of solutions in the cloud. Applying traditional security techniques is not sufficient.

For CSPs, it is important to have adequate senior leadership involved in all security matters to ensure that they are appropriately addressed.

Security Governance

Another critical success factor is that appropriate governance needs to be in place. That is, is an appropriate organizational structure in place to manage the organization facing the cloud computing solution? A risk assessment framework should be adopted to ensure that consistent and reasonable practices are applied. Defining security metrics will be key to both the CSP and the customer. Each will have different perspectives and it is important to ensure that both understand their responsibilities well and none rely on each other.

Key security policies that would become critical would be the handling of data, storage of data, communication policy, vendor management (including external connections), trust reporting (i.e., how to give assurance to third parties and customers of the reliability and security of the solution), and awareness policy (both for customers and for internal users to the boundaries of responsibilities around security).

Security Assurance

Another key aspect to overcome is for the CSP to provide assurance to its customers that their operations are secure and reliable. As we discussed in Chapter 8, SAS 70 is not an adequate reporting format and CSPs will need to develop a more transparent means of gaining the confidence of their customers.

Customers of CSPs need to perform their own audits and ensure that they have the right to audit for key operations. Clearly, this will become burdensome for CSPs, so they will need to develop more assurance by becoming compliant with standards such as ITIL, ISO 27001, and others to build up confidence from the market.

Security Management

Information governance, that is, the need to have controls over the life cycle of data as we illustrated in Chapter 7, is crucial for both the CSP and its customers. One of the biggest issues is the difficulty in tracking the exact location of data during processing times; therefore, having control over its creation, storage, use, and destruction is important. Leveraging data mining tools and providing sound IT operational practices will be key to managing data.

Developing capabilities around information asset security will be challenging to CSPs. As we discussed earlier, although host-level security can be addressed, host-to-host communication and its integrity are much harder to secure due to the volume and dynamic nature of how data travels through the infrastructure. Although traditional security scanners can be deployed, it is critical to have real-time reporting around them; therefore, an IT GRC solution would assist in providing management with a "dashboard" of key metrics to provide oversight of site security and reliability.

User Management

As we illustrated in Chapter 5, identity access management can be leveraged to assist the CSP in providing access more seamlessly to its customers. However, IAM solutions today need to be enhanced to deal with having multiple CSPs providing access to the same customer. Also, these solutions need to provide the ability for self-provisioning in such a multitenancy environment. User awareness will be key, and more education is needed for the customers of CSPs to understand how the security posture will be changed with the CSP.

Technology Controls

A number of new and exciting technologies can be applied to both the CSP and its customers. A central question to ponder is who should manage the keys as they relate to the encryption of data? Can the CSP be trusted and does it have the expertise to hold the keys? Other factors to address would be browser security, image stabilization, and how access can be controlled.

Technology Protection and Continuity

CSPs provide for a resilient system; however, there will be times, perhaps due to a failure by the ISP or telecommunications carrier, when the customer may not be able to access the CSP's environment. Although most CSPs will build resiliency and redundancy into the design of their services, it is inevitable that there will be some outages. It is essential for both CSPs and their customers to have robust business and disaster recovery plans. The responsibilities for certain tasks will not be clear, so it is important for both parties to recognize who will be responsible for which part of the business continuity plan and/or the disaster recovery plan. The testing of each plan will be critical here to ensure that the right level of coordination between the CSP, ISP, and customer as well as others exists.

Overall Guidance

Overall, both customers and CSPs need to work together to mutually agree on what aspects of security will be provided and monitored by both parties to manage the risks of leveraging cloud computing, and the traditional models of security have to be retooled to address the risks of cloud computing. It has been shown that the security around the CSP can be monitored and controlled; however, it will ultimately be the responsibility of the customers of the CSP to ensure that the appropriate measures are taken and that they cannot rely on the CSP to provide a secure and reliable environment without consultation and advice from the CSP's customers.

The Future of Security in Cloud Computing

Over the course of this book, we have discussed key drivers for adoption and potential barriers, including the inherent security concerns associated with cloud computing. Let's look forward and see what potential direction security may take in the areas we just discussed.

Infrastructure Security

There is without question a need for greater transparency regarding which party (customer or CSP) provides which security capabilities, as well as greater assurance over the CSP's capabilities and efforts. It is likely that there will be increased agreement on what security capabilities each party is to provide, as well as some level of standardization across CSPs regarding CSP security capabilities with respect to specific offerings in the SPI service delivery model. It is also likely that this standardization and agreement will be reflected in operational SLAs.

In the future, identity management should be adopted to address the interrelationships between systems, services, and people. As intercloud (i.e., cloud-to-cloud) communications come into existence, due to customer demands these interrelationships will take on even greater urgency.

Data Security and Storage

Due to the nature of cloud computing (e.g., multitenancy) and the volume of data likely to be put in the cloud, data security capabilities are important for the future of cloud computing. Because of that, coupled with today's inadequate encryption and key management capabilities, cryptographic research efforts, such as predicate encryption,[#] are underway to limit the amount of data that can be decrypted for processing in the cloud. Recently announced capabilities of fully homomorphic encryption to process encrypted data should be a huge benefit to cloud computing.[*] Future commercial viability of such capabilities would be a huge benefit to cloud computing. Similar research into large-scale, multi-entity key management should also be encouraged, as it would be of enormous benefit to cloud computing.

[#] Predicate encryption is a form of asymmetric encryption where encrypted data can be selectively decrypted by different individuals (or groups) without having to decrypt all of the encrypted data. See "Predicate Encryption Supporting Disjunctions, Polynomial Equations, and Inner Products," by Jonathan Katz, Amit Sahai, and Brent Waters, at *http://eprint.iacr.org/2007/404.pdf*.

[*] See *http://www-03.ibm.com/press/us/en/pressrelease/27840.wss*.

Identity and Access Management

Today, access governance within the enterprise is a constant struggle and requires constant customization. This is compounded by the fact that no single monolithic IAM solution is available to meet the basic use cases, such as SSO, within an enterprise. Although enterprises are deploying IAM solutions to address yesterday's problems, today your business units may be adopting cloud services in an ad hoc, viral fashion. Although user-provisioning project cost overruns and failures have reduced customer expectations, federation is viewed positively and web access management, enterprise SSO, audit, and compliance have become IAM drivers. Hence, enterprises will have to rapidly reevaluate the IAM strategy approach to address IAM use cases for cloud services. With the advent of cloud-based identity services, enterprises may adopt a hybrid IAM strategy where some aspects of IAM that require architectural change migrate to cloud services while the trusted source and processes stay within the enterprise trust boundary.

When it comes to the trusted source of identities, the standard practice within enterprises is to rely on a well-established, trusted source of identity registries (e.g., an enterprise HR database for managing the identities of employees, contractors, and partners). That practice and process architecture will be challenged by new enterprises that grow with cloud services and come to rely on "everything as a service." The trusted source model will be disrupted when HR services move from controlled enterprise boundaries to cloud services (e.g., Workday for HR services). In that IT delivery model, there are a few issues to ponder: how will the trusted source manifest when the HR service is delivered from the cloud? Can we trust those services to be the authority of identities? And what new connector services will be required to manage access control and compliance in the cloud?

The "identity-aware cloud service" is another thing to watch for. When identity becomes pervasive and portable across clouds (e.g., cross-domain authentication) a new level of granular access control can be deployed across the cloud. The cross-cloud security policies should be able to map sophisticated policies that go beyond a single cloud or domain (e.g., "user x can connect to service y that connects to service z").

Today's cloud APIs are squarely focused on cloud service deployment and management, including provisioning and managing the life cycle of cloud resources (computing, storage, network). In the future, we'll see APIs encompass cloud user access management and role life cycle management functions leveraging industry standards including SAML, SPML, and XACML.

In addition to user-to-service authentication, service-to-service authentication and authorization frameworks will emerge. These frameworks will aid in delegated authorization without disclosing credentials. We are witnessing the genesis of flexible frameworks such as Microsoft claims-based authentication and the mash-up of OpenID and OAuth—a hybrid model where OpenID is used for federated login with the OAuth authorization process. In that loosely coupled model, authenticated users can be assigned a more granular artifact for authorization—a claim. This model helps developers to design applications and services so that they aren't tied to a particular credential type or to a particular set of roles. This will allow developers to externalize authentication and authorization from the application. Claims-based authentication also gives users more control as it allows users to reveal an appropriate level of user attributes based on user consent.

In this era of business consolidation where mergers and acquisitions are the norm, identity and access management solutions will become dynamic and flexible to meet the needs of a merged corporate entity or divested entities. In this scenario, the agile cloud-based identity and access processes anchored on "trusted relationships between domains" will obviate the need for any major architectural or costly implementations to reflect the changed access landscape and support new entitlement requirements.

Security Management

Today, given that a large segment of early adopters (SMBs) are solely focused on cloud service business benefits such as reduction of operational expense, elasticity, and on-demand service delivery, CSPs do not have the necessary market impetus to compete on service management support differentiators and capabilities. Enterprise customer adoption and standardization of application delivery models (compute and storage) will drive the need for fine granular instrumentation that offers a customer-specific view for services in the cloud.

To achieve a consistent service quality coupled with repeatability and predictability, customers will have no choice but to turn to automation and standardization on service management frameworks. The purported benefits of scalability and elasticity of cloud services can only be accomplished with strong management capabilities including centralized monitoring, provisioning, and configuration management practices. These practices have proven to deliver quality service for enterprise users and will continue to play a role in the cloud.

Although CSPs may not be able to offer a comprehensive set of management features and services, we believe that independent service providers (including start-ups) will be able to exploit market opportunities to deliver new cloud management services. We are witnessing the early stages of these services (e.g., Amazon's cloud watch services that offer visibility into resource utilization, operational performance, and overall demand patterns, including metrics such as CPU utilization, disk reads and writes, and network traffic). Driven by customer demand, more of these types of services will emerge, offered by either the CSP or certified third-party specialists who customize their offerings on the service provider platform. Hence, we will witness the emergence of a new breed of security-as-a-service offering that addresses security management issues including logging, security event management, vulnerability management, and incident response (e.g., Qualys's service offering of vulnerability management as a service).

Similar to the management standards that were established during the client/server computing era (e.g., Common Information Model, Java Management Extensions, Simple Network

Management Protocol, and WS-Management), we will see the emergence of cloud management standards that facilitate unified management functions across CSPs. An example is a recent initiative from the Distributed Management Task Force standards body, called the Open Cloud Standards Incubator; the objective of the group is to standardize interactions between cloud environments by developing cloud resource management protocols, packaging formats, and security mechanisms to facilitate interoperability. (The scope of this activity is limited to the cloud resource management aspects of IaaS with some work touching on PaaS, including SLAs, quality of service, utilization, provisioning, and accounting and billing.) Another effort is driven by the Open Cloud Computing Interface workgroup, which is governed by the Open Grid Forum. The group's objective is to deliver an API specification for remote management of a cloud computing infrastructure, allowing for the development of interoperable tools for common tasks including deployment, autonomic scaling, and monitoring. The scope of the specification will be the high-level functionality required for the life cycle management of VMs (or workloads) running on virtualization technologies (or containers) supporting service elasticity.

In the future, we might see other standards organizations, such as ISO, the World Wide Web Consortium (W3C), the Organization for the Advancement of Structured Information Standards (OASIS), and the Internet Engineering Task Force (IETF) initiate new efforts to standardize management protocols that interoperate with many clouds. To accelerate enterprise cloud adoption, it is imperative that cloud management standards are created that will be supported by CSPs and that facilitate seamless interoperability across disparate clouds. Similar to the client/server era, standards will help to create an ecosystem of ISVs and service providers that provide customers with choice, flexibility, and greater agility by way of automation.

Privacy

It will be essential for the CSP to understand international privacy laws to comprehend how data can be transferred from one part of the world to the other. This was a challenge during the globalization of the world economy. It is unlikely that this will be resolved without some form of government intervention or the creation of a global privacy standard that will provide consistency across jurisdictions. Such standards will help define the way businesses can leverage cloud computing.

Once cloud computing becomes more mainstream, the standard audit reports (e.g., SAS 70 Type II and SysTrust) augmented by specific requirements around privacy and security (such as the AICPA/CICA Generally Accepted Privacy Principles—GAPP) may suffice the audit concerns regarding handling of data and its privacy concerns. In the meantime, most organizations will have to rely on on-site audits, physical inspections, and reviews of security architectures until cloud computing becomes an accepted practice.

Audit and Compliance

It is likely that each CSP will define its own processes and controls (i.e., compliance), and in the short term this does not present a problem. However, as CSPs start to connect to each other and provide cross-CSP solutions, a uniform compliance framework will become more important to ensure that appropriate security measures are being consistently applied. The adoption of the IT GRC program would a good starting point to gain agreement on the adequacy of security measures since the discussion will be based on standards relevant to the CSP and its customers.

Given the volume and multitenancy of cloud computing, the compliance program for CSPs needs to be more real-time and have greater coverage than most traditional compliance programs.

Impact of Cloud Computing on the Role of Corporate IT

As adoption of cloud computing continues to grow, there will be a greater shift of IT functions and jobs from traditional corporate IT departments to CSPs. This will result not only in a downsizing of corporate IT departments, but also in a commoditization of IT functions (e.g., which CSP provides the best of service *x*) and jobs. For organizations, this will likely mean hiring fewer specialized IT personnel. Those IT personnel who are hired will likely not be actual practitioners, but managers or supervisors of the IT services provided by CSPs. It is likely that organizational costs spent on IT will decrease, as falling hardware costs will have to be passed on to customers at least partially by CSPs because of competition and fewer in-house IT personnel with skills demanding higher compensation than many other jobs. In addition, a shift in organizational payment for computing services from a centralized IT budget to business unit budgets will lead to greater efficiencies in computing services used.

This will affect the IT profession itself. Custom applications will be developed less frequently, and only in very specialized cases (i.e., narrow or niche markets). Similarly, applications will likely be less customized. (However, there will be an increased demand for and increased competition from CSPs to provide greater personalization of applications offered by CSPs.) This will lead to fewer application developer positions. It is also likely that strong pressure by customers for open systems will result in fewer proprietary systems and fewer systems using proprietary languages, such as today's use of Apex by Salesforce.com or ABAP (Advanced Business Application Program) by SAP. Similarly, corporate IT departments are likely to hire far fewer system administrators, and such responsibility will shift to CSPs. And the growing number of servers maintained by CSPs will require a greater number of system administrators to be hired, in spite of increasing use of automated tools for configuration management. (Google alone is rumored to operate about 500,000 servers. And think about how many servers can fit into the 8 million square feet of data center space in which IBM Global Services operates?) There will also be a decrease in the number of network engineers needed by corporate IT departments, and again many of those jobs will shift to CSPs.

So, the future of corporate IT departments will see significant changes. First, the relationship between business units and corporate IT departments vis-à-vis CSPs will shift. Greater power will shift to business units from IT. Second, a number of functions performed today by corporate IT departments will shift to CSPs, along with corresponding job positions. Third, the functions performed by corporate IT departments will shift from those who do (i.e., practitioners who build or operate) to those who define and manage. And fourth, IT itself will become more of a commodity as practices and skills are standardized and automated. Dan Geer famously warned of a Microsoft monoculture. That has not occurred, but there will be less proprietary technology and less computing diversity simultaneously going forward.

Summary

Looking at cloud computing, it is important to step back and keep the big picture in view. What is really new here, and what changes impact security and privacy? Remember that cloud computing is a change in business models, and not a new technology. From an information security perspective, the single biggest change with cloud computing is the use of shared resources, or multitenancy. The impact of that change is that trust boundaries have moved. The real source of concern for information security practitioners is that it is not clear where those trust boundaries are now. With each level of the SPI delivery model the trust boundaries are different, and even within each level the trust boundaries change from provider to provider.

It is also important when looking at the security afforded by CSPs to keep your current (information security practitioner) perspective in mind. For information security professionals from large enterprises looking at the security afforded by CSPs, that security may very well look weak and even unacceptable in comparison with their current (large enterprise) security posture. However, for many information security professionals from SMBs looking at the security afforded by CSPs, that security may look acceptable and even better in comparison with their current (SMB) security posture. Where you "sit" may have a significant influence on your view of the security provided by CSPs.

That being said, going forward there is definitely a need for greater transparency by CSPs regarding their security practices, and to document those efforts through auditing for the benefit of their customers. To that end, the existing, commonly used auditing framework, SAS 70, is really no longer adequate for cloud computing audit purposes. Thankfully for all, that framework is now being updated to better reflect changed needs.

However, greater transparency alone will not be sufficient for improving the levels of security that are needed in cloud computing. There need to be significant improvements in security technology as well. Those improvements are needed in both preventive (proactive) controls and detective (reactive) controls.

IAM technology is really not acceptable in today's non-cloud computing environments. IAM today fails to provide an adequate solution in enterprise environments. Attempts to leverage today's IAM technology to the cloud are bound to fail spectacularly for the reasons we discussed in Chapter 5. Significant IAM improvements are needed for cloud computing, and hopefully the IDaaS business model will spur those changes. Failure to do so will hamper the growth of public cloud computing.

Similarly, today's (encryption) key management capabilities cannot even meet today's enterprise requirements. Expecting those same technologies to scale to the cloud, and to provide easy-to-use management of complex needs, is simply wishful thinking. A radical improvement in key management capabilities is needed to meet cloud computing demands. Failure to do so will hamper the growth of cloud computing.

With regard to security monitoring, SIEM technologies are barely able to meet today's large enterprise needs. It simply is not realistic to expect that today's SIEM solutions will be able to scale to the cloud level. Additionally, the whole approach to SIEM probably needs to be revisited with regard to its ability to handle intercloud monitoring. Cloud customers are already demanding cloud portability through an open cloud API, and will shortly be demanding to use multiple clouds simultaneously. That demand for multiple cloud use simultaneously will break today's approach to SIEM.

As more and more data is put into public clouds, customers will demand greater efforts by CSPs to protect their data. Those customers who happen to be large enterprises will be looking at their own DLP efforts, and demanding the same of their CSPs. With far greater data volume transfers than their current gateways handle, and an increasing volume of encrypted network traffic, it is doubtful that today's DLP solutions will prove effective in cloud computing.

Do these deficiencies in current information security technologies mean the demise of the technologies or of cloud computing itself? No, definitely not. However, these deficiencies do mean that many customers are likely to be unsatisfied with CSP security efforts in the short term. These current deficiencies also mean an opportunity for information security vendors—and for new information security start-ups looking to shake up the current approaches that today's technologies provide.

A great part of the concern today about cloud computing security and privacy is based on unfamiliarity—it's new, and not enough people understand it well enough to make informed judgments. Real security issues for and by CSPs absolutely exist today. However, better understanding, greater transparency, and better security technology capabilities going forward mean that the hue and cry of today over the cloud's lack of security will soon fade, and will become yesterday's concern.

SAS 70 Report Content Example

THE **SAS 70 TYPE II** REPORT INCLUDES THREE REQUIRED SECTIONS: the auditor's opinion, the service organization's description of controls, and tests of operating system effectiveness and the results of those tests. The report may also include an additional section with other information provided by the service organization (provided for informational purposes but not subject to audit).[*]

Section I: Service Auditor's Opinion

The following is example SAS 70 Type II audit opinion text for a scenario in which the service organization achieves the specified control objectives. The opinion would be modified to suit the circumstances of the specific audit.[†]

> <On Audit Firm Letterhead>
>
> To XYZ Service Organization:
>
> We have examined the accompanying description of controls related to the ABC application of XYZ Service Organization. Our examination included procedures to obtain reasonable assurance about whether (1) the accompanying description presents fairly, in all material respects, the

---

[*] For additional information, refer to AICPA Audit Guide Service Organizations: Applying SAS No. 70, as Amended.

[†] AICPA Auditing Standards, Audit Standards (AU) Section 324 – Service Organizations, subsection 324.54.

aspects of XYZ Service Organization's controls that may be relevant to a user organization's internal control as it relates to an audit of financial statements, (2) the controls included in the description were suitably designed to achieve the control objectives specified in the description, if those controls were complied with satisfactorily, and (3) such controls had been placed in operation as of <Date2>. The control objectives were specified by XYZ. Our examination was performed in accordance with standards established by the American Institute of Certified Public Accountants and included those procedures we considered necessary in the circumstances to obtain a reasonable basis for rendering our opinion.

In our opinion, the accompanying description of the aforementioned application presents fairly, in all material respects, the relevant aspects of XYZ Service Organization's controls that had been placed in operation as of <Date2>. Also, in our opinion, the controls as described are suitably designed to provide reasonable assurance that the specified control objectives would be achieved if the described controls were complied with satisfactorily.

In addition to the procedures we considered necessary to render our opinion as expressed in the previous paragraph, we applied tests to specific controls, listed in Section III, to obtain evidence about their effectiveness in meeting the control objectives, described in Section III, during the period from <Date1> to <Date2>. The specific controls and the nature, timing, extent, and results of the tests are listed in Section III. This information has been provided to user organizations of XYZ Service Organization and to their auditors to be taken into consideration, along with information about the internal control at user organizations, when making assessments of control risk for user organizations. In our opinion, the controls that were tested, as described in Section III, were operating with sufficient effectiveness to provide reasonable, but not absolute, assurance that the control objectives specified in Section III were achieved during the period from <Date1> to <Date2>.

The relative effectiveness and significance of specific controls at XYZ Service Organization and their effect on assessments of control risk at user organizations are dependent on their interaction with the controls and other factors present at individual user organizations. We have performed no procedures to evaluate the effectiveness of controls at individual user organizations.

The description of controls at XYZ Service Organization is as of <Date2>, and information about tests of the operating effectiveness of specific controls covers the period from <Date1> to <Date2>. Any projection of such information to the future is subject to the risk that, because of change, the description may no longer portray the controls in existence. The potential effectiveness of specific controls at the Service Organization is subject to inherent limitations and, accordingly, errors or fraud may occur and not be detected. Furthermore, the projection of any conclusions, based on our findings, to future periods is subject to the risk that changes may alter the validity of such conclusions.

The information in Section IV of this report is presented by XYZ Service Organization to provide additional information and is not a part of the XYZ Service Organization's description of controls placed in operation. The information in Section IV has not been subjected to the procedures applied in the examination of the description of the controls applicable to the processing of transactions for user organizations and, accordingly, we express no opinion on it.

This report is intended solely for use by the management of XYZ Service Organization, its customers, and the independent auditors of its customers.

Signed – Audit Firm Name

Date

Section II: Description of Controls

The service organization's description of controls typically includes narrative descriptions of the following components:

- Overview of operations
- Description of services provided by the service organization that are covered in the report
- Control objectives and supporting control activities
- Control environment, risk assessment processes, and monitoring processes
- Information systems and communication processes
- User control considerations (i.e., controls that users of the service organization should have in place to address their responsibilities with regard to controls over the service)

Section III: Control Objectives, Related Controls, and Tests of Operating Effectiveness

This section details the service organization's control objectives and supporting control activities that form the scope of the SAS 70 examination. This information is considered part of the service organization's description of controls and may be explicitly included in Section II of the report or incorporated by reference. Section III also details the test procedures performed by the auditor and the results of those test procedures. The following is an example of how the testing of control-specific activities is typically presented in the SAS 70 Type II report. It is not intended to represent a complete set of control activities to meet the specified control objective.

Control objective X: Logical access

Service Organization XYZ maintains controls to provide reasonable assurance that access to the ABC system and data is limited to properly authorized individuals

Description of controls	Auditor's tests of operating effectiveness	Results of auditor's tests of operating effectiveness
There is a formal process for granting and revoking access to XYZ information systems and services. Access to information systems is based on a valid business reason for access and is commensurate with the user's requirements. Privileged operating system access to production systems is restricted to authorized individuals	Inquired of relevant personnel and inspected the Security Policy to gain an understanding of the process for granting and revoking access to XYZ information systems and services Inspected a selection of users with administrative access to a selection of production servers to determine whether privileged accounts were allocated in accordance with XYZ's system access requirements Inspected user access lists for a selection of systems and compared with a selection of employees hired during the audit period to determine whether system access was granted based on job responsibilities Inspected user access lists for a selection of systems and compared with a selection of employees terminated during the audit period to determine whether system access was revoked per policy requirements	No exceptions noted
Procedures require that default operating system accounts, passwords, and other security parameters be changed in accordance with XYZ's operating system configuration standards	Inquired of relevant personnel and inspected XYZ's operating system build standards to gain an understanding of XYZ's operating system configuration standards Inspected user account configurations for a selection of servers to determine whether default account settings were changed in accordance with XYZ's operating system configuration standards	No exceptions noted
Authorized XYZ personnel are permitted to administer production servers and network devices by authenticating first to the ABC network, then to a bastion host, and then to the relevant server or network device	Inquired of relevant personnel and inspected security policies and procedures to obtain an understanding of administrator access restrictions Inspected firewall configurations to determine whether access to production servers and network devices is limited to specific hosts and networks	No exceptions noted

Description of controls	Auditor's tests of operating effectiveness	Results of auditor's tests of operating effectiveness
	Inspected the user access list for the bastion host to determine whether access is restricted to appropriate personnel	

This example is for illustrative purposes only and does not contain all the control activities that would be required to achieve the control objective.

Section IV: Additional Information Provided by the Service Organization

Other information that was not subject to audit may be included in this informational section of the report. For example, the service organization may choose to include a description of its business continuity/disaster recovery processes in this section of the report.

SysTrust Report Content Example

WITH A SYSTRUST EXAMINATION, THERE IS AN AUDITOR'S OPINION. In addition, the service provider provides a management assertion and a system description that are attached to the auditor's opinion to form the SysTrust reporting package. Optionally, the reporting package can also include a schedule of controls that the service provider has implemented to address the Trust Services criteria.

SysTrust Auditor's Opinion[*]

<On Audit Firm Letterhead>

To the Management of XYZ Service Provider, Inc.:

We have examined management's assertion that XYZ Service Provider during the period <Date1> through <Date2> maintained effective controls over the ABC System to provide reasonable assurance that its System was reliable based on the AICPA/CICA Trust Services Criteria for Systems Reliability. This assertion is the responsibility of XYZ Service Provider's management. Our responsibility is to express an opinion based on our examination.

A reliable system is one that is capable of operating without material error, fault, or failure during a specified period in a specified environment. The AICPA/CICA Trust Services Availability,

---

[*] American Institute of Certified Public Accountants (AICPA), Trust Services Principles, Criteria and Illustrations for Security, Availability, Processing Integrity, Confidentiality, and Privacy (Including WebTrust® and SysTrust®), 2006. Available at *http://www.webtrust.org*. [Trust Services Principles]

Security, and Processing Integrity Criteria are used to evaluate whether XYZ Service Provider's controls over the reliability of its System are effective.

Our examination was conducted in accordance with attestation standards established by the American Institute of Certified Public Accountants and, accordingly, included (1) obtaining an understanding of XYZ Service Provider's relevant system availability, security, and processing integrity controls; (2) testing and evaluating the operating effectiveness of the controls; and (3) performing such other procedures as we considered necessary in the circumstances. We believe that our examination provides a reasonable basis for our opinion.

In our opinion, management's assertion that XYZ Service Provider maintained effective controls over the reliability of its ABC System to provide reasonable assurance that, during the period <Date1> through <Date2>, based on the AICPA/CICA Trust Services Criteria for Systems Reliability, the System:

> Was protected against unauthorized access (both physical and logical)
> Was available for operation and use, as committed or agreed
> Processing was complete, accurate, timely, and authorized

was fairly stated in all material respects.

Because of inherent limitations in controls, error or fraud may occur and not be detected. Furthermore, the projection of any conclusions, based on our findings, to future periods is subject to the risk that the validity of such conclusions may be altered because of changes made to the system or controls, the failure to make needed changes to the system or controls, or a deterioration in the degree of effectiveness of the controls.

XYZ Service Provider's use of the SysTrust Seal constitutes a symbolic representation of the contents of this report and it is not intended, nor should it be construed, to update this report or provide any additional assurance.

Signed – Audit Firm Name

Date

SysTrust Management Assertion

<On Service Provider XYZ Letterhead>

Service Provider XYZ maintained effective controls over the security, availability, and processing integrity of its ABC System to provide reasonable assurance that:

> The System was protected against unauthorized access (both physical and logical)
> The System was available for operation and use, as committed or agreed
> System processing was complete, accurate, timely, and authorized

during the period <Date1> to <Date2>, based on the Trust Services Criteria for security, availability, and processing integrity established by the American Institute of Certified Public Accountants (AICPA) and the Canadian Institute of Chartered Accountants (CICA).

The attached System Description of Service Provider XYZ's ABC System identifies the aspects of the System covered by our assertion.

SysTrust System Description

The service provider's System Description typically includes narrative descriptions of the following components to provide clarity regarding the examination scope:

- Background
- Infrastructure
- Software
- People
- Procedures
- Data

SysTrust Schedule of Controls

If desired, the service provider may include a detailed schedule of controls that describes the controls it has implemented to achieve the Trust Services Criteria. An extract of such a schedule is shown here for illustrative purposes.[†]

Security principle		
The system is protected against unauthorized access (both physical and logical)		
Criteria reference	**Security criteria**	**XYZ's description of controls**
1.0 policies	The entity defined and documented its policies for the security of its system	
1.1 policies	The entity's security policies are established and periodically reviewed and approved by a designated individual or group	The company's documented systems development and acquisition process includes procedures to identify and document authorized users of the system and their security requirements
		User requirements are documented in service-level agreements or other documents
		The chief security officer (CSO) reviews security policies annually and submits proposed

[†] Trust Services Principles.

Criteria reference	Security criteria	XYZ's description of controls
		changes for approval by the information technology standards committee
1.2 policies	The entity's security policies include, but may not be limited to, the following matters: • Identifying and documenting the security requirements of authorized users • Allowing access, and determining the nature of that access and who authorizes such access • Preventing unauthorized access • Developing the procedures to add new users, modify the access levels of existing users, and remove users who no longer need access • Assigning responsibility and accountability for system security • Assigning responsibility and accountability for system changes and maintenance • Testing, evaluating, and authorizing system components before implementation • Addressing how complaints and requests relating to security issues are resolved • Developing the procedures to handle security breaches and other incidents • Providing for allocation of training and other resources to support its system security policies • Providing for the handling of exceptions and situations not specifically addressed in its system security policies • Providing for the identification of and consistency with applicable laws and regulations, defined commitments, service-level agreements, and other contracts	The company's Information Security Policy contains the elements set out in criterion 1.2
1.3 policies	Assuming responsibility and ensuring that accountability for the entity's system security	Management has assigned responsibilities for the maintenance and enforcement of the company security policy to the chief security

Criteria reference	Security criteria	XYZ's description of controls
	policies, and changes and updates to those policies, are assigned	officer (CSO). Others on the executive committee assist in the review, update, and approval of the policy as outlined in the executive committee handbook
		Ownership and custody of significant information resources (e.g., data, programs, and transactions) and responsibility for establishing and maintaining security over such resources are defined

This schedule is for illustrative purposes only and does not contain all the criteria for the Security Principle.

Open Security Architecture for Cloud Computing

WITH PUBLIC CLOUD COMPUTING, PART OF YOUR INFRASTRUCTURE AND YOUR TRUST boundary moves to a third-party provider. Maintaining consistent security across boundaries is complex and challenging for information security professionals. Evolving public cloud services will likely be complex webs and dependent on not only providers but also providers to providers. In fact, the SaaS service you receive may be provided by another IaaS provider (e.g., backup services using Amazon's S3). The chain of dependencies may not be obvious, and the current lack of transparency from cloud service providers (CSPs) will make it difficult to comprehend the risks that come with the benefits. Most importantly, the lack of industry-standard controls to assess cloud risks, and lack of a baseline to benchmark the consumed cloud services, can result in operational inefficiencies and weaken compliance management.

You must carefully consider a number of control areas before you move computing operations to a CSP, since services provided are not under direct control of the customer. Risk management in cloud computing is an evolving area, and standards are being debated by the community. Given the current lack of agreed upon standards across providers, it is unlikely that customer requirements for mitigating controls to manage risk will translate into the control framework of CSPs. Therefore, it is unlikely that CSPs will directly implement controls specified by customers. It is more likely that CSPs will refer their control framework to existing standards such as SAS 70, SysTrust, and ISO 27001.

The Open Security Architecture cloud computing pattern is an attempt to illustrate core cloud functions, the key roles for oversight and risk mitigation, collaboration across various internal organizations, and the controls that require additional emphasis. For example, the Certification, Accreditation (CA), and Security Assessments (SA) series increase in importance to ensure oversight and assurance given that the operations are being "outsourced" to another provider. SA-1/4/5 (System and Services Acquisition) is crucial to ensure that acquisition of services is managed correctly. CP-1 (contingency planning) helps to ensure a clear understanding of how to respond in the event of interruptions to service delivery. The Risk Assessments controls are important to understand the risks associated with services in a business context—but may be challenging to implement, depending on the supplier and the degree of visibility into their operations. The pattern also provides a view into activities that are shared by security architects, security managers, and business managers—that is, they need to collaborate and jointly agree on the controls required to mitigate risk.

We believe that risk assessment, controls, and compliance management frameworks will continue to evolve with cloud computing delivery models (SaaS, PaaS, IaaS), business models (public, private, hybrid), provider maturity, and the degree of visibility into their operations. Hence, readers are encouraged to frequently revisit this and other evolving frameworks, and adjust their internal risk models and processes in managing mitigating controls.

The following figure shows one model, from the Open Security Architecture (*http://www .opensecurityarchitecture.org*) group, of what the relationship of these controls looks like in public cloud computing.

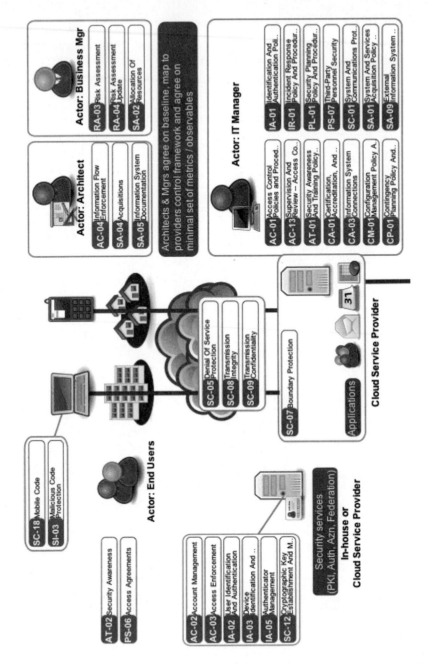

Architects & Mgrs agree on baseline, map to providers control framework and agree on minimal set of metrics / observables

Actor: Business Mgr

RA-03	Risk Assessment
RA-04	Risk Assessment Update
SA-02	Allocation Of Resources

Actor: Architect

AC-04	Information Flow Enforcement
SA-04	Acquisitions
SA-05	Information System Documentation

Actor: IT Manager

AC-01	Access Control Policies and Proced..
AC-13	Supervision And Review -- Access Co..
AT-01	Security Awareness And Training Policy
CA-01	Certification, Accreditation, And ..
CA-03	Information System Connections
CM-01	Configuration Management Policy A..
CP-01	Contingency Planning Policy And..

IA-01	Identification And Authentication Pol..
IR-01	Incident Response Policy And Procedur..
PL-01	Security Planning Policy And Procedur..
PS-07	Third-Party Personnel Security
SC-01	System And Communications Prot..
SA-01	System And Services Acquisition Policy ..
SA-09	External Information System ..

Actor: End Users

SC-18	Mobile Code
SI-03	Malicious Code Protection

AT-02	Security Awareness
PS-06	Access Agreements

AC-02	Account Management
AC-03	Access Enforcement
IA-02	User Identification And Authentication
IA-03	Device Identification And ..
IA-05	Authenticator Management
SC-12	Cryptographic Key Establishment And M..

Cloud Service Provider

SC-05	Denial Of Service Protection
SC-08	Transmission Integrity
SC-09	Transmission Confidentiality

SC-07	Boundary Protection

Applications

Security services (PKI, Auth, Azn, Federation)

In-house or Cloud Service Provider

(Continued.)

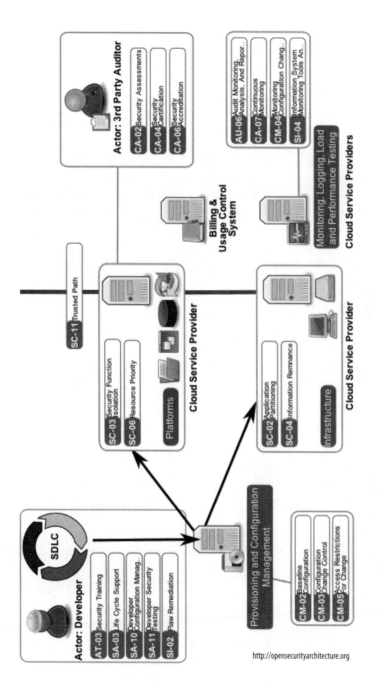

Actor: 3rd Party Auditor

- CA-02 Security Assessments
- CA-04 Security Certification
- CA-06 Security Accreditation

Cloud Service Providers

- AU-06 Audit Monitoring, Analysis, And Repor...
- CA-07 Continuous Monitoring
- CM-04 Monitoring Configuration Chang...
- SI-04 Information System Monitoring Tools An...

Monitoring, Logging, Load and Performance Testing

Billing & Usage Control System

SC-11 Trusted Path

Cloud Service Provider

- SC-03 Security Function Isolation
- SC-06 Resource Priority

Platforms

Cloud Service Provider

- SC-02 Application Partitioning
- SC-04 Information Remnance

Infrastructure

SDLC

Actor: Developer

- AT-03 Security Training
- SA-03 Life Cycle Support
- SA-10 Developer Configuration Manag...
- SA-11 Developer Security Testing
- SI-02 Flaw Remediation

Provisioning and Configuration Management

- CM-02 Baseline Configuration
- CM-03 Configuration Change Control
- CM-05 Access Restrictions For Change

http://opensecurityarchitecture.org

The following text explains the figure. It was taken from the Open Security Architecture website at *http://www.opensecurityarchitecture.org/cms/library/pattern_landscape/251-pattern-cloud-computing*.

Legend

Services provided by the cloud computing environment are not under direct control and therefore a few control families become more significant. Controls in the CA series increase in importance to ensure oversight and assurance, given that the operations are being "outsourced" to another provider. SA-1/4/5 are crucial to ensure that acquisition of services are managed correctly. CP-1 helps ensure a clear understanding of how to respond in the event of interruptions to service delivery. The RA controls are very important to understand the risks associated with the service in a business context, but may be challenging to implement, depending on the supplier and the degree of visibility into their operations.

Description

Cloud computing can be defined as the provision of computing services via the Internet such as:

- Applications (software-as-a-service, or SaaS)
- Platforms
- Infrastructure (IaaS)
- Process orchestration and integration

The cloud model is of great interest to service providers because it likely represents the next great wave of innovation sweeping across the Internet and presents tremendous business opportunities for those who can successfully define and implement the new paradigm. End users are interested because services are reasonably priced and can be accessed from any browser, giving access to the computing environment from any location and making collaboration much easier. Corporate IT departments are interested because the model reduces capital investments, removes constraints on power and space, may deliver much faster development and implementation times, and promises to simplify the management of complex environments.

So should it be a simple decision to scrap the legacy environments and move to the cloud? Well, for many use cases, especially private end users and Small to Medium Enterprises (SMEs), the risk versus reward is strongly in favor of adopting relevant new cloud services as they become available. However, for large organizations, especially those in regulated sectors, the decision is not so simple.

Key Control Areas

There are a number of control areas that you must consider carefully before you move computing operations to cloud services:

Contractual agreements

Who owns the data, what rights or recourse do you have for security breaches or incidents, what happens when you want to move to another provider?

Certification and third-party audits

Is the provider certified, e.g., SAS 70 (remember the scope of a SAS 70 will determine how must trust you can place in it), and can you request independent audits of the facilities and operations?

Compliance requirements

Do they meet your organisations compliance needs? E.g., data privacy, safe harbor. Where are the operations located, and where would your data reside? Be aware that providers will need to obey law enforcement regulations in their operating locations, and may be obliged to disclose data without your consent to government and law enforcement agencies if requested.

Availability, reliability, and resilience

What happens when the service is not available? What are the points where you need additional resilience for access?

Backup and recovery

In the event of a physical or logical disaster, what are the Recovery Point and Recovery Time Objectives (RPO/RTO) that you will need and they will provide?

Service levels and performance

What do they offer, and what do you need? What happens if the service is below expectations? Remember a service may be available but have an unacceptable performance level or response times.

Decommissioning

Will data be securely deleted once it is no longer needed? What about the virtual machines or processes you are using? Will fragments reside client-side in your browser that you need to be aware of?

A key activity that is shared by the architect, the security manager, and the business manager is to jointly agree on the controls required. They should:

- Agree on the control baseline applicable to this cloud sourcing activity/service.
- Confirm how this translates into the control framework of the cloud provider because, unlike regular supplier contracting, it is very improbable that the cloud provider will directly implement the controls specified by the customer. It is more likely that the cloud

service provider will refer to his standard (PCI DSS-adherent, NIST-adherent or ISO-adherent) control framework.

- Decide on additional risk mitigating controls.

You will likely need supporting services if your process is comprised of a number of cloud services. Some of the important ones to consider are:

- Security (OpenID, .NET Access Control, PKI), billing (DevPay)
- Load monitoring and testing (SOASTA, Hyperic)
- Provisioning and configuration management (RightScale)

This is an evolving area, and standards for integration are still emerging. Maintaining a security context across a number of separate cloud providers can be a real challenge! Especially when you consider that you likely want to use roles to manage authorisation to different functions. There is a good case for maintaining your own directory and federation services that you will use to provide authentication across in-house and cloud services. Where possible, it is recommended to abstract the authentication and authorization services behind industry standard interfaces such as SAML.

Cloud services will likely be complex webs, and the service you receive may in fact be provided by another cloud provider (e.g., Box.net uses Amazon S3). This became apparent when an Amazon S3 outage affected a number of services that had been built using Amazon for storage. The chain of dependencies may not be obvious, so make checks according to the criticality of your requirements. If creating custom code elements, the developer constantly needs to consider code refactoring to keep the code base as simple as possible and hence mitigate what is frequently the biggest overall IT risk: complexity.

Examples

Applications/SaaS include:

SaaS
> Salesforce.com, Google Docs, Facebook, LinkedIn, Doodle

Platform service providers include:

Content
> SpringCM, Xythos On Demand, Google Base

Platform-as-a-service
> Force.com, Google App Engine, Bungee Labs Connect, Etelos, Intiuit QuickBase, LongJump, Apprenda SaaSGrid, Oracle Platform for SaaS, MS Azure

Data
> Amazon S3, Box.net, Google Base, Amazon SimpleDB, TrackVia, Microsoft SSDS

Infrastructure as a service include:

Cloud providers
IBM Blue Cloud, Joyent, GoGrid, Sun Grid, Amazon EC2

Examples of Integration and Orchestration include:

Integration
Boomi, Mule On Demand, OpSource Connect (OSB), Amazon SQS, Microsoft BizTalk Services

Orchestration
ProcessMaker, Appian Anywhere, Skemma, Intensil

Billing and contract management
OpSource/LeCayla, Aria, eVapt, Amazon DevPay, Zuora

Security
OpenID, OAuth, Ping Identity

Cloud deployment
rPath, CohesiveFT, VMware, Xen, Parallels, BEA WebLogic Server VE, 3tera AppLogic, Elastra Cloud Server

Assumptions

Cloud computing is an evolving area, and it is expected that this pattern will be revised within a year to reflect developments. It is likely that for large corporations a prudent and realistic strategy will be to deploy for test and development environments, which give some benefits without the downside of exposing production data sets.

Typical Challenges

- Trustworthiness of partner—how to establish and track?
- Lack of certainty on many aspects of controls required.
- Compliance.
- Ability to move to other providers.
- Authentication and authorization across multiple providers and systems.

Indications

The organization will provide some or all of their computing environment via cloud services. The organization has constraints on existing power or space, a desire to reduce capital expenditure, a need to provision services rapidly, big variations in computing demand, and collaboration with a wide range of B2B partners.

Contraindications

Lack of understanding of your compliance needs or inability to confirm how the supplier will meet your requirements.

Resistance Against Threats

Untrustworthy supplier, eavesdropping, impersonation, data theft, lack of performance, and logical and physical disasters are addressed by this pattern. Consider checking supplier applications for cross-site scripting (XSS) attacks, which can be used to log keystrokes, capture data, and propagate web application worms such as Samy. Feed injection for RSS and Atom can allow an attacker to compromise applications, if feeds are not properly secured.

References

MS Azure presentation gives useful information on threats and broader considerations when using the cloud:

> *http://www.slideshare.net/davidcchou/microsoft-cloud-services-architecture-presentation?type=powerpoint*

Developer perspective:

> *http://blog.smashedapples.com/cloud_services/*

Hoff's security blog covers cloud security along with many other topics:

> *http://rationalsecurity.typepad.com/*

Google Apps Type II SAS 70:

> *http://googleenterprise.blogspot.com/2008/11/sas-70-type-ii-for-google-apps.html*

The cloud security blog from Craig Balding is a nice technical and news resource:

> *http://cloudsecurity.org/*

All other major vendors have their own literature and approaches—just search on Google!

Relevant technologies that underpin cloud service provision:

- AJAX (Asynchronous JavaScript with XML) is a mechanism for exchanging data between browser and server without refreshing the page.
- RSS (Really Simple Syndication) allows publication of and subscription to frequently changing content.

- JSON (JavaScript Object Notation) is a lightweight method to pass serialised data when using JavaScript and provides an alternative to XML.
- Flash/Flex/Air/Silverlight/Gears are client-side programming and runtime execution environments that provide a richer browser experience.
- SOAP (Simple Object Access Protocol) is a method for remote procedure calls using XML over HTTP.
- REST (REpresentational State Transfer) is a simple architectural style that transfers state information via HTTP resource requests.

Related patterns: Identity management

Classification: Cloud computing

Release: 08.02

Authors: Phaedrus

Reviewer(s): Tobias, Spinoza

Control Details

AC-01 Access Control Policies and Procedures (*http://www.opensecurityarchitecture.org/cms/library/08_02_control-catalogue/23-08_02_AC-01*)

AC-02 Account Management (*http://www.opensecurityarchitecture.org/cms/library/08_02_control-catalogue/24-08_02_AC-02*)

AC-03 Access Enforcement (*http://www.opensecurityarchitecture.org/cms/library/08_02_control-catalogue/25-08_02_AC-03*)

AC-04 Information Flow Enforcement (*http://www.opensecurityarchitecture.org/cms/library/08_02_control-catalogue/26-08_02_AC-04*)

AC-13 Supervision And Review—Access Control (*http://www.opensecurityarchitecture.org/cms/library/08_02_control-catalogue/35-08_02_AC-13*)

AT-01 Security Awareness And Training Policy And Procedures (*http://www.opensecurityarchitecture.org/cms/library/08_02_control-catalogue/167-08_02_AT-01*)

AT-02 Security Awareness (*http://www.opensecurityarchitecture.org/cms/library/08_02_control-catalogue/168-08_02_AT-02*)

AT-03 Security Training (*http://www.opensecurityarchitecture.org/cms/library/08_02_control-catalogue/169-08_02_AT-03*)

AU-06 Audit Monitoring, Analysis, And Reporting (*http://www.opensecurityarchitecture.org/cms/library/08_02_control-catalogue/175-08_02_AU-06*)

CA-01 Certification, Accreditation, And Security Assessment Policies And Procedures (*http:// www.opensecurityarchitecture.org/cms/library/08_02_control-catalogue/160-08_02_CA-01*)

CA-02 Security Assessments (*http://www.opensecurityarchitecture.org/cms/library/08_02_control -catalogue/161-08_02_CA-02*)

CA-03 Information System Connections (*http://www.opensecurityarchitecture.org/cms/library/08 _02_control-catalogue/162-08_02_CA-03*)

CA-04 Security Certification (*http://www.opensecurityarchitecture.org/cms/library/08_02_control -catalogue/163-08_02_CA-04*)

CA-06 Security Accreditation (*http://www.opensecurityarchitecture.org/cms/library/08_02_control -catalogue/165-08_02_CA-06*)

CA-07 Continuous Monitoring (*http://www.opensecurityarchitecture.org/cms/library/08_02_control -catalogue/166-08_02_CA-07*)

CM-01 Configuration Management Policy And Procedures (*http://www.opensecurityarchitecture .org/cms/library/08_02_control-catalogue/152-08_02_CM-01*)

CM-02 Baseline Configuration (*http://www.opensecurityarchitecture.org/cms/library/08_02_control -catalogue/153-08_02_CM-02*)

CM-03 Configuration Change Control (*http://www.opensecurityarchitecture.org/cms/library/08_02 _control-catalogue/154-08_02_CM-03*)

CM-04 Monitoring Configuration Changes (*http://www.opensecurityarchitecture.org/cms/library/ 08_02_control-catalogue/155-08_02_CM-04*)

CM-05 Access Restrictions For Change (*http://www.opensecurityarchitecture.org/cms/library/08_02 _control-catalogue/156-08_02_CM-05*)

CP-01 Contingency Planning Policy And Procedures (*http://www.opensecurityarchitecture.org/ cms/library/08_02_control-catalogue/142-08_02_CP-01*)

IA-01 Identification And Authentication Policy And Procedures (*http://www .opensecurityarchitecture.org/cms/library/08_02_control-catalogue/181-08_02_IA-01*)

IA-02 User Identification And Authentication (*http://www.opensecurityarchitecture.org/cms/ library/08_02_control-catalogue/22-08_02_IA-02*)

IA-03 Device Identification And Authentication (*http://www.opensecurityarchitecture.org/cms/ library/08_02_control-catalogue/182-08_02_IA-03*)

IA-05 Authenticator Management (*http://www.opensecurityarchitecture.org/cms/library/08_02 _control-catalogue/184-08_02_IA-05*)

IR-01 Incident Response Policy And Procedures (*http://www.opensecurityarchitecture.org/cms/ library/08_02_control-catalogue/135-08_02_IR-01*)

PL-01 Security Planning Policy And Procedures (*http://www.opensecurityarchitecture.org/cms/library/08_02_control-catalogue/89-08_02_PL-01*)

PS-06 Access Agreements (*http://www.opensecurityarchitecture.org/cms/library/08_02_control-catalogue/119-08_02_PS-06*)

PS-07 Third-Party Personnel Security (*http://www.opensecurityarchitecture.org/cms/library/08_02_control-catalogue/120-08_02_PS-07*)

RA-03 Risk Assessment (*http://www.opensecurityarchitecture.org/cms/library/08_02_control-catalogue/86-08_02_RA-03*)

RA-04 Risk Assessment Update (*http://www.opensecurityarchitecture.org/cms/library/08_02_control-catalogue/87-08_02_RA-04*)

SA-01 System And Services Acquisition Policy And Procedures (*http://www.opensecurityarchitecture.org/cms/library/08_02_control-catalogue/51-08_02_SA-01*)

SA-02 Allocation Of Resources (*http://www.opensecurityarchitecture.org/cms/library/08_02_control-catalogue/52-08_02_SA-02*)

SA-03 Life Cycle Support (*http://www.opensecurityarchitecture.org/cms/library/08_02_control-catalogue/53-08_02_SA-03*)

SA-04 Acquisitions (*http://www.opensecurityarchitecture.org/cms/library/08_02_control-catalogue/54-08_02_SA-04*)

SA-05 Information System Documentation (*http://www.opensecurityarchitecture.org/cms/library/08_02_control-catalogue/55-08_02_SA-05*)

SA-09 External Information System Services (*http://www.opensecurityarchitecture.org/cms/library/08_02_control-catalogue/59-08_02_SA-09*)

SA-10 Developer Configuration Management (*http://www.opensecurityarchitecture.org/cms/library/08_02_control-catalogue/60-08_02_SA-10*)

SA-11 Developer Security Testing (*http://www.opensecurityarchitecture.org/cms/library/08_02_control-catalogue/249-08-02-SA-11*)

SC-01 System And Communications Protection Policy And Procedures (*http://www.opensecurityarchitecture.org/cms/library/08_02_control-catalogue/61-08_02_SC-01*)

SC-02 Application Partitioning (*http://www.opensecurityarchitecture.org/cms/library/08_02_control-catalogue/62-08_02_SC-02*)

SC-03 Security Function Isolation (*http://www.opensecurityarchitecture.org/cms/library/08_02_control-catalogue/63-08_02_SC-03*)

SC-04 Information Remnance (*http://www.opensecurityarchitecture.org/cms/library/08_02_control-catalogue/64-08_02_SC-04*)

SC-05 Denial Of Service Protection (*http://www.opensecurityarchitecture.org/cms/library/08_02 _control-catalogue/65-08_02_SC-05*)

SC-06 Resource Priority (*http://www.opensecurityarchitecture.org/cms/library/08_02_control -catalogue/66-08_02_SC-06*)

SC-07 Boundary Protection (*http://www.opensecurityarchitecture.org/cms/library/08_02_control -catalogue/67-08_02_SC-07*)

SC-08 Transmission Integrity (*http://www.opensecurityarchitecture.org/cms/library/08_02_control -catalogue/68-08_02_SC-08*)

SC-09 Transmission Confidentiality (*http://www.opensecurityarchitecture.org/cms/library/08_02 _control-catalogue/69-08_02_SC-09*)

SC-11 Trusted Path (*http://www.opensecurityarchitecture.org/cms/library/08_02_control-catalogue/ 71-08_02_SC-11*)

SC-12 Cryptographic Key Establishment And Management (*http://www.opensecurityarchitecture .org/cms/library/08_02_control-catalogue/72-08_02_SC-12*)

SC-18 Mobile Code (*http://www.opensecurityarchitecture.org/cms/library/08_02_control-catalogue/ 78-08_02_SC-18*)

SI-02 Flaw Remediation (*http://www.opensecurityarchitecture.org/cms/library/08_02_control -catalogue/40-08_02_SI-02*)

SI-03 Malicious Code Protection (*http://www.opensecurityarchitecture.org/cms/library/08_02 _control-catalogue/41-08_02_SI-03*)

SI-04 Information System Monitoring Tools And Techniques (*http://www .opensecurityarchitecture.org/cms/library/08_02_control-catalogue/42-08_02_SI-04*)

AAA

Authentication, Authorization, and Accounting is a system used to control what computer resources users have access to and to keep track of the activity of users over a network.

Active Directory

A directory service from Microsoft.

Apex

An on-demand platform from Salesforce.com. Apex provides a set of features for building business applications using a proprietary language called Apex code.

API

An *application programming interface* is a series of software routines and development tools that comprise an interface between a computer application and lower-level services and functions (such as the operating system, device drivers, and other software applications). APIs serve as building blocks for programmers putting together software applications. In the context of cloud computing, APIs are sets of web services

methods for accessing/manipulating cloud resources.

ASP

An *application service provider* is a business that provides computer-based services to customers over a network.

Asymmetric encryption

The use of two different keys, first for encryption (public key) and then for decryption (private key) of data.

Authentication

The act of confirming the identity of an individual or system.

Authorization

The act of specifying access rights to resources or functionality.

AWS

Amazon Web Services is a collection of infrastructure web services delivered over the Internet by Amazon.com.

CCID

The Cloud Computing Incidents Database (CCID) records and monitors verifiable, noteworthy events that affect cloud computing providers, such as outages, security issues, and breaches, both as they are happening and on an ongoing historical basis.

CSP

A *cloud service provider* is a provider of cloud computing services.

DLP

Data loss prevention refers to systems that identify, monitor, and protect data-in-use, data-in-motion, and data-at-rest through deep content inspection and with a centralized management framework.

DMZ

A computer or small subnetwork that sits between a trusted internal network, such as a corporate private LAN, and an untrusted external network, such as the public Internet.

DoS, DDoS

Denial of service, or *distributed denial of service*, is a type of network-based attack that attempts to make computer or network resources unavailable to their intended users.

EC2

The *Elastic Compute Cloud* is an AWS commercial web service that allows customers to rent computers on which to run their own computer applications.

EU

The *European Union* is an economic and political union of 27 member states, located in Europe.

Federated identity

A practice for establishing trust with multiple parties by sharing user identity and attributes with multiple parties with multiple trust levels.

GLBA

The *Gramm-Leach-Bliley Act* was enacted by the U.S. Congress in 1999 and requires that financial institutions perform risk management of non-public information,

implement an information security program, including periodic monitoring and testing of the program, and update safeguards as needed with changes in how information is collected, stored, and used.

GRC

Governance, Risk, and Compliance is an increasingly recognized term that reflects a way in which organizations can adopt an integrated approach to these three areas.

HIPAA

The *Health Insurance Portability and Accountability Act* was enacted by the U.S. Congress in 1996 and requires entities that process protected health information to comply with security and privacy requirements.

Hybrid cloud

An environment consisting of internal or external providers where an organization may run non-core applications in a public cloud, while maintaining core applications and sensitive data in-house in a private cloud.

Hypervisor

A software/hardware platform virtualization system that allows multiple operating systems to run on a host computer concurrently.

IaaS

Infrastructure-as-a-service is the delivery of computer infrastructure as a service.

IDaaS

Identity-as-a-service refers to the practice of delivering identity management as a service.

IdM, IAM

Identity management or *identity and access management* is the management of the identity life cycle.

IdP

An *identity provider* is a service provider that creates, maintains, and manages identity information and asserts identities to other service providers within a federation.

IDS

An *intrusion detection system* is software or hardware designed to detect unwanted attempts at accessing, manipulating, or disabling computer systems, mainly through a network such as the Internet.

ISMS

An *Information Security Management System* is a set of policies concerned with information security management as defined by the ISO/IEC 27001 standards.

ISP

An *Internet service provider* is a company that offers its customers access to the Internet.

ITIL

The *Information Technology Infrastructure Library* is a set of concepts and policies for managing IT infrastructure, development, and operations.

Key management

Provisions made in a cryptography system design that are related to the generation, exchange, storage, safeguarding, use, vetting, and replacement of keys.

LDAP

Lightweight Directory Access Protocol is an application protocol for querying and modifying directory services running over TCP/IP.

Least privilege

The least-privilege principle requires that in a particular abstraction layer of a computing environment, every module or individual user must be able to access only such information and resources that are necessary for a legitimate purpose.

Liberty ID-FF

The *Liberty Alliance Project Identity Federation Framework* supports the development of identity-based, identity-consuming, and standard web services, in addition to clients of such services. The Liberty Alliance Project was formed to develop technical specifications that would solve business process issues including single sign-on, federation, and consent.

Metadata

Data about other data, of any sort in any media. An item of metadata may describe an individual datum, or content item, or a collection of data including multiple content items and hierarchical levels (e.g., a database schema). In data processing, metadata provides information about or documentation of other data managed within an application or environment.

NIST

The *National Institute of Standards and Technology* is a standards organization and measurement standards laboratory and is a non-regulatory agency of the U.S. Department of Commerce.

OATH

Open Authentication is a collaborative effort of IT industry leaders aimed at providing an architecture reference for universal, strong authentication across all users and all devices over all networks.

OAuth

An open authorization protocol standard that lets users give third-party websites limited access to their data without giving away their passwords. The OAuth protocol enables websites or applications (consumers) to access protected resources from web services (service providers) via an API, without requiring users to disclose their service provider credentials to those consumers.

OpenID

An open, decentralized, free framework for a user-centric digital identity. OpenID eliminates the need for multiple usernames across different websites, simplifying your online experience.

OTP

A *one-time password* makes it more difficult to gain unauthorized access to restricted resources, as opposed to a static password.

PCI

Payment Card Industry is a general term that collectively describes the debit, credit, prepaid, e-purse, ATM, and POS cards and associated businesses.

PCI DSS

Payment Card Industry Data Security Standard is a standard from the PCI Security Standards Council developed to ensure financial data security standards for entities that process credit card transactions.

PKI

Public Key Infrastructure is a set of hardware, software, people, policies, and procedures needed to create, manage, store, distribute, and revoke digital certificates.

Private cloud

An offering that emulates public cloud computing, but on a private network.

Public cloud

A cloud service that is hosted, operated, and managed by a third-party vendor from one or multiple data centers, and offered to multiple customers.

RBAC

Role-based access control is an approach to restricting system access to authorized users based on roles for various job functions.

REST

Representational State Transfer is a style of software architecture for distributed hypermedia systems such as the Internet.

S3

Simple Storage Service is an online storage web service from AWS.

SaaS

Security-as-a-service refers to the practice of delivering traditional security applications as an Internet-based service.

SaaS

Software-as-a-service is a model of software deployment whereby a provider licenses an application to customers for use as a service.

SAML

Security Assertion Markup Language is an XML-based standard for exchanging authentication and authorization data between security domains—that is, between an identity provider (a producer of assertions) and a service provider (a consumer of assertions).

SAS 70

Statement on Auditing Standards No. 70 was developed by the American Institute of Certified Public Accountants (AICPA) to provide a mechanism for service organizations to complete one audit of their controls, resulting in a report that could be provided to their customers and their customers' auditors.

SDLC

Software Development Life Cycle is the process of developing information systems through investigation, analysis, design, implementation, and maintenance.

SIEM

Security incident and event management is a tool used on organizational data networks to centralize the storage and interpretation of logs, or events, generated by other software running on the network.

SLA

A *service-level agreement* is a part of a service contract where the level of service is formally defined.

SOA

Service-oriented architecture is a collection of services with the underlying structure supporting communications between services. Service orientation aims for a loose coupling of services with operating systems, programming languages, and other technologies that underlie applications.

SOAP

Simple Object Access Protocol is a protocol specification for exchanging structured information in the implementation of web services in computer networks.

SOD

Segregation of duties is the concept of having more than one person required to complete a task, and is one of the key concepts of internal control.

SOX

The *Sarbanes-Oxley Act* was enacted by the U.S. Congress in 2002 in response to incidents of significant financial reporting fraud; it requires public companies to certify the effectiveness of internal controls over financial reporting.

SPI

An acronym standing for the three major services provided in public cloud computing: SaaS, PaaS, and IaaS. SPI is a commonly agreed-upon framework for describing the cloud computing service delivery model.

SPML

Service Provisioning Markup Language is an XML-based framework for exchanging user, resource, and service provisioning information between cooperating organizations.

SSH

Secure Shell is a network protocol that allows data to be exchanged using a secure channel between two networked devices.

Strong authentication

Associated with two-factor authentication or, more generally, multifactor authentication.

Symmetric encryption

Use of a single secret key for both the encryption and decryption of data.

SysTrust

An audit framework that was developed by the AICPA and Canadian Institute of Chartered Accountants (CICA) to provide a mechanism for service providers to complete an audit based on a predefined set of criteria for security, availability, processing integrity, and confidentiality.

Two-factor authentication

A system wherein two different factors are used in conjunction to authenticate individuals.

Virtualization

The creation of a virtual (rather than actual) version of something, such as an operating system, a storage device, an application, or network resources.

VPC

An acronym that stands for *vulnerability, patch, and configuration* management.

VPN

A *virtual private network* is a computer network in which some of the links between nodes are carried by open connections or virtual circuits in some larger networks (such as the Internet), as opposed to running across a single private network.

WebDAV

Web-based Distributed Authoring and Versioning is a set of extensions to Hypertext Transfer Protocol (HTTP) that allows users to edit and manage files collaboratively on remote World Wide Web servers.

XACML

eXtensible Access Control Markup Language is a declarative access control policy language implemented in XML and a processing model, describing how to interpret the policies.

XAML

eXtensible Application Markup Language is a declarative XML-based language created by Microsoft that is used to initialize structured values and objects.

We'd like to hear your suggestions for improving our indexes. Send email to *index@oreilly.com*.

ERP (enterprise resource planning)
  benefits of, 230
  interoperability and, 31
  matching investments to revenue, 228
  SaaS support, 230
  SOX considerations, 186
  start-ups and, 28
EU (European Union)
  data privacy considerations, 154
  defined, 294
EU Directive, 155, 162–163
Eucalyptus software, 56
European Union (see EU)
eXensible Access Control Markup Language (see XACML)
eXensible Application Markup Language (XAML), 298
eXtensible Markup Language (see XML)
external clouds (see public clouds)

F

FBI, 156, 157
Federal Information Processing Standards (FIPS), 67
Federal Information Security Management Act (FISMA), 159
Federal Rules of Civil Procedure (FRCP), 155
Federal Trade Commission, 154
federated identity (see identity federation)
filtering
  email, 218, 220
  web content, 221
FIPS (Federal Information Processing Standards), 67
firewalls
  data security and, 66
  IaaS VPC management, 136
  MSSP support, 218
  network access control and, 128
  network-level security, 42
  virtual server security and, 47
FISMA (Federal Information Security Management Act), 159
five 9s of uptime, 70
fixed quotas, 121
FRCP (Federal Rules of Civil Procedure), 155
FTP over SSL (FTPS), 62
FTPS (FTP over SSL), 62

G

GAPP (Generally Accepted Privacy Principles) standard, 146, 199
Garfinkel, Simson, 38
Gartner forecast, 240

Generally Accepted Privacy Principles (GAPP) standard, 146, 199
GlassFish server, 211
GLBA (Gramm-Leach-Bliley Act)
  compliance management and, 101
  defined, 294
  Financial Privacy Rule, 160
  Safeguards Rule, 160
GoGrid, 14
Google
  availability management, 115, 118
  OpenID support, 89, 91
  services overview, 205, 214
Google App Engine
  authentication considerations, 102
  domain name support, 42
  language support, 57
  quota system, 121
  services overview, 205
Google Apps
  SaaS support, 54
  SAML support, 96, 97
  SSO process, 83
Google BigTable, 62, 120
Google Docs, 54
Google GData API, 87
Google Health, 161
Governance, Risk, Compliance (see GRC)
Gramm-Leach-Bliley Act (see GLBA)
GRC (Governance, Risk, Compliance)
  benefits for CSPs, 171–172
  defined, 294
  key components, 170
  program implementation, 172–174
GSA MSO (Managed Service Organization), 96

H

Health Insurance Portability and Accountability Act (see HIPAA)
health monitoring
  IaaS support, 124
  PaaS support, 122
  SaaS support, 120
HIPAA (Health Insurance Portability and Accountability Act)
  compliance management and, 101
  defined, 294
  IAM support, 75
  Privacy Rule, 160, 190
  retention and destruction principle, 152
  Security Standards, 188–192
HITECH Act, 161, 191
host-level security
  data security and, 66
  IaaS considerations, 45

infrastructure security
   application level, 49–59
   concluding thoughts, 245–247, 260
   host level, 44–49, 66
   network level, 36–43, 70
infrastructure-as-a-service (see IaaS)
integrity (see data integrity)
internal clouds (see private clouds)
International Auditing and Assurance Standards
      Board (IAASB), 197
Internet service providers (see ISPs)
interoperability, enterprise barriers for, 31
intrusion detection, 139
intrusion detection systems (see IDSs)
intrusion prevention systems (see IPSs)
Invisible Things Lab, 46
IP addresses
   security risk factors, 38
   VM support, 42
IPSs (intrusion prevention systems)
   data security and, 66
   IAM support, 73
ISAE 3402 standard, 197, 201
ISMS (Information Security Management System),
      113, 196, 295
ISO/IEC 17799 standard, 192
ISO/IEC 20000 standard, 112
ISO/IEC 27001 standard
   audit considerations, 199
   comparison, 113
   comparisons, 200–201
   defined, 196, 295
   IT/security control objectives, 175
ISO/IEC 27002 standard
   access control, 113, 125
   comparison, 113
   host-level security and, 44
   IAM practices, 75
   incident response, 113
   IT/security control objectives, 175
   monitoring support, 113
   VPC management, 113, 130
ISPs (Internet service providers)
   availability management and, 117
   defined, 295
   email filtering, 218
   evolution of, 3
   privacy considerations, 158
IT department
   case study, 230–234
   COBIT considerations, 192
   governance factors, 235
   GRC program implementation, 173
   IAM practices, 75, 106
   illustrative control objectives, 174–178

   impact of cloud computing, 225–237, 256, 264
   incremental control objectives, 179–180
   incremental spending growth, 240
   potential threats of using CSPs, 228–230
   privacy responsibilities, 145
   project risk assessment, 171
   trust boundaries and, 73, 109
IT Governance Institute, 185
IT Service Management (ITSM), 112
ITGCs (information technology general controls),
      185
ITIL (Information Technology Infrastructure
      Library)
   access control, 113, 125
   availability management, 113
   COBIT support, 192
   defined, 295
   IAM support, 75
   IT case study, 233
   security management and, 110
   VPC management, 113
ITSM (IT Service Management), 112

J

J-SOX, 186
Java language, 57, 205
JavaScript Object Notation (JSON)
   access control, 128
   API support, 15
Jericho Forum, 5
Jericho Systems, 91
JSON (JavaScript Object Notation)
   access control, 128
   API support, 15

K

Kaminsky Bug, 41
Kaminsky, Dan, 41
Kerberos authentication, 128
key management
   control objectives, 180–182
   data security and, 69
   defined, 295
   IaaS considerations, 103
Key Management Interoperability Protocol
      (KMIP), 69
key performance indicators (see KPIs)
Kloxo control panel, 46
KMIP (Key Management Interoperability
      Protocol), 69
KPIs (key performance indicators)
   defining, 171
   monitoring progress via, 174
   viewing control weaknesses, 172

L

laws and regulations
  compliance management, 101
  CSP compliance, 182–192
  federal, 155–162
  illustrative control objectives, 178
  international, 162–164
  privacy implications, 155
  U.S. legal orders, 157
LDAP (Lightweight Directory Access Protocol)
  authentication and, 76
  defined, 295
  IAM support, 77, 81
least-privilege principle
  access control and, 127
  application-level security and, 58
  defined, 295
  IAM practices, 100
Liberty Alliance Project
  defined, 295
  identity federation and, 81
license fees, 18
litigation hold, 156
logging, control objectives, 179
Lxlabs, 46

M

MAC (Media Access Control) address, 158
MACs (message authentication codes), 69
malicious file execution, 50
malware, 219, 220
managed security service providers (MSSPs), 218
managed security services (MSSs), 218
MapReduce web service, 205
Mather, Tim, 145
Media Access Control (MAC) address, 158
Merrill Lynch, 240
message authentication codes (MACs), 69
metadata
  data security and, 66
  defined, 295
Microsoft
  Geneva claims-based authentication
    framework, 103, 106
  IAM guidance, 92, 104, 105
  OpenID support, 89, 91
  services overview, 214
Microsoft Azure Services Platform, 91, 103, 105, 206
Microsoft Health Vault, 161
milw0rm website, 46
mobile computing, 177
monitoring
  control objectives, 177, 180

CSPs and, 169
GRC support, 171, 172
health, 120, 122, 124
IAM guidance, 105
KPI support, 174
security management and, 113, 143
SysTrust framework, 198
user activity, 74, 100
MSSPs (managed security service providers), 218
MSSs (managed security services), 218
multitenancy
  availability management and, 119
  cloud identity administration and, 94
  data security and, 62, 65
  defined, 8
  PaaS support, 20, 56
  SaaS support, 19, 55
  virtualization and, 14

N

Nagios tool, 119, 122, 124
NAIC Model Audit Rule, 186
NANOG (North American Network Operators
    Group), 40
National Industrial Security Program Operating
    Manual, 64
National Institute of Standards and Technology (see
    NIST)
National Security Letters (NSLs), 156, 157
NDA (non-disclosure agreement), 44, 54
NetSuite, 118
network access policies, 136, 177
network connectivity
  access control and, 128
  enterprise barriers for, 31
  PaaS considerations, 122
Network Layer Reachability Information, 39
network-level security
  data availability and, 70
  ensuring access control, 38–39
  ensuring data confidentiality, 36
  ensuring data integrity, 36
  Internet-facing resources and, 39–41
  mitigating risk, 42
  private clouds and, 36
  public clouds and, 36
  replacing zones/tiers with domains, 42
  risk factors, 36
NIST (National Institute of Standards and
    Technology)
  COBIT support, 192
  Federal Information Processing Standards, 67
  on private community cloud, 81
  purpose, 5, 295
  Special Publication 800-57, 69

Tim Mather is an experienced security professional currently pursing a graduate degree in information assurance full-time. He is a frequent speaker and commentator on information security issues, and serves as an advisor to several security-related start-ups.

Most recently, he was the chief security strategist for RSA, The Security Division of EMC, where he was responsible for keeping ahead of security industry trends, technology, and threats. Prior to that, he was vice president of technology strategy in Symantec's Office of the Chief Technology Officer, where he was responsible for coordinating the company's long-term technical and intellectual property strategy. Previously at Symantec, he served for nearly seven years as chief information security officer (CISO). As CISO, Tim was responsible for development of all information systems security policies, oversight of implementation of all security-related policies and procedures, and oversight of all information systems audit-related activities. He also worked closely with internal product groups on security capabilities in Symantec products.

Prior to joining Symantec in September 1999, Tim was the manager of security at VeriSign. Additionally, he was formerly manager of information systems security at Apple Computer. Tim's experience also includes seven years in Washington, DC, working on secure communications for a classified, national-level command, control, communications, and intelligence (C^3I) project, which involved both civilian and military departments and agencies.

Tim is a Certified Information Systems Security Professional (CISSP) and a Certified Information Systems Manager (CISM). He holds master's degrees in national security studies from Georgetown University and in international policy studies from the Monterey Institute of International Studies. Tim holds a bachelor's degree in political economics from the University of California at Berkeley.

Subra Kumaraswamy has more than 18 years of engineering and management experience in information security, Internet, and e-commerce technologies. He is currently leading an Identity & Access Management program within Sun Microsystems. Subra has held leadership positions at various Internet-based companies, including Netscape, WhoWhere, Lycos, and

Knowledge Networks. He was the cofounder of two Internet-based startups, CoolSync and Zingdata. He also worked at Accenture and the University of Notre Dame in security consulting and software engineering roles.

In his spare time, Subra researches emerging technologies such as cloud computing to understand the security and privacy implications for users and enterprises. Subra is a founding member of the Cloud Security Alliance (*http://www.cloudsecurityalliance.org/*) as well as cochair of the Identity & Access Management and Encryption & Key Management workgroups. Subra has a master's degree in computer engineering and is CISSP certified.

Shahed Latif is a partner in KPMG's advisory practice based in the company's Silicon Valley office. He has more than 23 years of experience working with global Fortune 1,000 companies focusing on providing business and technology solutions across a variety of areas, and he has worked with many of the Fortune 500 high-tech companies in Silicon Valley. Shahed spent 10 years in the London office of KPMG working in the financial sector consulting group, information risk management group, and assurance practice. He has worked with large global companies, which gave him the opportunity to work in Africa, Asia, and Europe. He is currently KPMG's information security leader for the Western Region of the United States, and helps all clients implement security, privacy, and continuity solutions.

Shahed regularly speaks on technology topics at industry forums around the world, including Africa, Asia, and Europe as well as the United States. He is a regular lecturer at Stanford University and has given a variety of speeches on governance risk and compliance, identity access management, raising security awareness, and incident response.

Shahed is a member of the Institute of Chartered Accountants in England & Wales and a member of the San Francisco chapter of the Information Systems Audit and Control Foundation. He received a bachelor's degree in managerial and administrative studies, majoring in finance and computer science, from the University of Aston, Birmingham, in the United Kingdom.

He is also an active Boy Scout Leader in the Meridian District and has coached boys' soccer teams for the past five years.

COLOPHON

The cover image is from Getty Images. The cover fonts are Akzidenz Grotesk and Orator. The text font is Adobe's Meridien; the heading font is ITC Bailey.

Get even more for your money.

Join the O'Reilly Community, and register the O'Reilly books you own.It's free, and you'll get:

- 40% upgrade offer on O'Reilly books
- Membership discounts on books and events
- Free lifetime updates to electronic formats of books
- Multiple ebook formats, DRM FREE
- Participation in the O'Reilly community
- Newsletters
- Account management
- 100% Satisfaction Guarantee

Signing up is easy:

1. **Go to: oreilly.com/go/register**
2. **Create an O'Reilly login.**
3. **Provide your address.**
4. **Register your books.**

Note: English-language books only

To order books online:

oreilly.com/order_new

For questions about products or an order:

orders@oreilly.com

To sign up to get topic-specific email announcements and/or news about upcoming books, conferences, special offers, and new technologies:

elists@oreilly.com

For technical questions about book content:

booktech@oreilly.com

To submit new book proposals to our editors:

proposals@oreilly.com

Many O'Reilly books are available in PDF and several ebook formats. For more information:

oreilly.com/ebooks

O'REILLY®

Spreading the knowledge of innovators   www.oreilly.com

Buy this book and get access to the online edition for 45 days—for free!

Cloud Security and Privacy
By Tim Mather, Subra Kumaraswamy & Shahed Latif
August 2009, $34.99
ISBN 9780596802769

With Safari Books Online, you can:

Access the contents of thousands of technology and business books

- Quickly search over 7000 books and certification guides
- Download whole books or chapters in PDF format, at no extra cost, to print or read on the go
- Copy and paste code
- Save up to 35% on O'Reilly print books
- **New!** Access mobile-friendly books directly from cell phones and mobile devices

Stay up-to-date on emerging topics before the books are published

- Get on-demand access to evolving manuscripts.
- Interact directly with authors of upcoming books

Explore thousands of hours of video on technology and design topics

- Learn from expert video tutorials
- Watch and replay recorded conference sessions

To try out Safari and the online edition of this book FREE for 45 days,
go to *www.oreilly.com/go/safarienabled* and enter the coupon code LIZBKFH.
To see the complete Safari Library, visit safari.oreilly.com.

Spreading the knowledge of innovators   safari.oreilly.com